24/7 INNOVATION

A Blueprint for Surviving and
Thriving in an Age of Change

Stephen M. Shapiro

McGraw-Hill

New York   Chicago   San Francisco
Lisbon   London   Madrid   Mexico City
Milan   New Delhi   San Juan   Seoul
Singapore   Sydney   Toronto

Library of Congress Cataloging-in-Publication Data

Shapiro, Stephen M.
    24/7 innovation / by Stephen M. Shapiro.
        p.   cm.
    Includes bibliographical references.
    ISBN 0-07-137626-7
    1. Organizational change.   2. Organizational change—Management.   3. Organizational
effectiveness.   4. Creative ability in business.   I. Title: Twenty-four/seven innovation.
II. Title

    HD58.8 .S477   2001
    658.4'063—dc21   2001031719

McGraw-Hill

A Division of The McGraw·Hill Companies

1 2 3 4 5 6 7 8 9 0   DOC/DOC   0 9 8 7 6 5 4 3 2 1

ISBN 0-07-137626-7

*This book was set in Times New Roman by McGraw-Hill's Professional Book
Group composition unit, Hightstown, N.J.*

Printed and bound by R. R. Donnelley & Sons Company.

This book is printed on recycled, acid-free paper containing
a minimum of 50% recycled, de-inked fiber.

Contents

Appendixes

Acknowledgments

This book is about innovation. And throughout, I make the point that innovation comes from focusing on interdependencies. It's about connecting the dots. As Steve Jobs once said, "Creativity is just having enough dots to connect." And so I would like to thank many of the individuals and companies who provided me with enough "dots" to create this book. I am indebted to some individuals who provided me with great examples of innovation from within their own organizations: Jay Rosser of Koch Industries, Mark Livesey and Alan Challis of WilliamsF1, Ruy Shiozawa of Global Village Telecom Brazil, Dr. Trevor Gibbs of GlaxoSmithKline, Finn Johnson of Mölnlycke Health Care, Tom Stathos of PPL, and Aartjan Paauw of Universal Leven. I would also like to thank the many innovative organizations that provided me with some great content and agreed to be included in the book: Invensys, Sun Microsystems, BC Hydro, Fiat, VEW Energie AG, Electrabel, the Real Estate Assessment Center of the U.S. Department of Housing and Urban Development, and countless others.

I also owe a debt of gratitude to the numerous people from Accenture who took time from their busy schedules to serve as liaisons between me and their clients: Carlos Rust, Johan Karlberg, Peter Henderickx, Stefano Andreello, Alun Evans, Brian Sprague, Harold de Bruijn, Mani Vadari, Robert Spenser, Filip Thon, and Garret Wu.

Marcin Tworek once said, "Creativity is great, but plagiarism is faster." And in pulling together this book, I did "steal with pride" from friends and colleagues. Although I reference their work in the places where it is used, I want to offer a special up-front thank-you to: Brad Kolar, Mark Haffner, Joe Wootten, Bill Hughes, Martha Batorski, Gail Odom, Lex Pater, Dave Ferrin, Chris Adams, and Andy Neely (Cranfield University).

I also want to thank the many other people who helped me pull this book together and make it a reality: Mike Johnson, a great writer and editor, who worked days, nights, and weekends to convert my random thoughts into coherent prose; Tim Hindle, who provided the first cut of the manuscript; Brad Kolar, Mark McDonald, Mark Nassi, Frank Nugent, Mimi Wallk, Francis Pederit, Bill Petrarca, Nick Lawrence, and my dad, Allan Shapiro, who took the time to read and review the book and provided me with wonderful suggestions; Peter Roberts, Marc De Kegel, Pat Mullaney, Barry Patmore, Bob Farwell, Bill Stoddard, and Ron Anderson, who have been leaders in Accenture's Process practice over the years, and all of whom provided ideas and support for this book; Ela Aktay, Jane Palmieri, Jeffrey Krames, and all of the great people at McGraw-Hill who made this a reality; Laura Roberts, Kim Badland, Kelly Wink, Cheryl Wroth, Eda Colbert, Deborah Gaul, Vera Lattimore, Sam Geal, and Judith Reeson, who each contributed in his or her own way in pulling this together; Dr. Michael Hammer and Steve Stanton for their contributions to the world of business and with whom I had the great pleasure of working a few years ago. A debt of gratitude is also owed to Mike Bell and Mike Stimak, formerly of Unisys, who many years ago took a chance and hired me for an engineering co-op assignment, an experience that has had a profound impact on my career and my life. And most importantly, on a personal note, I am eternally grateful to my parents, grandfather, and sister for the love and support they have given me throughout my life. They are my biggest fans.

Finally, I would like to thank all the rest of the colleagues, clients, and friends who have contributed to my life and this book over the years. If I were to thank everyone, the acknowledgments would be as long as the book itself. My sincerest gratitude to all.

Introduction

I always knew there would be the likelihood of a good book after 15 years of consulting with major companies around the world. The pace of business expansion was unprecedented during this period, and the changes have put managers into a whirl of uncertainty. This uncomfortable situation demands sharp reflexes and creative thinking just to stay even. In fact, the only way to compete today is by accepting that we are in a permanent state of evolution. Admittedly, there is nothing entirely new about this. As the pre-Socratic philosopher Heraclitus said, "All is flux. The sun is new each day."

What is the key to long-term, sustainable success in these rapidly changing circumstances? This book is an attempt to answer that question, and the answer is simple: perpetual innovation. The business world, like life itself, never stops reinventing itself.

In the static world of previous years, traditional business success could often be attained through efficiency and effectiveness. Get to a dominant position in the marketplace and ride it. But in today's age of change, as soon as you achieve success, someone is nipping at your heels, learning your unique strengths, and planning to take a portion of your market. The only way to succeed is to have the ability to change—rapidly and repeatedly. This requires perpetual innovation from you and your entire staff at all times.

But it became clear to me in my consulting activities that most companies are stuck in outmoded ways of thinking. I am always amazed at the high quality of people employed by companies around the world. And I am even more amazed at how little most companies tap into the creative potential of these employees. Rigid policies, prescriptive processes, political infighting, and fragmented organizations have stifled innovation for too long.

Innovation 24 hours a day 7 days a week is no mystery: It's the ability of an organization and the people in it to come up with new ideas to satisfy the changing whims of ever-fickle customers without any special stimulation and without interruption. I am not referring to the backroom sources of innovation we have all known and loved in the past. I am referring to pervasive innovation. Innovation throughout the organization, everywhere, every day, by everyone—24/7, as we say in modern parlance—to the point where innovation is as natural as breathing.

Innovation is not random. In fact, much like jazz in the world of music, it emerges best when there is a structure to nurture it. I have been playing the saxophone since I was seven years old, and although I play all types of music, jazz is my passion. I love jazz because it is heavy on innovation ("improvisation" in musical terms). Just as innovation is not random, improvisation is not random. There is a simple structure to jazz, like 12-bar B-flat blues. It has a rhythm, chord progression, and tempo. As *Jazz: The Rough Guide* says, "Improvisation is the art of playing without premeditation, rather than necessarily 'making it up as you go along.' ... Most jazz performances are less than 100 percent improvised, and some may be less than 5 percent improvised and still be good jazz: it is the spirit (or illusion) of spontaneity which communicates."[1] Businesses, like jazz ensembles, need simple structures to foster innovation to emerge. But jazz is much more than just improvisation, it is the fruit of the activity of a group of people. It is not a solitary pursuit. Jazz musicians play solos with their band, but they rarely give concerts on their own. Jazz is a social activity, and so are businesses.

Unfortunately, many businesses are run more like classical symphony orchestras than jazz bands. The classical musician plays a long, elaborate composition written by someone else, a composition that leaves little room for interpretation. The composer (often someone long dead) has written elaborate compositions (detailed work flows), placed them neatly in binders, and expected the employees (the musicians) to follow them by rote.

This difference is "box" thinking versus "line" thinking. When people say you need to think "out of the box" to be innovative they are right, but for the wrong reasons. The boxes that most people operate in are focused on activities, computers, people, or departments within a company. But it is the lines, the interconnections and interdependencies between the boxes, where innovation emerges. Innovative thinking comes from making connections. Connections between boxes. Connections between ideas. Connections between companies. Or connections between industries. Focusing on the lines frees an organization to improve within the guidelines of the simple structure. I revisit this concept of box versus line thinking throughout the book, as I believe it to be one of the fundamental elements of success.

The power of focusing on the lines and connections is illustrated in a conversation I heard between two colleagues, Brad and Lisa. They were talking about why some people seem to be more innovative and insightful than others. Brad, who is one of the most lateral thinkers I know, asked Lisa, "When you are learning or reading or experiencing something new, what is the main question in your mind?" Her response was, "I ask, what does this mean?" And that is what most people would say. Most people first try and understand the situation, and then see how that relates to other things they know. Brad said his first question is always, "What is this like?" He compares it to other things he knows. From that he can then derive meaning. And in doing so, he is able to leverage relationships from the domain with which he is familiar and translate them to the new domain. This is what appears as an "insight" to someone else. It is not about intelligence or knowledge. It's about being able to understand quickly. Even with little knowledge on a given topic, an innovative person is able to connect the dots, and leverage something else he already knows about. This is what organizations need to do. Connect the dots.

In the subtitle of this book—*A Blueprint for Surviving and Thriving in an Age of Change*—the term "blueprint" is something called a Capability. A Capability is a combination of people, processes, and technology that together deliver business performance as defined by the strategy.

To tell this story, I open with a chapter on the value and power of 24/7 innovation, then move on to five chapters focused on each of the components of a Capability. I start with process, the backbone of a company. I show how process can be an enabler of an innovative organization. And this is not process as it was once understood. As Jerry Hirshberg, founder and president of Nissan Design International, once said, "The widely held assumption was that an error-free process would more reliably lead to error-free results. As it turns out, this was not an error-free position."[2] Investing heavily in detailed process flows not only reduces flexibility, but it also fails to give you the results you want. In Chapter 3, I move on to the all-important subject of culture. I show what an innovative culture looks like, discuss how to get the most from your employees, and offer approaches for getting there. In Chapter 4, I move on to customers and strategies. How can a company view the customer as an extension of the business ("hire the customer") and potentially create additional sources of revenue through new ventures? In the chapter on technology, I get beyond the e-commerce hype and discuss how companies are using technology in innovative ways and how technology can foster innovation. The last blueprint element is performance measures. Although performance measures are typically viewed as an inhibitor of innovation, this chapter shows how companies can use measures as a way of freeing the organization and helping entrepreneurial spirit emerge.

Chapters 7 and 8 are about specific techniques for improving your chances of success, namely, targeting and simulation. The former helps focus innovation investments to maximize returns, while the latter tests innovations before they see the light of day. The final chapter, Chapter 9, describes the road a company can take that leads to pervasive innovation—the stages a company can and should go through to reach the ultimate destination, an alliance-based organization.

I have also included a Prologue and an Epilogue. The Prologue is about the past—how we got into our present fix. It is a brief historical account of business over the last few centuries with an emphasis on how past approaches have stifled innovation. The Epilogue, on the other hand, looks to the future. I provide some innovative frameworks that can serve as foundations for rapid change within organizations in years to come. Finally, in the appendixes, I provide four case studies of companies that are doing innovative work, then offer some diagnostic tools.

You will probably notice that most of the examples I use in the book are of companies that are not based in the United States. This may be a little surprising, since in my experience, most business books have focused on U.S. corporations. Although I am American, I moved to London in 1999. I was thrilled to find such a fertile ground for innovative ideas over here, and felt compelled to highlight the interesting work of European companies.

Publishing a business book is a risky proposition these days. Companies that were "excellent" at the time of writing may have fallen from their perch. And in some respects writing a book which describes best practices for innovation but which also says that best practices are insufficient is slightly ironic. But to try and copy what another company is doing lock, stock, and barrel is just another form of box thinking. Instead, connect the dots. Make connections. Read about what the companies in this book have been doing and then consider some of them in the context of your own business situation. And then try and use these models to create new ideas for fostering innovation.

Thriving in this age of change is no easy feat. It requires changes everywhere and from everyone in the organization. To fail to move in this direction is the equivalent of signing your company's death warrant. Survival through perpetual and pervasive innovation is a must. Because it is only through 24/7 innovation that a company can hope to achieve and sustain a leadership position in today's competitive marketplace.

Stephen M. Shapiro
London/New York
E-mail: Steve@24-7Innovation.com
Web site: www.24-7innovation.com

FROM BOXES
TO LINES

1. *Out of clutter find simplicity.*
2. *From discord find harmony.*
3. *In the middle of difficulty lies opportunity.*

ALBERT EINSTEIN, HIS THREE RULES OF WORK

In writing this book, I felt that a historical perspective on business would provide an interesting and useful context for my arguments, especially for readers who are a bit vague on the past contributions of people like Frederick Taylor, W. Edwards Deming, and Dr. Michael Hammer. But as a colleague of mine once said to me, he has read so much about Taylor that he feels he can "claim him as a dependent on my taxes." So it is with some trepidation that I go ahead with this Prologue. Yes, most of this is historical, but it provides the essential context for what comes next in business—an era of innovation such as we have never seen.

Although businesses over the years have used innovative approaches for improving their productivity, this has often been done at the expense of individual innovation. Innovation has been driven from the top, rather than being pervasive throughout the organization. The goal has been to create a well-oiled machine that turns employees into robots to remove all variability. To help illustrate what I mean, I find it useful to think of a business as being, quite simply, a pattern of boxes and lines. The "boxes" can be tasks, people, departments, computers, or units within a business. The "lines" are the interrelationships and dependencies that connect those boxes together. It seems to me that too often businesses have focused on the boxes rather than the lines. Remember the wall of Post-it Notes during the peak of reengineering? Remember the huge investments in computers that never paid off? Decades of new ideas for improvements have left many businesses tied up in knots.

One reason for this fragmentation is that organizational theories have often mirrored the science or technology of the day. The shift from an agrarian to an industrial economy, and the accompanying changes in technology and the way that products were manufactured, led to a focus on tasks, machines, and the things that make up machines, that is, what happens "inside the boxes." It is not surprising that Frederick Taylor concentrated on improving human performance by dividing work into small, discrete sets of activities around the machines they were performed on. And only managers, the people with "intelligence," designed these work activities. It was assumed that workers had neither the requisite intelligence nor the time, so they were told to get on with doing what they were told to do. This seemed appropriate at a time when the workforce was largely uneducated.

Then came the shift to the information age in the 1960s and 1970s, and computers focused on applications that processed information. But, unfortunately, computers can't think, and therefore prescriptive solutions were developed so that computers could process information within clear boundaries. But this forced out innovation and led to a renewed focus on automating tasks, albeit the tasks were different. The organization of businesses naturally began to reflect this approach, leading to the 1990s era of "reengineering"—a very industrial, nuts-and-bolts term in itself. Business process reengineering (BPR), although focused on connections across functions, still maintained a box focus. In this case, the box was the process. The focus was still on the box, but more was on the information and the process within the box. And although processes are an important part of a business, they are only one dimension.

The current shift in technology is the most exciting yet—the convergence of the Internet, the World Wide Web, e-mail, telecommunications, and computer networks. And as a result, our business models are beginning to focus on the lines (i.e., interdependencies). This leads us into the era of collaboration, integration, and innovation that I will be exploring and advocating in this book. The key is not to use technology in isolation, but as a tool to connect the boxes.

The past 100 years of business management and technology have, for the most part, focused on automation, mechanization, and the routinization of work, at the expense of innovation. There has been too much focus on improving the boxes (processes, departments, individuals, computers, databases, etc.). Fortunately, we now are seeing a change.

As I said in the introduction, I am a jazz saxophonist. And the concept of lines versus boxes is exactly what jazz is all about. The key in jazz is to let each player (a "box") express his or her own individuality through improvisation (a form of innovation) in the context of a simple chart comprised of chord structures and rhythm (the "lines"). There are few limits to what a jazz musician can do with his or her solo. The only "control" is the framework. The musician is given the freedom to express his or her own individuality. Jazz is very much about the musician, the human factor.

In the business world, we are now seeing the reintroduction of the human factor. This is a development that has evolved out of necessity. Today's world is one of uncertainty, unpredictability, and change. Indeed, as it is often said, change is the only constant. And machines, computers, and prescriptive compositions do not afford companies the flexibility they need to survive and thrive. They may get to the top today with their best practices, great ideas, and what they consider to be innovative thinking. But their competitors are nipping at their heels and may leapfrog over them tomorrow. Companies have begun to realize that they need innovative business models that leverage technology so that their people can make the best use of their innate creativity. This means focusing on the lines (flows, coordination, dependencies) of the business that allow for innovation and adaptability to emerge from within and across the boxes.

This is a challenging proposition for most companies. This requires no less than having good jazz scores (operating models and processes), played by good jazz musicians (employees), playing high-quality instruments (technology) in the right way, so that the audience (customer) enjoys the performance. And central to all of this is improvisation (innovation). Musicians read a score. But when they come to play that score they improvise their solo parts, partly because they feel that it improves the music, partly because they are responding to the improvisation of someone else within the group, and partly because they are responding to audience reaction. Once this procedure has begun, it can take the music far away from the original score and send it on a journey that was never dreamed of by its composer. This is the form of perpetual innovation that companies need in order to evolve continuously to meet customer and market needs in this age of change.

My suggestion, and the theme of this book, is that companies must find a way to achieve 24/7 innovation—all day, every day—in order to survive in an increasingly daunting competitive environment. Tomorrow's companies will need pervasive innovation—creative thinking everywhere, by everyone. We are witnessing the start of the next evolutionary phase of business innovation.

Surviving and Thriving in an Age of Change

C H A P T E R

1

INNOVATION FOR COMPETITIVE ADVANTAGE

"Creativity is thinking up new things. Innovation is doing new things."

THEODORE LEVITT

One of the few certainties of today's business environment is that it never stands still. Only one approach to this unsteady state of affairs makes sense: perpetual innovation—the constant shifting of strategies and tactics to reshape the business and take competitors by surprise. The winners will be the companies that find ways to release their innovative potential and apply it to the way they think and the way they work. In this opening chapter, we illustrate the value of innovation to today's businesses and examine the concept of Capabilities as its tool, with five key components: strategy, measurements, processes, people, and technology. Taken together, the Capability approach can become the blueprint for change that catapults a company—large or small, old or new, high-tech or low-tech—to leadership of its sector

7

and helps it stay there. Done well, the implementation of Capabilities in an organization can bring about revolutionary change that is strategic, pervasive, and daunting to competitors. The innovative company is envied by all and valued by the financial markets.

I play golf—not well, but I play golf. My handicap is in double digits. For me to shoot par would be a dream. But for Tiger Woods, par would be a nightmare. I am reminded of this comparison when I see companies that are satisfied to focus on their understanding of "par," otherwise known as best practice. It was once an admirable aim, but is not sufficient today. Your competitors are more like Tiger Woods than they are like me. Par won't keep you alive in the current environment.

Smart businesses are learning to push farther. They know that best practice will not get them where they want to be. Not so long ago, it *was* possible for a company to set the industry standard or best practice, then sit back and watch weaker rivals try to catch up. But businesses are now in a greater state of flux than ever before in the history of commerce. Global competition has reached a stage where no sooner has one firm achieved excellence than so too have its imitative rivals. For example, everyone used to talk about Wal-Mart's supply chain prowess as a competitive advantage, but now it is a requirement for any successful business. There is no time to pause for a breath. The only way a company can hope to stay ahead now is by being continuously entrepreneurial and innovative, by creating processes and capabilities that allow innovation to flourish and become a core strength. Only then is it possible to escape from the game of follow-the-leader, of shooting for par.

Innovation is both a means to an end *and* an end in itself. It should be a firm's core capability that delivers superior value—generating growth and delivering high returns. At the same time it is a stand-alone state of mind that investors look for in public companies. Firms perceived as adept at innovation benefit from the "innovation premium," the extra value that analysts factor into the shares of the most flexible companies merely because they are consistently able to renew, reshape, and refocus their energies to meet new competitive challenges. Analysts say this premium can amount to as much as one-fifth of the underlying value of a company's shares.

Companies in the twenty-first century can hope to be innovative all the time only if they shift their innovative thinking out of the laboratory and take it to the broad base of the entire organization. A culture of innovation must be nurtured like a living organism, permeating everything the company does, all the time, including the design and operation of its processes. To be perpetually responsive to today's fast-changing markets requires a radically new approach to designing businesses.

But what does it mean to be continually innovative? Innovation has traditionally been thought of as something separate and discrete, brought into the organization, as it were, from outside, from the laboratory. No more. The businesses that show the way in this century will be built not around a lot of heads and hands, but around a lot of hearts, around motivation, dedication, and commitment to creative thinking. This new energy is not the exclusive province of start-ups. Any mature company can develop the same taste for renewal because, let's face it, there are really only two reasons people aren't innovative all the time. Either they aren't motivated to be innovative, or they aren't perceived as "competent" in innovation. Both of these problems can be solved, as we shall see in the chapters ahead.

PROCESS AND INNOVATION
Process has become a major part of business vernacular since the birth of business process reengineering (BPR). When businesspeople use the word *process*, they often mean definable groups of activities or efforts focused heavily on an individual process. In a flowchart, they are the boxes—the discrete components of the business. However, this limited view often led companies to believe that computers could solve their problems. It was, they thought, just a matter of speeding up the processing of data, and for that all they needed was more sophisticated (i.e., more expensive) hardware and software, which in fact added to the rigidity of the business. They tended to look upon the individual processes within the organization as if they were self-contained units.

By applying Braess's Paradox[1] to this business analogy, we find that an improvement to a subsystem has a 25 percent chance of improving the system as a whole, a 50 percent chance of not affecting the system at all, and a 25 percent chance of having a negative effect on the system. Not very good odds. In fact it is the lines connecting the boxes on a flowchart, the interdependencies, that are critical to the performance of a business. What you do inside of each box is less important than how the boxes fit together.

If we look at how companies attempted to improve their businesses in the past decade or two, it seems that many became process junkies. So obsessed were they with the idea of BPR that they threw process reengineered solutions at almost every problem in sight. Abuses were rife. When the reengineering consultants finished their work, they often left behind volumes of process maps. I once got a call from a manager who boasted of his 1500 pages of process flows and wanted to know what I thought. To his dismay, I had to tell him I was not impressed. Who could ever implement such a complex design? He had seen the trees (and killed several in printing the processes), but the forest was nowhere in his field of vision. He had not thought of the next steps: coordinating the processes, coming up with innovative ideas and insights, and finding some talented people to fit it all together into a smoothly running business.

This must ring a bell with every manager and consultant who has ever shuffled Post-it Notes around on a wall trying to analyze and improve work flows. The obsessives among us create elaborate binders of process flows in the expectation that the organization's employees will read them, understand them, and forever after perform the process in the same way. This might seem sensible, but the truth is that doing isolated things more efficiently, faster, and cheaper is not necessarily better for the organization as a whole.

There is a video I use when running seminars that illustrates this point. Called the *Four-Hour House*, it shows a world-record competition held a number of years ago in which participants had to build a three-bedroom house from scratch (with no prefabrication of any sort) in less than four hours.[2] It's an amazing video to watch, one filled with excellent techniques for compressing time. The winning team was able to do it in 2 hours 45 minutes, including landscaping! Admittedly it took 350 people to build the house, but it is still incredible to watch. I then ask, "Is this a good business process?" After pondering the question, most people agree that it is not, and for a variety of reasons. Okay, maybe there is the quality problem. My mother, who is an interior designer, says she would never live in that house because the corners are probably not perfectly squared. Others wonder if the hasty construction could produce a house safe enough to live in.

But aesthetic and safety issues aside, this is still not how a good business should operate. Consider a city made up of four-hour houses. Beautiful streets lined with these houses, and all of them with "For sale" signs in front of them. Have we really improved anything? No. In fact, all we have done is create a greater inventory problem.

I used the Four-Hour House example once with a client that makes electronic equipment. At one point, the person responsible for the order-to-cash process jumped up and said, "Hey, that's us! We have invested so much in developing our equipment faster than anyone else, we can produce our components in four hours, while our competitors take two weeks. But what do we do? We put the finished goods in the warehouse." For me this is the perfect example of an argument I have had over the years with experts in logistics and warehousing strategies. They would claim to be able to make the most efficient warehouses in the world. I claim that often the goal should be to eliminate the need for warehouses altogether. Here, a single-minded focus on the house-building box meant that box was never connected to other boxes, such as the sales process.

PERVASIVE INNOVATION

Most importantly, the close contact and coordination between different parts of the business create a climate of open communication and cooperation that in turn will allow cross-functional innovation. When this happens, the company begins to develop innovation as its core competence. By focusing on the interdependencies rather than the prescriptive aspects of isolated activities or traditional processes, the worker gains the flexibility to define how to do the work within the context of those links. The process starts by making sure that people know why they are doing their work, who they are doing it for, and when it must be completed. The emphasis is *not* on how the work is to be done.

But moving a company to this stage of performance is both complex and far-reaching, and it touches every aspect of work—who does it, how it's done, how it's measured, how it's rewarded, and who's in charge. What's more, doing it right requires revolutionary change, and therefore innovation is often treated as a threat by those who are comfortable with the status quo.

Like good jazz, businesses can operate within constraints that resemble sheet music, allowing for creativity within simple structures. This jazz metaphor seems particularly appropriate to the loose–tight combinations we should strive for in seeking innovative solutions. My own background as an amateur sax player has actually helped me evolve my thinking about how to develop business innovation within such fixed structures. I'm a believer in improvisation at work and at play.

What I'm describing here is a way of bringing healthy change into a company and making it part and parcel of the firm's culture. As "change movements" go, this is a sophisticated one. Innovation is becoming a permanent feature—not a management fad—in successful companies. There must be a state of perpetual innovation for all employees, from the CEO on down. The concept of 24/7 innovation differs from earlier change movements (such as business process reengineering, total quality management, and just-in-time inventory management) in several important respects:

1. It is strategic. Innovation is targeted at the critical parts of the business that differentiate it from its competitors.

2. It is pervasive. The idea of innovation has to permeate every aspect of an organization, from its structure to its management. The quest for better ways of doing things has to become part of the corporate psyche.

3. It is holistic, acknowledging the "oneness" of things—the interdependence of all aspects of the business.

4. It is focused on creating value. We are not talking about cost cutting and streamlining without regard for the impact they have on customers and other stakeholders. We are talking about focusing on delivering value to stakeholders in general, and to customers in particular.

5. It emphasizes governance. I do not mean supervision or management. I'm referring to the leadership of a business that sets the standard for other companies to follow.

6. It uses technology as an enabler, rather than an answer. In the past, companies often chose their technological solutions and then found ways of designing the business around them. Although technology can and should inspire new business models, in innovative organizations, technology is the tool of business requirements, not the other way around.

7. It recognizes the critical role of people. Innovation is carried out by people, for people. Success comes from an uncompromising commitment to an organization's people. People are clearly the vital link at every level of the business.

SURVIVAL OF THE FITTEST

One way of stimulating innovation is to force internal competition. A simple Darwinian approach can be effective—only the ideas or products that are most successful survive. Those that are less successful may be changed, cannibalized, or jettisoned altogether. Procter & Gamble has used this approach for many years. They allowed products from different divisions to go head to head against one another, creating healthy competition and avoiding complacency. Likewise, companies use this survival of the fittest model to stimulate innovation.

Prior to being acquired by RWE AG in 2000, VEW Energie AG, a Germany-based utility, had sales revenue of approximately $2.5 billion, 5300 employees, and 850,000 customers. VEW recently restructured the business within its Networking unit, which is responsible for transmission and distribution. When they redesigned the business capabilities, they restructured them in a very innovative way. Instead of putting maintenance, switching, construction, and operation together, they chose to place service, maintenance, and construction into one unit. Switching and operations (including inspections) were put in another unit. This created a company within a company with the required infrastructure to reach a competitive position. Since other companies offer maintenance and related services, this unit could, in the future, be constantly compared to outside competition on price and quality. The head of the internal service provider unit or, later, the asset manager will be free to handle the service capability internally or go outside. This keeps the internal unit on their toes as they are no longer necessarily the sole source. And the internal service provider should be able—in the future—to offer competitive products on the external market.

Another company, Invensys, a global electronics and engineering firm, also takes a Darwinian view of business, although not to an extreme. In a recent Accenture study of 32 companies in the electronics and engineering industry, Invensys was identified as the leader in the area of portfolio management. They have been able to reconfigure their portfolio to focus on smart products via selective purchases of automation and of technology businesses. They were also identified as leaders in the area of global diversity, with over 50 percent of their business coming from sales outside of their home region. One of the ways this is achieved is by allowing only the strongest, most profitable, highest-growth areas of business to dominate; those that are withering on the vine are lopped off. Invensys acquires and disposes of new operations as needed, with one caveat. Before jettisoning the poor performers, the company does provide support in the form of quality and lean enterprise techniques, such as Six Sigma, a statistical approach to minimizing errors developed by Motorola, to help them improve. Only when such tightening of operations fails to bring the business around is the final decision made to divest. There is more on the Invensys story in Chapter 2 and Appendix A.

FREE MARKETS AND KOCH INDUSTRIES

Another company that lives and breathes free market philosophies is Koch Industries. Koch (pronounced "coke") is one of the most interesting companies I have come across in my career as a consultant. It is indeed the real thing—a customer-focused innovative organization that believes deeply in the tenets of the free market.

The company is privately owned and, with a $40 billion annual turnover, is the second largest privately held company in the United States. If Koch Industries were public, it would rank twenty-first in the Fortune 500.

Koch Industries is a conglomerate with a wide range of interests. But what is interesting is not so much *what* the company does as it is the original way the company goes about it, which is governed by a management philosophy that Koch calls market-based management (MBM). Market-based management provides employees with both an intellectual framework for interpreting the world and a system with which to put the company's ideas and strategies into action.

Market-based management is the brainchild of Charles Koch, who developed it in conjunction with professors from George Mason University. Charles, the company's chairman and CEO, says he picked up a book in 1962 about the Austrian school of economics and has never looked back. The school, which included such influential economists as Friedrich Hayek, preached the benefits of free markets and described free economies as systems of spontaneous, unplanned order. That struck a chord with Charles, and he spent the next two years "almost like a hermit, surrounded by books."

Out of his seclusion grew the idea of MBM (although old-timers insist that the firm was practicing MBM long before Charles put a name to it). It started with a realization that, as Hayek claimed, if central control was a "fatal conceit" in an economy, then it was also a fatal conceit in a firm. Charles chipped away at the command-and-control style of structure that existed in his family's business, and in its place he asked employees to run their businesses as if they owned them. He is constantly urging employees to adopt innovative ways of thinking and to abandon the command-and-control attitudes that almost inevitably have been drilled into them by their schools and/or their previous employers.

This developed into both a philosophy (encapsulated by the idea that the free market is an information system whose power in society can be drawn inside a company) and a system. The system is based on giving employees a set of rights, responsibilities, and rewards which will best enable them to reach their potential and which will continually revolutionize the way value is created for their customers.

Today, Koch Industries consists of a network of employee-entrepreneurs who work within a framework of appropriate incentives (appropriate to each individual, that is) and decision-making powers. Anyone brought in specially to do a job within the group is immediately given the authority to spend money and to move people when and where he or she chooses.

Charles Koch believes that a few individuals at the top cannot possibly plan and coordinate all a firm's activities, nor can they have all the knowledge necessary to run a thriving business. Market-based management is his alternative, a system with six key elements:

1. *The Mission.* What an organization must do in order to be successful. At the core of this is the desire to provide value to the customer.

2. *Values and Culture.* The guidelines and norms that influence the actions of all the firm's employees. Central to this is the idea that employees think of themselves as owners of their part of the business.

3. *Roles and Responsibilities.* The decentralization of decision making as far as possible, based on the best local knowledge and information. With the right to make decisions comes a well-defined responsibility: the responsibility to admit that you're wrong when you are.

4. *Compensation and Motivation.* Motivating employees to use their personal knowledge and energy in order to improve products, services, and (ultimately) results.

5. *Knowledge Sharing.* Generating and using knowledge from all the organization's employees. Pervasive knowledge sharing helps managers do the best possible job of identifying opportunities, solving problems, and making decisions.

6. *Internal Markets.* Bringing the price system of the free market inside the organization. This is done by applying internally the prices and services that employees actually use in their daily work. Koch allows any two units within the organization to account for an internal transaction at the prices they would seek in the open market, even if these prices differ. This of course is done in conformance with generally accepted accounting procedures (GAAP). This creates internal accounting problems, but these are ironed out at the center. The important point is that it ensures that units are rewarded appropriately for cooperating with each other. The company reckons that up to 50 percent of its profit comes from such initiatives.

How does this work in practice? One way it was used was to challenge assumptions and change the rules of the game within the company's trucking unit. Faced with disappointing performance from this unit, Koch's Canadian oil business implemented MBM principles to realign incentives among its truckers. The status quo was for truckers to use whatever company truck they had been assigned for their deliveries. Reasoning that people take better care of what they own, Koch offered the truckers the financing to buy their own rigs. The truckers had the opportunity to make more money this way, along with the incentive to do preventive maintenance, to take better care in treacherous driving conditions, and to make all of their deliveries promptly and safely. Moving from company-owned trucks to employee-owned trucks led to dramatic increases in efficiency, on-time deliveries, and profits. This is one of many examples of innovation at Koch Industries that are scattered throughout this book.

How does Koch, a privately held organization, motivate its employees in this age of stock options where companies in the "new economy" live or die by their ability to lure the best and the brightest with the carrot of equity? Koch Industries certainly seems to be at a disadvantage. They have a limited ability (or desire) to lure people with options. Only Charles Koch, his brother David, and a Houston investor, E. Pierce Marshall, own any voting shares. A small number of employees are offered rights to buy nonvoting shares. But for the most part, Koch relies on cash as a reward.

Top executives have been known to receive million-dollar bonuses, but most incentives are more modest affairs. A couple of years ago, the company budgeted $30 million for expansion of a pipeline it owned in Minnesota. A team of company employees then decided to try and do the job themselves for less. Within a couple of months they had increased the pipeline's capacity by 15 percent and spent just over $1 million. Koch immediately gave them all a check averaging 15 percent of their annual salary.

While Koch may be unwilling to use the full panoply of the equity markets in its MBM system, Charles Koch himself says, "The power of using the market system as a model for management systems has been only partially tapped. I believe there are tremendous opportunities to develop and apply market-based management." On the evidence of Koch Industries, MBM is a fertile source of innovation.

THE MIGRATION TO 24/7 INNOVATION
In companies still grappling with organizational issues, it's managing the interdependencies that will be the key. Any advantage to be gained from ever-more-sophisticated technology in the process boxes is largely ephemeral. It vanishes on a time scale that is getting shorter and shorter because such improvements become rapidly available to competitors. As my colleague Paul Nunes puts it, "Process-execution advantages diminish over time. In contrast, the relational assets inside an organization are harder to copy and thus provide the greater competitive advantage."

Much has been written about the woes associated with functionally driven, siloed organizations that are saddled with hand-offs, internal rivalries, delays, quality problems, and lack of ownership. In these functionally bound organizations, functions naturally drive the business. There is very little that links the silos together, and there is usually minimal focus on customers and other stakeholders. Instead, efforts are internally focused and, often, on only one piece of the business.

In our daily lives all of us bump up against business practices that have not made the leap out of their stovepipes. For example, we're all familiar with the credit card company that continues to send us sales literature for months after we've signed up for one of its cards. If only the sales department in the organization would inform marketing that we're hooked, it could stop casting its flies before us and save considerable cash by eliminating wasteful and annoying mail shots.

Organizations move through a series of stages as they work their way toward an alliance-based network (See Figure 1-1). To be sure, there is a migration under way. Over the last half dozen years many companies have begun to move toward a more process-focused orientation. The first step in this evolution is to become process-*sensitive*. At this stage, processes serve as a kind of veneer; they are acknowledged, but functions still dominate. This is a good first step, but rarely are massive benefits achieved. And, unless there is a strong commitment to moving forward, gains made at this stage tend to be unsustainable. So companies often push toward a more process-*driven* organization. Processes become the primary driver of the business; functions continue to exist, but in a subordinate role. Conventional wisdom says that the ultimate step in the transformation is to be process-*dominated*. Here, processes are the business. Functions are often reconstituted as centers of excellence, where the emphasis is on skills building around functional disciplines.

Although many consider process domination the final destination for an organization, it must be remembered that processes are only one component of what makes a business successful. Technology, applications, information, organization, skills, and culture are just a few of the other critical components. Rethinking processes without an integrated view of how these other components fit together leads to suboptimization and further fragmentation. The result would be just another kind of a box focus (e.g., "process," "technology") whereas the lines between the boxes (e.g., how technology enables or inspires the processes) are the real differentiators. Components cannot be considered in isolation. For example, redesigning a process without considering how e-commerce can enable or even drive new business models would be a missed opportunity. I am reminded of projects where there was a tech team, a process team, an application team, an e-commerce team, and a change management team, all working away in

FIGURE 1-1. Organization models: From a functionally bound to an alliance-based network.

Alliance-Based Network

Service Delivery

Customer Relationship

Product Development

Noncore Capabilities
assigned to alliance partners

Alliance partners

Capability-Based Network

Service Delivery

Customer Relationship

Product Development

Processes dissolved
by Capabilities

Process-Dominated

Service Delivery

Customer Relationship

Product Development

Processes are the business

Process-Driven

Service Delivery

Customer Relationship

Product Development

Processes drive the business

Process-Sensitive

Finance

Manufacturing

Marketing

Processes are acknowledged,
but functions dominate

Functionally Bound

Finance

Manufacturing

Marketing

Functions drive the business

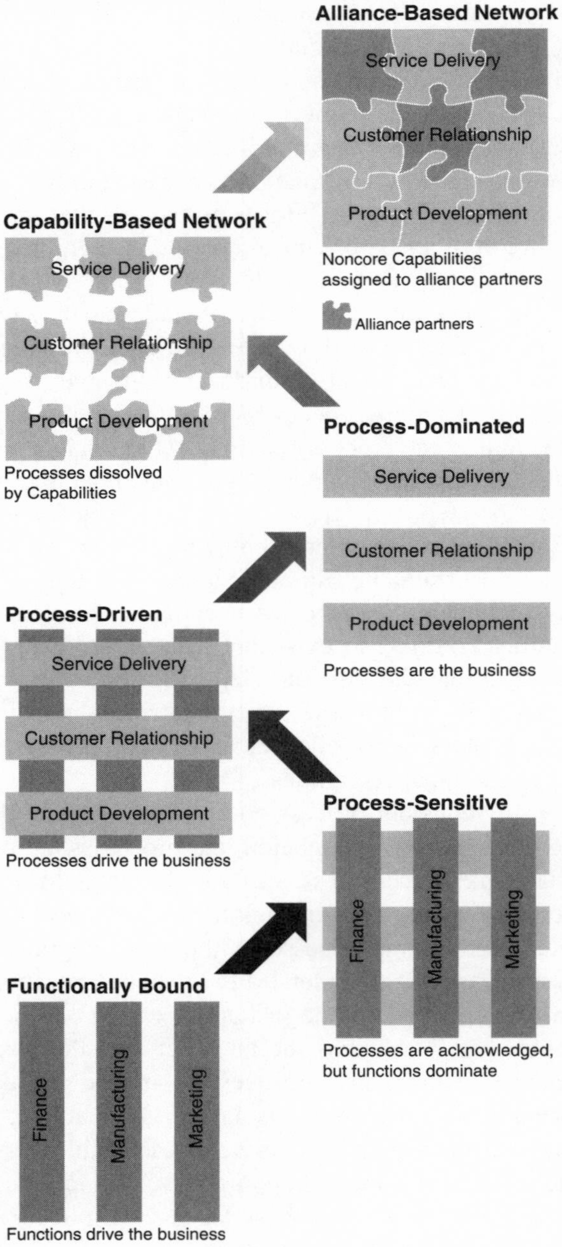

semi-isolation with very little to glue them together. The problem with such models is that application decisions are often made independent of the needs of the process. The e-commerce team is likely to be off on its own developing technological solutions without understanding how they fit in to the overall business requirements. One day senior management wakes up and finds that each team has developed great ideas that don't fit together.

THE CONCEPT OF CAPABILITIES

The challenges of integration raised the need for a new model that goes beyond a company's processes, a model that takes a holistic view of a business, integrating all of the critical components. This requirement evolved into the concept of a *Capability*. Capabilities enable an organization to perform optimally in activities that typically require processes, people, and technology. Capabilities derive from an explicit strategy, and they deliver measurable results.

Companies have many Capabilities. Some are focused on production, distribution, or sales, and some are support-oriented and focused on finance, human resources, or information technology (IT). Sometimes they are within a particular process and sometimes they span processes. And they almost always span departments or functions.

All Capabilities are comprised of five components, each of which is analyzed in detail in subsequent chapters. (See Figure 1-2.)

FIGURE 1-2. The components of a Capability.

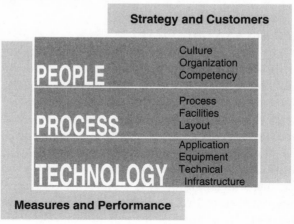

- *Strategy and customers* (e.g., differentiators, financial drivers, points of contact)

- *Measures and performance* (e.g., financial measures, customer measures, operational measures)

- *Process* (e.g., how work is performed, where work is performed)

- *People* (e.g., accountabilities, skills, behaviors, jobs, roles, incentives)

- *Technology* (e.g., applications, information, hardware, networks, and technical infrastructure)

It is the combination and interrelation of the components of a Capability that make it a critical concept. No one piece can be designed or executed in isolation. And for this reason, it is imperative that companies go beyond process management and move toward Capability-oriented management.

A key component of Capability thinking is to consider sourcing strategies for each Capability. As I tell clients: "Do what you need to do world class and find others to do everything else." Companies must focus on the Capabilities that distinguish them in the marketplace, and find alliance partners for other less critical ones. I discuss the concept of targeting high-value Capabilities in Chapter 7.

As companies focus on Capabilities and address sourcing strategies and alliances, the ultimate destination for many will be as alliance-based networks. An *alliance-based* organization is a global company with a mix of owned and allied Capabilities. Capabilities are arrayed in such a way that results can be measured, managed, and integrated. Related and dependent activities must be kept in alignment. All of this needs to be overlaid with a single leadership and culture and linked via a common IT platform.

INNOVATION AS A CAPABILITY
This is a book on innovation. And yes, innovation is very much a Capability in its own right. For an organization to be innovative, all aspects of a Capability must be considered and must be well honed. And as the level of sophistication in the innovation Capability increases, so does the value the organization reaps. (See Figure 1-3.) Most people are at the "innovation as an event" level. They have brainstorming sessions or hold contests to generate new ideas. If the idea is a good one, there is some value added to the organization. In some cases, the idea may even lead to tremendous value (such as 3M's invention of Post-it Notes). However, there is generally a huge amount of transformation between the idea generated in an event and its realization. At a more sophisticated level, innovation is more than an

event and becomes part of a process. That is, the organization has a structure in place to define problems, generate and evaluate ideas, and develop action plans to implement those ideas. The result is a realistic, deliverable solution based on an organizational problem. However, the problem with both of these is that innovation is reactionary and discrete. It only occurs when someone decides it is time to innovate. Innovation as a Capability, however, creates exponential value. In the innovation-as-Capability world, people innovate not only to solve the problems that are presented to them, but in everything they do. They continuously or even radically improve their products, processes, and organization.

Innovation as a Capability is comprised of the five components that make up all Capabilities:

Strategy and Customers. A strategy is needed to decide when, where, and how innovation will be used within the organization. Some companies use innovation when in crisis mode only. "We have a major customer who is threatening to leave us if we cannot get him his shipment today. What are we going to do?" Of course this level of reactive innovation does little to differentiate a company from the competition, and just delays the sinking of the ship. Innovation must be pervasive and perpetual: everyone, everywhere, all of the time. Innovation must be seen as the key currency within the company.

Measures and Performance. Innovation, as with any Capability, needs to be measurable. But what is being measured? Should innovation be measured in a negative way, such as scapegoating for failure to solve a complex problem? Or should innovation be a core measure, one which determines career progression and compensation for everyone in the company? What kind of measures are used? Are they focused on business outcomes and results?

FIGURE 1-3.   Levels of innovation.

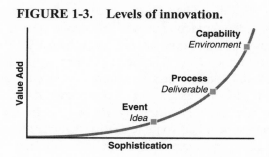

Process (and Infrastructure). Is innovation random and subject to divine intervention, or is there a standard model used for targeting, generating, and selecting innovative ideas? Is divergent thinking encouraged before converging on best ideas? Is the physical environment stale, businesslike, and siloed, or is it conducive to innovative thinking and collaboration?

People. Is the culture one of "praying that it will work," or is it one that values innovation and deems it necessary for success? Is innovation viewed skeptically as "phony-creative," or is innovation done without thinking about it? Is innovation led by the "last one to step back," or is everyone accountable? Are innovation skills regarded as being the property of a select few who show curiosity, or are innovation skills valued above all others within the organization?

Technology. Are groupware tools used to help enable collaboration among employees, customers, and suppliers? Are decisions made based on gut feel, or are they supported by real data? Are ideas lost in the ether of the organization, or are they maintained in idea banks to facilitate the capture and dissemination of innovative thinking?

The chart in Appendix B, "Innovation Capability Maturity," can be used as a simple diagnostic tool to help an organization assess where it is today in innovation. Of course not all companies have the capacity to become innovative immediately, but the chart can help set targets and define a path forward. Don't assume, however, that for all companies being more sophisticated is always better. Many companies can do very well, depending on size and complexity, with low-tech, simple solutions. Small start-ups survive very well without PowerPoint and complex collaboration tools. They rely on white boards, flip-charts, e-mail, and lots of personal encounters. Even larger companies can benefit from simple approaches.

Innovation does not exist only to create products. The great 3M, the Minneapolis-based manufacturer, invariably comes near the top of any list of America's most admired companies. Yet in the early 1990s, when 3M's performance was a role model for much of corporate America, senior managers were prepared to admit that the company needed to set out on a systematic search for its own excellence. It had, they felt, taken its eye off its customers and their needs. Traditionally, 3M had emphasized product innovation. But management had come to realize that excellent products alone were not enough. "If you were overwhelmingly differentiated," said one of the company's senior executives, "sometimes in the past you could get away with sloppiness in other areas. But not anymore." The new environment forced 3M to get creative in examining every link in its supply chain—from procurement to delivery to the consumer's needs.[3]

Innovation is a must, because employees aren't computers and (to the great frustration of some) the environment in which companies operate is highly unpredictable. Customers are demanding and perplexingly fickle, and they want us to do things that our detailed work-flow binders can't help us with. How, then, can we satisfy them? We must look elsewhere. That is why jazz is the perfect metaphor for business activity. And I am not the only one who has been struck by the appropriateness of the jazz metaphor in the context of business innovation. In 1996, John Kao wrote *Jamming*, which used jazz as a theme for creativity. And in *The Social Life of Information*, the authors, John Seely Brown, director of Xerox's Palo Alto Research Center (PARC), and Paul Duguid describe some work done by two Xerox technicians trying to repair a client's machine. To paraphrase the authors: "The afternoon resembled a series of alternating improvisational jazz solos, as each took over the lead, ran with it for a little while, then handed it off to his partner, all against the bass-line continuo of the rumbling machine, until it finally all came together."[4] That is the way the two technicians found a solution to their client's problem, a solution they would never have found by simply following the book.

But for me, jazz is more than just creativity. It is bringing a company together in such a way that there is coordinated action throughout. Just as with jazz, this requires simple structures that enable innovation to take place in a harmonized and collaborative fashion. These simple structures are process's role in fostering innovation. They provide the framework for freedom inside the structure.

What the jazz musician adds of his own accord is not pulled out of thin air. It is based on fundamental rules about chord progression and chord structures. Likewise, what the business invents in order to improve any given Capability has to be founded on certain basic ground rules. The players in a business have to be able to innovative at any minute of the day while literally "on their feet." Innovation is crucial to the pursuit of business excellence. It is as important as improvisation is to jazz.

At a large conference in France, I once provided a physical demonstration of the analogy between jazz improvisation and business innovation. After discussing ways to stay loose in business, I called a small group of jazz musicians from backstage where they had been awaiting their cue. I had commissioned them for this very short gig but had never played with them or even met them. I strapped on my tenor sax and said only this to the band: "Twelve-bar B-flat blues." We took off into the unknown and produced a terrific 15 minutes of pure musical invention. I think my audience got the message. Conversely, had I wanted to demonstrate a more traditional process orientation, I would have reached for my bassoon and we would have played something classical, not deviating one note or one beat from the score.

But hold it right there, some might say. Does that mean letting employees make up things—do something that is not in the policy manuals and procedures? My goodness! Can we risk it? And the answer has to be, "Yes of course we can." Customers won't hang around these days while companies work through their own internal procedures. They demand choice, and can go elsewhere in ways they were never able to in the past.

Customers have more consumer power than ever before for three reasons, all largely, but not solely, driven by e-commerce. First, there is greater competition due to reduced barriers to entry. Second, the cost and effort of switching from one company to another have been greatly reduced. And third, customers have more knowledge than ever before because the Internet has made information on prices, ratings, and alternative products widely available.

Employees have to be trusted to search intelligently for improvements on their own initiative. But they do need guidance, training, and the tools to implement whatever solutions they come up with. It's not a straight choice between imposing rigid structures on employees and allowing them total freedom. It's a matter of finding the right balance.

RADICAL VERSUS INCREMENTAL INNOVATION

If companies are counting on innovation to add value, what sort of innovation should it be? The sort that completely reshapes a company, or the sort that leads to more modest increases in efficiency? Should it be incremental or radical? I would not suggest that radical innovation by itself is best or even sufficient. To me, the ideal combination is small innovations, applied at the right time, on top of radical innovation of the operating model.

The distinction mirrors the difference between "research" and "development." In the traditional concept of pure research, scientists and engineers search in isolated laboratories for dramatic discoveries that will take the progress of their own organization (and, they hope, also of society) a distinct step forward. On another patch, developers are looking to progress by means of a series of tiny steps, making small improvements in something that already exists—be it a product or a process. These small innovative developments, when combined, have the power to make a big difference.

Incremental innovation takes something that is already there and makes it better. The design of cars provides a good example. Cars are usually marketed as new models when they are in fact no more than a previous model with a few new features and a slightly different look. Or, in the business travel market, an incremental innovation might be the shift of business from a retail outlet to the Internet. A radical innovation in that same market, however, would involve looking at the overall picture and the way business travel is changing. The radical innovator might see the threat to business travel that could come from desktop-based video conferencing, and might then develop a very different business strategy, one that includes making a major investment in a video-conferencing product. Radical innovation requires no less than a redefinition of the organization's business model, its cost structure, and its markets.

When combined, radical and incremental innovation will enable a company to change its operating model and sustain a competitive advantage over time. Often, this requires no less than continually reinventing the company. My colleagues and I said for many years that the only path to sustainable success is made by changing the rules of the game in order to either create new markets or transform existing markets. We used Figure 1-4 to illustrate this point. We also said that value is in the "margins." But we had only anecdotal evidence to support this statement. Then, in 1997, Gary Hamel, visiting professor of strategy at the London Business School, provided quantitative research to support this hypothesis. He found that between 1986 and 1996 there were only 17 companies out of the Fortune 1000 that saw their shareholder return grow at an annual average rate of 30 percent or more.[5] Their secret? As we could have predicted, 16 of them had

FIGURE 1-4.   Creating or transforming markets for success.

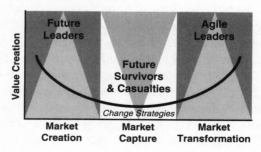

either created new markets or transformed existing ones. The seventeenth reengineered its way to spectacular shareholder value. Hamel predicts that "the ability to reinvent the basis of competition within existing industries and to invent entirely new industries…will be the next fundamental competitive advantage for companies around the world." This requires radical and incremental innovation every day, everywhere, by everyone.

And the key word in that last sentence is "everyone." It is a myth that innovation is something best left exclusively to one type of person, the "creative type." Everyone can be innovative—in different ways and under different circumstances. The "people" element will be discussed in Chapter 3.

COORDINATION WITH CUSTOMERS

A key premise of this book is that innovation requires coordination throughout the business. Once the lines that connect the parts of the business together have been clearly delineated, managers and employees are free to improvise within those constraints. One key line that needs to be considered is the relationship between the business and its customers. To say this is a critical path is to restate the obvious, yet neglect of this relationship is all too common, even in some of the most experienced international companies. The values and needs of the customer must be thoroughly understood and incorporated into the business design. Unfortunately, new technology can be a curse, making a process worse rather than better and locking the company into a way of doing business that will be hard to change. Finally, customer feedback and measurement go hand in hand with the evolutionary nature of this relationship.

Consider this simple story about the man who decided to try the pioneering, much-trumpeted online service of a major supermarket chain. He had invited 10 family members for lunch on Christmas Day, including his sister who was flying in from more than a thousand miles away. For the occasion he ordered almost $500 worth of food and drink, including a turkey, and paid for it with his credit card. From the options given to him by the supermarket Web site he chose to have his goods delivered on the morning of December 23.

The morning came and went, but his food did not arrive. So he called the supermarket, only to be told that their last pre-Christmas delivery day was December 22. He explained that the company's Web site had offered him December 23. "Well it shouldn't have," was the abrupt reply.

After further lengthy phone calls, the supermarket firmly told him that it would not be delivering his order. Furious, he went to the supermarket's main rival, and lugged back on foot (he did not own a car) the necessary victuals for the meal. As bad luck would have it, by the time he got to the other supermarket, they had no defrosted turkeys left.

The hapless customer e-mailed his story back to the original supermarket, but after two months, he had still not received a reply. It is logical to assume that the supermarket's failure to listen to the feedback from this customer was not an isolated case. But even if it was, the company's reaction could prove to be an expensive mistake, for the customer told his story to a national newspaper.[6] Now, not only will the customer and his family be sure to shop elsewhere, but many of the newspaper's readers are likely to think twice about using that online service.

All that damage could have been avoided if the employee to whom the customer complained had been flexible enough to break the rules. Even if the general manager himself had to collect the order and send it round in his chauffeur-driven car, the company would have been better off.

An innovative business is not one that installs new computers and online solutions, and then ignores the people, or just trains people how to use computers and information systems. Quite the contrary. An innovative business has everything to do with people and is concerned with technology mainly as a means to the end of making people more valuable. Contrary to the hype in today's new economy, the technology is not the differentiator. Of course, you need technology, but it's how you use it that really counts.

It is clear by now that we are not talking about business in a stable state. No firm is in a position to stop thinking about how to make improvements, not 3M, not the industrial portfolio groupings, not the big supermarket chains. The volatility of markets and the wider choices that customers enjoy today make complacency tantamount to business suicide. And as attractive as technology can be, it will never provide the flexibility that people can—the people who create the products and offer them to the marketplace. In a changing business, any corrective steps must go beyond the traditional divide-and-conquer solutions of the past and tackle the key relationships within and outside the business. By designing Capabilities and freeing up the potential for innovation, businesses can evolve in a way that will confront the competition of the twenty-first century. With the proper framework installed around a culture of innovation, a company can make the most of its human capital. Conversely, failure to do so may cause a seemingly sound company to wither away.

The Blueprint

2

PROCESS-ENABLED INNOVATION

"In our business, the three kinds of lies are lies, damn lies, and benchmarks."

CHICO MARX

Sparking innovation in an organization has its spontaneous side but it is not a random activity, like lightning. Innovation should be fostered by managing the interaction of processes and encouraged through a culture of constant questioning. To provide some direction, in this chapter I will discuss a framework and offer some guidelines for poking and prodding the flab of the organization. The framework is structured around seven dimensions of potential change. At the end of such an exercise, you should emerge with new and original ideas for improving the processes and their interrelationships. Companies taking this approach are in a state of perpetual change. In many ways, this makes them competitively unassailable.

N ow that I've had a chance to discuss the world of innovation in general, it is time to dive into each of the blueprint elements one at a time. The first element I will discuss is process. As a starting point, let's get clear what I mean by *process*. It is a way of organizing a company's activities and resources that establishes cross-functional coordination throughout the firm. This kind of coordination makes often-isolated pieces of the business work smoothly together to achieve a company's goals while also allowing for and even fostering innovation. Designed well, processes create value for customers, employees, shareholders, and all other stakeholders around an enterprise.

In a recent meeting on process with clients, I asked for definitions of this much-abused word. And I got a string of uninspired answers such as "detailed work flows," "repeatability," "road maps" and other terms indicating an unbending, prescriptive approach to organizing work. This kind of thinking is the antithesis of innovation, so I steered the clients in a new direction—toward the freedom that good process can bring to an organization. Immediately the energy level perked up and we began to break free. We concluded that good processes must be capable of creating high-performance businesses and that high performance is about far more than cutting out the fat in the processes. Managers must start with far higher goals than improving efficiency. Their processes must be about delivering exceptional value, setting a new standard for performance, and even in some cases redefining the competitive environment.

In a world where competitors can so easily imitate yesterday's invention, the key differentiator, the key competitive advantage, will be the ability to innovate continuously. Today it doesn't matter so much what companies invent; they need to become the sort of organization able to invent and reinvent, to keep the innovation treadmill rolling. This is what gives leading companies their strength, their staying power, and their value. They live in a state of perpetual innovation, a kind of innovation that is not confined to R&D but takes place in every area of the company—in every process, and in the mind of every employee.

Process innovation is about generating, evaluating, and implementing creative solutions that enable the company to achieve and renew its business across the board. But such innovation does not just happen. It emerges when people ask the right sort of questions about the work they are performing and about the ways those tasks might be improved.

As I've said, business innovation, like jazz improvisation, is far from random. What's needed is the business equivalent of a score—not an elaborate one, but one that includes some simple structures that enable innovation to emerge when it is most needed. Some of my colleagues and I came up with a helpful framework for sparking innovation. We call it the *Seven Rs*, a handy mnemonic that has worked well with many clients. It consists of a series of questions that can be bundled into seven categories. Each category refers to a different dimension of process and business change.

1. *Rethink*, the first R, is concerned with the rationale and assumptions behind a company's processes. These are the "Why?" questions, such as, "Why are things done the way that they are?"

2. *Reconfigure*, the second R, is about the activities involved in the processes. Here the aim is to find new answers to the sort of questions that begin with "What?" An example of a reconfigure question is "What activities can be eliminated?"

3. *Resequence* concerns the timing and order in which work takes place. Here the innovation comes from asking "When?" questions. "When do particular tasks need to be done?" "Can tasks be reshuffled to better effect?"

4. *Relocate* looks at the location of the activities and the physical infrastructure in which they take place. It asks questions that begin with "Where?" "Where could a given activity take place so that it would need less transport between suppliers and/or customers?"

5. *Reduce* addresses the frequency (how much, how often) of particular activities. It asks, for example, "How much of the activity needs to take place, and how often?" Sometimes the creative answer to such questions involves a higher frequency, not a lower one. More can sometimes mean less—but the reverse can also be true.

6. *Reassign* is about the performers of process work, the people who carry out the tasks. It involves coming up with new answers to questions that begin with "Who?" "Who carries out a given activity?" "Could someone else possibly do it more effectively?"

7. The final R stands for *retool*, and it focuses on the technologies and competencies that enable work to be done. It looks for new answers to questions that begin with "How?"—questions such as "How can technology transform this process?" It involves inquiring, for example, into ways the Internet might be able to transform traditional processes into electronic processes, so-called e-processes.

By frequently asking these seven types of question—"Why?" "What?" "When?" "Where?" "How often?" "Who?" and "How?"—and looking for

new answers—designers and front-line workers will find themselves stim-
ulated to come up more or less continually with fresh approaches to old
processes, and occasionally with completely new ones.

In practice, a change made to one dimension of a process typically
affects several others. For example, if work is reassigned (under the sixth
R) to a new supplier, the work will probably also need to be relocated (our
fourth R) to a new geographical place—namely, the premises of the new
supplier. At the same time, the process might also be retooled (our seventh
R) with new technology in order to link the organization to the new supplier
and the supplier's systems. Of course, this is not always true. Sometimes
forcing unnatural combinations can lead to even more innovative results, as
we shall see in some of the examples below.

Working within the framework of the Seven Rs cannot guarantee creativity, but it does help challenge old ideas and generate new ones. In the
first instance, the key to successful innovation is the quantity of ideas generated, not the quality. Or at least this holds true in situations where you
have time to evaluate and select alternatives. There is rarely one clear-cut
way of improving things, be it a commercial process, a household chore, or
a musical score.

So it is better to think "and" rather than "or," and avoid jumping to con-
clusions too quickly. The elements of one idea can often be combined creatively with elements from another. Good ideas are seldom mutually
exclusive. It is also helpful to separate the generation of ideas from their
evaluation. Sometimes the most outlandish idea turns out to be the right
one. A noted example is the famous 1980s' advertisement in the United
States featuring the California Dancing Raisins singing "I Heard It through
the Grapevine." This was generated out of an exercise in which participants
were asked to describe the "worst" idea they could come up with. This was
it, and it turned out to be a hit. Another is the Heineken beer catch phrase:
"It reaches parts that other beers can't reach." This slogan was very nearly
discarded at a meeting with the company's advertising agency. After much
wrangling, they decided to give it a try. It caught on, especially in Europe,
and now is part of the language in Britain.

A technique we often use is called *morphological analysis*, a fancy-
sounding name for a simple technique: select some or all of the Seven Rs
and come up with various answers to each that might solve your problem,
then randomly mix and match various combinations. For example, if we
were to redesign supermarket checkout, we might look at Reassign, Relocate, and Resequence—the typical combination for checkout to be done by
the cashier, at the cash register, after all of the purchases are made. Let's try

a different combination. What if the customers did the scanning at their shopping carts as they selected items? In fact, Safeway in London is experimenting with a checkout system in which customers do scan in prices as they select items off the shelves and then pay for their purchases by credit card. Random audits help prevent theft or miscounting. Some of the most creative ideas come from the most unnatural combinations. My research group at Accenture developed what we call the Morph-O-Magic Slot Machine, which is fun to use and facilitates morphological analysis. (See Figure 2-1.) You simply enter in different parameters (e.g., in the shopping example above, Reassign may include customers, checkout clerks, the butcher, the security guard, or the cleaning lady) for a subset of the Seven Rs, pull the handle, and see what random combination comes up. Many combinations do end up being losers. But when you get a winner, the payoff can be huge. And using this approach is a great way to uncover implicit assumptions about a business. When you generate combinations that are different from what has been done in the past, people will almost surely say, "Hey, we can't do that because…" You then begin to uncover the underlying assumptions. This is where real innovation can emerge. You get the idea. So go wild and try lots of interesting combinations.

FIGURE 2-1.   Morph-O-Magic Slot Machine.

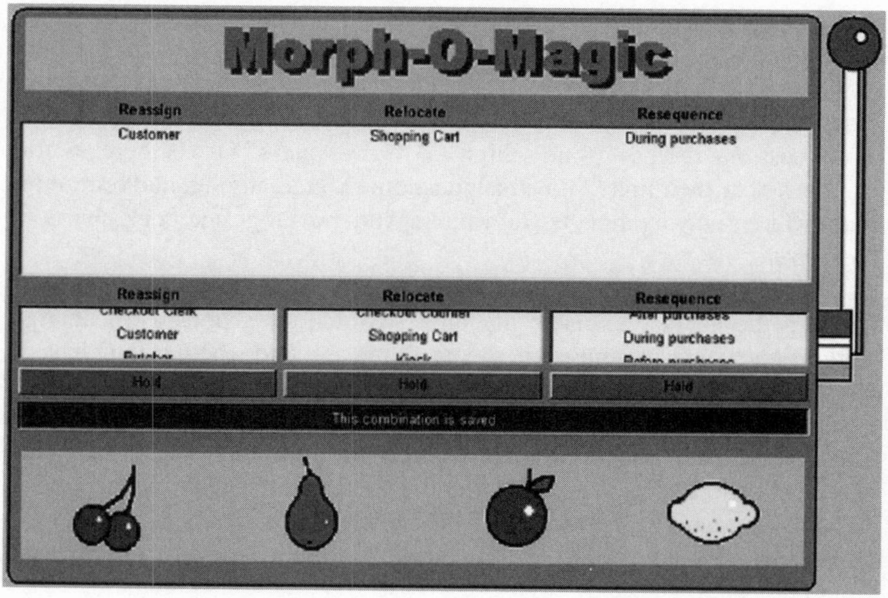

But don't fall into the "more complex is more innovative" trap. Usually the opposite is true. In the movie *Roxanne*, Steve Martin heads up a volunteer fire department, and at one point a cat gets stuck in a tree.[1] The firemen try to get it down with harnesses, ladders, ropes, and other "technologies." They fail miserably (and hilariously). Martin then comes around with a can of tuna fish, which when opened persuades the cat to hurry down for its meal. Simplicity itself.

The examples in this chapter range from well known to obscure, tried-and-true to new, and incremental to radical. But regardless, I think they are all good ideas to consider for redesigning your processes. They are only the tip of the iceberg of what a company can do to be innovative. But they are a start. The following sections, which look at each of the Seven Rs in greater detail, should be read in conjunction with the chart in Appendix C, "Applying the Seven Rs." These summarize the business circumstances in which it is most appropriate to ask particular questions. It's helpful to scan this list early on in an improvement effort in order to find the statements that most closely fit your organization's situation.

R1: RETHINK

Throughout this book, I refer to the fact that we are architects of companies and industries. An architect is not a "reengineer." To illustrate this point, I often ask clients what is the difference between an optimist, a pessimist, a reengineering consultant, and an architect? The optimist looks at a half-filled glass of water and sees it as half full. The pessimist looks at the same glass and sees it as half empty. The reengineering consultant sees too much glass. Cut off the top. Downsize. An architect looks at the same glass and asks questions such as "Who's thirsty?" "Why water?" Or "Is there another way to satisfy the thirst?" It is this questioning, challenging, and rethinking that differentiates architects from those who rearrange the deck chairs on the *Titanic*.

The key is to challenge the status quo and bring underlying assumptions to the surface. This is the only way to drive significant change. Rethinking asks why things are the way they are, and whether they have to be that way. Rethinking is especially critical in today's age of rapid change. It is no longer good enough to get really superb at what you do. As soon as you rest on your laurels, someone else will come along and copy your source of differentiation and potentially take the lead. CDNOW.com understands this point only too well. This company was the leader in online CD sales until six weeks after Amazon.com decided it wanted to branch out from books into CDs.

Rethinking is a bit different than the other Rs because challenging an assumption does not necessarily lead to a solution. With the other Rs, the improvement lies in the answers to the questions. With rethinking, that is not the case. It does, however, lead to more creative thinking because once the constraints of the past have been lifted, the imagination can flow in all sorts of new directions. Then the other six Rs can be used to generate new process designs that address the assumptions brought to the surface by consideration of the results of the Rethink step. In addition, asking questions associated with the other six Rs is sure to uncover additional assumptions. The action is a circular one: each step feeds into the next one, which in turn feeds off the previous steps.

The first thing to be sure of when rethinking a process is that you are solving the root cause of the problem (assuming that it is a problem you are solving). The key is to avoid wasting time chasing symptoms. A symptom, such as poor sales or high inventory, for example, has many potential causes, just as a sore throat can indicate a number of different diseases.

Take the case of an airline that had the sort of high costs associated with carrying an excessively large inventory of spare parts. The initial assumption might have been that the airline should make improvements in its inventory-management processes. But in this case the real problem was that the airline was using its own planes to move the parts around. It was looking at this as a way of obtaining free transportation and cutting logistics costs. In practice, however, the airline soon found that its spare parts were being left on the tarmac because, as soon as there was revenue-producing freight to be carried, the freight got priority. To compensate for these self-imposed delays in delivering parts, the airline was compelled to hold excess inventory. The best solution to this company's problem lay not in streamlining its warehouse operations, but in improving the way parts were transported.

Next, a company must see if things are being done a certain way because that's just the way things have always been done. Once the reasons for doing things in a certain way have been articulated, they can be probed and challenged. And then they can either be discarded or accepted as unavoidable constraints on the organization's efforts to innovate. Quite often, the reasons are no longer very compelling. In the 1960s, Britain's considerable engineering industry was almost run into the ground because it was managed by people who were focused on production, not profit. "If anybody wanted us to make something that hadn't been made before," said Sir Jack Scamp, former director of GEC, "we regarded it as a compliment. If anybody asked whether it was going to be worthwhile in terms of profit, the reply would have been, 'Well, somebody has to do it.'" Subsequently, there was a major shift toward shareholder value. And GEC has managed to transform itself into the high-tech company Marconi.

Sometimes the most powerful barriers to changing the way work is done are invisible: hidden assumptions about the way work is being done. They are so ingrained in organizations that the people who work there are no longer aware of them—if they ever were. But it is important to uncover these rules and assumptions and to analyze whether they can be broken. And if they can be broken, the next step is to look at the new possibilities that might be opened up by doing so.

Process Pipelining

One assumption that is particularly commonplace and that often gets in the way of the ability to see alternative ways of doing things is the one-size-fits-all assumption. This is the idea that for efficiency's sake, or some similar reason, a process has to be carried out in exactly the same way every time that it is performed. This was the problem at a leading life insurance company, an organization that manages 2.5 million policies. The company was aware that its processes needed improvement. Its handling of claims was slow and its processing costs were very high. At first, the company thought it needed to do something radical, to abandon its current way of doing things completely and start afresh. But when it looked at the problem more closely, it found that the claims-handling process itself wasn't that bad; the one-size-fits-all design of the system was creating the inefficiencies. Every claim was being put through the same rigorous procedures. The company's mistake had been to design a single process so that it could accommodate the most complicated cases.

Management decided to abandon the underlying assumption that all claims were equal (or, at least, that all claims had to be treated equally) and to employ a technique called *process pipelining* (see Figure 2-2). This involves scaling a process down rather than changing it altogether, and then segmenting its inputs according to their level of complexity. A simplified version of the process is used for very straightforward cases, and somewhat less simple versions are matched to cases according to degree of complexity. The full process is reserved for the most difficult and time-consuming cases.

This company has also pipelined its call centers by segmenting calls on a customer-service basis (i.e., any event that can be completed within 3 minutes) and a cost basis (i.e., the event must be simple enough to require

FIGURE 2-2.   Process pipelining.

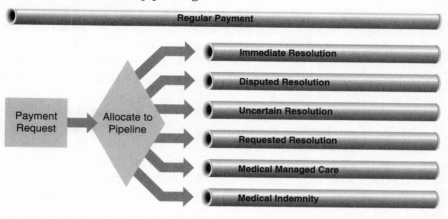

a given level of competence which in turn relates to salary). Applying these criteria allowed 60 percent of events to be performed by the cheapest resources within the organization whereas, in the past these were subject to an average response time completed by a higher-skilled individual.

In the area of new business, underwriting decisions have been analyzed and pipelined to the degree that allows some 70 percent of these to be completely automated. This allows applications to be routed electronically from the sales force straight through to the administration system. In return, this results in a significant reduction in workforce and greater customer satisfaction.

To find out if a process is suitable for pipelining, companies need to carry out an analysis of the cases that the process is designed to handle, and to relate those cases to the separate tasks that make up the process. If certain types of special cases require only a subset of all the tasks that are normally carried out, the process may indeed be suitable for pipelining.

An Ancient Legacy

Everyone knows the old expression "When you ASSUME you make an 'ASS' out of 'U' and 'ME.'" Well, here is some Net lore that helps illustrate the point.[2] The story goes that the design of one of the most advanced technologies in the world has been hampered by specifications dating back to the Roman Empire. When you look at a space shuttle sitting on the launch pad, you'll see two big booster rockets attached to the sides of the main fuel tank. These are the solid rocket boosters (SRBs) that are made at a factory in Utah. The engineers who designed the SRBs might have preferred to make them a bit wider, but the SRBs had to be shipped by train from the factory to the launch site. The railroad from the factory runs through a tunnel in the mountains. The SRBs have to fit through that tunnel. The tunnel size is (partly) determined by the rail gauge, and the U.S. standard railroad gauge is 4 feet 8.5 inches.

But why is that? Mainly because that's the way they were built in England. And the English built them this way because the first railroads were built on the same tracks as the horse-drawn tramways. The trams used that gauge because they were made from wagon parts (jigs and axles) that were designed to fit the ruts in the roads that were originally created by war chariots in Imperial Rome. And so we see that the U.S. railroad gauge is based on the specifications for Roman war chariots. So the next time you're handed a spec sheet and wonder what horse's ass came up with the numbers, you may be on the right track: the 4 feet 8.5 inch wide Roman war chariot was designed to be just wide enough to accommodate the rear ends of two war horses.

The point is that over the years companies hand down policies and practices that become standard operating procedure even though no one knows *why* they are following them. They are accepted as truth, when in fact there may be little logical reason for continuing them. Ironically, the war chariot story is itself an example of this point. The power of the Internet has allowed this tale (and other examples of Net lore) to be read by millions of people, who may believe and repeat it as fact without bothering to question its validity.

When the Rethink stage is complete, it is time for redesign. The remaining six Rs are described in varying levels of detail in the following sections. The sixth and seventh of the Rs, Reassign and Retool, have chapters dedicated to them.

R2: RECONFIGURE

The issue of whether to reconfigure a process centers on the nature of the work being done and on the question of whether all of it is really necessary. Reconfiguring is about analyzing the steps and activities that are being performed and then deciding how similar outcomes might be achieved through different means—by changing the steps, perhaps, or by eliminating some of them altogether. Reconfiguring goes to the heart of process innovation. Although it often leads to incremental changes, it can also drive radical change.

Be sure to challenge the process. Ask whether there is a way a given step could be done more cheaply. Or more quickly. Or just better. Or maybe there is a method that means you don't have to do it at all. Design everything from the customer's point of view. What attributes must the process have in order to produce the outcomes that the customer desires? Don't be constrained by what *is*, by the state of things today. Determine what really needs to be done in order to achieve the desired outcome. Innovation is all about finding new ways to deliver a desired outcome, but it does assume that the specified outcome is the correct one. Once you've made absolutely certain that the outcome you have identified is the outcome you really need, you can assume that everything else can vary.

Think out of the box; that is, try to practice the sort of lateral thinking promoted by Edward de Bono, noted author on innovative thinking. Consider starting with a *tabula rasa*, a completely clean sheet of paper. If a current process is very bad at delivering outcomes, don't just tweak it. Go back to the drawing board and think about it again from scratch. Ask, "What would be the perfect solution if we were starting to do this with an entirely new company?" Then ask, "What are we most afraid our competitors will do to us?" Then beat them to it.

Question Time

Following are a few useful questions that might help you think of ways to reconfigure a process.

Can the entire activity be eliminated?
One question that always needs to be asked is whether or not the process itself is valuable enough to justify continuing with it. How does it contribute to the overall value that the organization provides to its customers? Should it be tinkered with so that it provides more value, or should it be eliminated altogether? As Peter Drucker put it, "There is nothing more useless than to do efficiently what shouldn't be done at all."

Frequently cited examples here are in the area of procurement, where companies, most notably Ford Motor Company, have instituted a program of "evaluated receipts" where for selected suppliers and carriers, payment is rendered upon presentation of an invoice. No invoice and receipt matching is performed. Toyota took this one step further by arranging to pay its suppliers only for what it uses, not for what it receives. This means that items are tracked only once when they are used. When a car leaves the plant, Toyota knows the car has four tires, and that is when payment for the tires is issued.

Companies need to make sure that customers and profitability dictate decisions and not just policy. At one bank, for example, a policy allowing 90-day loan renewal cycles was not cost-efficient, but it was policy, so that's how they operated. They also had a policy of requiring a written change of address from customers. No one knew why it had been instituted or what good it did, but it was part of their process. Review all policies to see whether they add value for customers and stakeholders. If they do not, drop them.

An interesting example is a U.K.-based retailer that sells a variety of household goods through catalog showrooms. Most catalog showrooms have big warehouses in the back where they store the products, but this company has eliminated the distributed warehouse. Instead, it has trucks that drive around the city distributing items as they are requested. Only the most frequently ordered items are kept locally, thus reducing duplicate inventory being stored in each outlet.

How can duplication be reduced by putting quality controls at the source?
One way of improving a process is to stop problems at the source. Catching problems as early as possible avoids costly and time-consuming rework. If errors are allowed to affect customers, it creates dissatisfaction. The impact of quality problems is enormous. This is one of the reasons for growing interest in quality initiatives such as Six Sigma.

However, rigorous statistical approaches are not the only way of increasing quality. One example is Mölnlycke Health Care (MHC), one of Europe's leading manufacturers and suppliers of single-use products for surgical interventions and wound management. The products consist mainly of sterile items for use in surgery such as patient drapes, staff clothing, surgical dressings, and advanced wound care products.

Previous management was heavily influenced by the desire to be ISO9000-certified, as required by the U.S. Food and Drug Administration. The quality department would define business processes in great detail, then hand those designs to the line that was expected to execute them. And as the company prepared to reenergize the business, it planned to continue to use this methodical and detailed approach everywhere within the business. However, as MHC began to move forward, they realized that this practice was stifling innovation. "Nonbusiness" people were telling the line how to run operations.

So MHC decided to define the processes to different levels of detail. Those processes that needed ISO certification would be defined at a detailed enough level to meet those requirements. For all other processes, a less-detailed, less-prescriptive approach was used, providing only the simple structures necessary to ensure coordination. Much to everyone's satisfaction, this change released a great deal of creative energy. Quality moved from being a responsibility of the quality department to being a responsibility of every individual who executed a process.

One example was product development, which is critical to this industry. The old way, as defined in the binders of process flows, involved a chain of activities done in sequence by specified sub-groups. The new, simplified model defined product development as an activity performed by a team that has joint responsibility for the result from start to finish. Now product development no longer ends at product definition. It ends three months after the marketing companies have started selling the new products.

The development teams at MHC now have responsibility for R&D, but they also have responsibility for the factories, the development of marketing materials, and everything required for successful launch. Historically, only 15 percent of MHC's new products had been launched on time. Now nearly 70 percent launch on time.

How can intermediaries and non-value-adding work be eliminated?
An international company with a press list of 1500 publications worldwide had been spending thousands of dollars a month distributing its news through a third party. But the growth of the e-mail phenomenon suddenly made it possible to create this same distribution list on a simple desktop PC. With a few keystrokes the same objective could be accomplished at virtually no expense. The third-party service company was soon scrambling to reinvent itself.

How can best practices from other industries be borrowed and improved upon?
As I mentioned in the previous chapter, matching best practices within your industry only brings you to par. However, there is a great opportunity to "steal with pride" from other industries. Some of the more well-known examples include the case of Motorola learning delivery-management techniques from Domino's Pizza, a company

that delivers pizza in 30 minutes or less, and Xerox improving its warehouse productivity by analyzing methods employed by L.L. Bean, a United States–based catalog retailer.

Other interesting examples include a medical center that realized that patients judged their hospital experience not only on the quality of care but also on how much time, hassle, and paperwork were involved. The hospital used the Marriott hotel group to help redesign its admitting process. And there is the famous case of the airline that used the best practices of an Indianapolis 500 pit crew to help develop faster turnaround in its maintenance processes.

R3: RESEQUENCE

The third of the Seven Rs is Resequence. Here the central issue is one of timing. When is the work to be done? What are to be the sequence, the timing, and the interdependencies between one set of tasks and another? Can these be altered in ways that will improve the way the tasks are accomplished?

When activities have been performed in a particular sequence for many years, it is easy to assume that the order is immutable—that certain steps *must* be performed before others. Yet there are often far fewer such dependencies than at first meet the eye. Varying the timing and the sequence of work can be a powerful lever, not just for designing a faster process but also for designing one that allows for more customization, lower costs, and fewer errors.

There are four primary ways of resequencing activities.

1. They can be brought forward on the basis of an organization's accurate prediction of its future needs.
2. They can be postponed because the organization wants to wait until better information becomes available.
3. They can be shifted so that they are carried out in parallel with other activities.
4. They can be reshuffled to eliminate existing dependencies.

Question Time

When thinking about resequencing, there are a number of questions that can help spark off ideas for the process designer.

How can predicting future demand increase efficiency?
A process designed around a strong capability for predicting usage or demand can enable faster response times. For example, a company

can start the build process in advance of receiving orders—as in the case of fast-food restaurants that prepare burgers in advance of the lunchtime rush hour. Accurate prediction can also improve customer service by reducing the chances of running out of stock. Some companies' orders peak at year-end, when business customers are using up the year's budget and buying new equipment. In this situation, demand outstrips supply and the ability to replenish stocks. Prediction is a good way of keeping up with the orders by making more than is needed so that production can keep up with demand. Of course this can lead to obsolescence and high inventories, so this approach should be used only when necessary or when the inventory costs are low enough to justify the potential increase in service levels.

One place where predicting helped enormously involved an American hospital's admissions procedure. Before accepting a patient—and beginning to move them to the hospital—the institution formerly verified the availability of rooms, a step that took a considerable amount of time and sometimes resulted in the loss of a patient to another hospital. The organization came to realize, however, that in practice there were nearly always enough vacant beds for patients who were referred to it. As a result, the hospital changed its procedures and began to admit patients immediately upon request. It then found and prepared a room for them while they were still in transit.

Predicting to increase efficiency is a widespread practice. For example, 25,000 copies of this book are being printed on the assumption (hope) that at least that many copies will be sold. It would be impractical to print them on demand. Of course, new technologies, such as the invention of e-books, are changing that model. And speaking of technology, today's computer chips are able to "predict" what they will be asked to do next, which increases their efficiency. This is one of the ways in which Intel has been able to continue to boost processor speeds.

Can postponing an activity increase flexibility?
A process that postpones the making of key decisions until better information is available (for example, building to order rather than in anticipation of an order) can often meet customer needs more precisely. It can also reduce costs by minimizing inventory size.

This next one example, a famous one, is a powerful case of postponement at work. Benetton, the Italian clothing company that sells its garments through 6000 small boutiques in 120 countries, uses a delayed-decision technique to get around the difficult problem of rapidly changing fashion.[3] The clothes at Benetton are, for the most part, relatively similar. The distinguishing characteristic, as suggested by Benetton's tag line, the United Colors of Benetton, is in the colors. And as anyone in the fashion industry knows, predicting which color will be successful is nearly impossible. Who would have thought lime green would be popular last year? So, rather than manufacture garments from predyed yarn, Benetton makes many items of clothing in a neutral color. It then decides what colors to use according to customer demand. As it becomes clear which colors are currently popular, the company dyes items just before they are shipped to the shops. Doing this involves a considerable amount of innovation, for it is not technically easy to dye garments after they have been knitted or woven. Most manufacturers still dye the threads before putting a garment together.

As a result of Benetton's revolutionary system, the company can use electronic systems to order on short notice those garments that match their customers' rapidly changing tastes, and they can be sure to receive the garments in their shops before that taste has moved on to something else. Thus, Benetton uses this approach mainly near season's end, when the risks of prediction are highest. It still uses prediction techniques at the start of a new season when the risk of unsold stock is lower.

The delayed-decision concept is used by most businesses dealing with colors. Paint manufacturers, for example, now provide stores with pigments and tools that enable them to provide hundreds of combinations that can be mixed on demand. At cosmetic counters, you can get blush, lipstick, and eyeliner blended on the spot to meet your individual needs.

McGraw-Hill uses this concept as part of their custom publishing textbook program. Professors specify exactly what they want in their textbook, and McGraw-Hill then reconfigures existing material on the subject into a book, which it produces in runs of as few as 25—all within a week.

Key decisions about what to make, ship, order, etc., can be made at several different points in a process. In general, the later the decision is made the greater the flexibility of the outcome. Counterbalancing the benefits of procrastination, however, is the fact that making decisions earlier in a process often improves efficiency.

How can carrying out activities in parallel reduce time invested?
A process that has many activities going on in parallel—rather than in a sequence of lengthy linear tasks—compresses time to the benefit of the customer. Carrying on activities in parallel can also help to reduce errors. Complementary activities provide feedback about potential problems sooner rather than later, and more frequently.

Interdependencies between processes are important areas to examine for opportunities for improvements through resequencing. It is often assumed that one activity cannot be started before another one ends. Rarely is this the case, and when it is not true, parallel processing may be an opportunity. Consider the house-building competition described in Chapter 1. In order to build the house in 2 hours 45 minutes, the roof and walls were built in parallel with the foundation. Of course, in the case of the house, a crane—typically not used when building a house— was needed to lift the finished roof onto the new structure.

Concurrent product development is a result of parallel processing. One company's sequential product-development process used to begin when its marketing department developed an idea. The idea was then handed on to the engineering department, which designed the requirements for the new product. The engineers then passed on their specs to the tooling and manufacturing departments.

On a number of occasions, the employees responsible for tooling and manufacturing had to ask the engineers for revisions based on what could and could not be done with the manufacturing equipment that was available. The engineering department then had to go back to the marketing department to ask whether the necessary modifications were acceptable to them. And so the whole process got spun out into a seemingly endless shuffling of minor modifications backward and forward. Typically, there were several such iterations, and they inevitably slowed down the whole product-development process hugely.

Eventually, a new process was designed around a repository of shared data that allowed all of the steps to take place in parallel. A design could be reviewed simultaneously by all of the departments during the design phase itself. Suggested revisions—suggestions could be made at any time, by anybody—could then be incorporated as the design progressed. The ability to manufacture the product was thus, in a very real sense, built into the design from the very beginning. Not surprisingly, overall product-development times were reduced sharply.

How can the number of interconnections and dependencies be minimized?
With the Internet, work is no longer dependent on time or geography. New ways of operating emerge when you look at how activities can be distributed globally.

A good example of this can be found at IBM, where Java-based software is developed around the clock.[4] This was done by questioning one of the most fundamental business dependencies: the working day. When one shift of developers finished their day, they forwarded their work (via the company's network) to another location that was just beginning its working day. There, a second shift picked up the project until, at the end of their day, they forwarded it again on to another location, and so on. This freed the developers from the age-old constraints of the 9 to 5 working day.

R4: RELOCATE
In the Relocate dimension, the fourth of the Seven Rs, the focus is on the question of where work is done. The issues are location, distance, and physical infrastructure, and the overall aim is to minimize distance and maximize communication between the people involved in a process. This reduces the costs associated with travel times, hand-offs, late error detection, reworking, and quality problems.

There are several changes to bear in mind when thinking about the future location of work:

1. The definition of workplace has changed. This is part of a deep change in modern society. In the past, most work was carried out at fixed, permanent locations—usually the plant or the office of the individual's employer. But as the industrial economy continues to be replaced by the knowledge-based "weightless" economy, the primacy of fixed assets (like offices) is fading. Advances in IT have accelerated this change.

2. Organizations are becoming more "permeable." In the past, any work that took place on a company's premises was done by the company's employees only. But as organizations begin to ask where it makes most sense to do their work, these once strict boundaries are breaking down. Today's more permeable organizations often have customers, suppliers, and temporary workers all working together on their site.

3. Virtual organizations are increasingly common. If new information technology has changed anything, it has changed the capacity for

work to be done at remote locations. Large numbers of today's workers, whether they are permanent employees or temporaries, are equipped to work not just at home but also in the back of their car, from specially adapted vans, or from airport lounges. Professionals such as radiologists are able to read X rays immediately, even when they are in locations far from the hospital where the images originated. And, as a recent Accenture advertisement shows, even surgery can be done remotely.

4. New work requires new facilities. A change in the nature of work often requires a change in an organization's physical infrastructure as well. Many innovative processes today rely on teamwork for their proper execution, and teamwork requires a special type of physical facility to nurture it. It needs space that encourages fast communications and high levels of interaction, which means sharing space and sharing access to information. It implies the creation of "generic" space that can be used at any time by any member of what will inevitably be a constantly changing team. More and more offices are designed with increased team space and "hot desks" for individuals.

5. People are learning to say "no" to travel. Since almost all travel time is non-value-added time—whether it's a professional flying from city to city for meetings or a worker moving along to the next point on an assembly line—companies are increasingly looking for ways to design travel time out of their processes. Some use technology such as desktop video conferencing or collaboration tools. But they have to be careful not to infringe on value-adding travel time—of which there is some. For many people, for example, the journey to work is time they allocate to reading newspapers or to catching up on work-related documents.

Question Time

Following are some of the questions that process designers need to ask in order to spur themselves to think creatively about the opportunities for relocation.

How can modularity enable flexibility?
In an age of change, physical assets can sometimes become a liability. Banks are finding that their existing branch structures are a disadvantage in today's increasingly virtual environment. When physical assets are a necessity, the key is to make sure that they can be

quickly modified and adapted to meet changing business needs. Modularity is one approach for building in this flexibility.

One company I want to highlight in this book is Electrabel, the Belgian energy provider. Electrabel, with revenues of $6 billion and 15,000 employees, is Belgium's largest company. It is also the fifth biggest utility in Europe. The company's core businesses are the generation of electric power and the distribution of electricity, natural gas, water, and cable television. As with all utilities, deregulation is creating uncertainty and tough competition. Flexibility was critical in the design of their new distribution center. Addressing uncertainty about the future was critical, especially given the long lead times for the building of such facilities. The new center had to allow for the possible outsourcing of distribution activities in the future. And so, although the center had to be constructed on a site together with an administrative building for Electrabel, separate entries and exits to the two buildings, separate parking lots, and separate electricity/water/data connections to the network were created to allow for a future potential separation. The only thing that still needs to be done should such a separation take place is install a fence between the two buildings. The distribution center was also designed so that future expansion, both in activities and in the volume of materials to be stored, would not have an impact on operations. Modularity is a form of innovation in that it provides the flexibility to address future changes.

Flexibility was also the key word when looking at the materials-handling equipment used. Although there was a strong push from some Electrabel executives to go for a fully automated warehouse—because another business unit of Electrabel had just constructed one—the development team succeeded in showing that this would not allow for future changes in customer expectations. So the concept chosen was one of flexible automation, where bottlenecks could not arise because of the machinery, and the focus was on the quality of deliveries—whatever the level of operations.

Can this activity be moved closer to the customer or supplier in a way that will improve the overall effectiveness of the process?
Sometimes, physical distance is a major barrier to communication. And of course, when dealing with tangible items, physical distance increases the time it takes to move and ship goods. Bringing groups or companies that are dependent on one another physically closer together can often improve effectiveness, reduce transport times, and improve quality.

At Volkswagen's Resende plant in Brazil, major suppliers assemble components inside the plant. They then install those components in trucks and buses. This way of working brings about high-quality, accurate just-in-time delivery. It also helps in the coordination of cost-cutting initiatives.

Can an activity be moved closer to related activities in a way that will improve communication?
This question is similar to the previous one in that it is focused on bringing people physically closer together. However, this is more about intracompany communication. Although it has been around for a number of years, the Chrysler Technology Center (CTC) is still a great example of how buildings can be designed to foster communication. The CTC is designed along two dimensions. The first dimension is the platform, the type of car that is being designed. The second dimension is the part of the car being designed, such as the engine, chassis, and body. Each floor of the building represents a platform, so all people working on one type of car are located together. If you were to slice the building vertically, you would find that all of the people working on engines would be in one part of the building. This way, while walking the stairs or riding an elevator, you are likely to bump into someone working on the same part of the car, albeit for a different platform. The center is designed with a very open structure with lots of glass so that people can see the other people around them. This enables impromptu meetings to be held in the numerous meeting rooms. Everything is designed to facilitate communication, reduce lead times, and foster innovation.[5]

Can reducing traveling times and distance decrease cycle times?
In addition to improving communication, moving all related work activities closer together can significantly reduce time by reducing the movement of goods or, as in the case of the next example, the movement of people.

In the mid-1990s, Accenture revolutionized the way some hospitals were run by using a technique called patient-focused care. This is another example of taking best practices from one industry and bringing them to another. Here, cellular production techniques were borrowed from the manufacturing industry and brought into health care. Using this approach, all activities are focused around the item being built, or in this case, the patient being treated. So rather than the patient moving from nurse to nurse, room to room, and doctor to doctor, everything comes to the patient. Nurses would now arrange for all tests during a single patient visit, replacing the need for patients to make repeat visits for each test. Rather than dedicating operating rooms to specific procedures, they are now multifunctional, handling a wide range of operations. And all of the medical experts required to handle a patient are brought to the patient, rather than moving the patient around the hospital. Hospitals moved several centralized support functions (such as X ray) into small focused hospitals-within-a-hospital. Previously, much time and effort was spent in scheduling and moving patients to and from these centralized support departments and attending to them while they waited for service. The focused facility eliminates much of the movement time; it also simplifies scheduling, enabling patients to be served quickly as they are moved from their bed to the nearby service area.

How can a virtual organization be created that makes fewer demands on centralized physical assets?
Given that physical assets are rapidly becoming liabilities, companies are identifying new ways of making the most of their office space. Accenture has, in nearly all of its offices, adopted the hot-desking approach. Private offices have been replaced by unassigned cubicles, each of which is equipped with a table, chair, phone, and network connection. In some offices, people register for a specific cubicle at the reception desk. In others, the receptionists are outsourced from a hospitality company. In others, anyone can sit down at a free desk and get to work. Project rooms house all the files and materials pertaining to a given client. And all employees have "virtual" telephone extensions that enable them to be reached anywhere that there is a phone. The only thing lacking in hot-desk space is the personalized family photo. And it will probably not be long before workers can call up a virtual version of that onto the screens that are standard equipment in such spaces.

A number of traditional financial institutions are also trying hard to make fewer demands on physical assets. Many banks, for example, have moved into providing PC- and phone-based services. Some are providing "supermarket banking," opening small branches inside supermarkets and the like. All these developments diffuse the bank's business out to where its customers are. Nowadays far less happens at head offices or in the traditional branch. Technology is almost compelling banks to become virtual. And there is a growing number of truly virtual banks, where there are no physical branches at all. One example is Netbank; due to its low overhead costs, Netbank claims to offer 3.5 times the average rates on its interest-bearing accounts. But there is a downside to this model, since there are no branches for customers to visit when the need arises. There are numerous examples of clicks-and-mortar banks, such as FirstDirect in the United Kingdom, a division of HSBC, that offer a hybrid solution. Customers get most of the benefits of a virtual bank (e.g., higher interest rates and the ability to completely manage their accounts through the Internet), but they can still go to branches for some transactions.

How can a supplier store goods on behalf of its customers?
Instead of managing and storing your own inventory, it is often beneficial to have your supplier do this for you. Much has been written about General Electric's (GE) Direct Connect, a "virtual" inventory system that has helped GE hang on to a large proportion of its customers. In order to keep up with the giant superstores that were their competition, small independent retailers carrying GE appliances had to maintain large inventories. To reduce this inefficiency, GE introduced a virtual inventory system. Products are kept in GE's warehouses rather than in the stores, and small retailers can check the stock and place their orders via a computer system that gives them instant access to GE's order entry system. Orders are then shipped directly from the warehouse to the final customer. As a result, small retailers are able to offer the full range of GE appliances while keeping only a few samples on their premises. Everyone benefits. Customers have access to a larger range of units with higher levels of availability. Dealers no longer have to maintain costly inventory. And GE has a greater number of dealers out there aggressively selling GE products.

R5: REDUCE

Despite its name, the Reduce dimension encourages managers to explore what kinds of process improvements are possible if the frequency of activities varies—either upward or downward. Depending on the desired process outcome, either way—reducing or increasing—might be the right way to go. It is all about frequencies, volumes, resources, and information, determining how much of each is really necessary and appropriate to achieve a desired outcome.

Less (controls) can sometimes be more (savings). A large entertainment company, for example, used to require approval for any expenditure over $500. This delayed production schedules while assistants were busy trying to track down executives to get their approval for relatively minor expenses. So the company raised the limit to $5000, eliminating the vast majority of approvals and speeding up production schedules significantly. To some executives' surprise, expenses did not go through the roof as a consequence, in part because budget reports were designed so that they could flag unfavorable trends at an early stage.

And sometimes, more (information) can be more (insight and revenues). Data warehousing and data mining are enabling the capture and analysis of greater quantities of information. With this information, companies are able to more effectively target marketing promotions.

Question Time

Here are some questions that might spark ideas for process innovation in this area.

How can critical resources be used more effectively?
Critical resources need to be used properly. For example, in a manufacturing plant, that may mean finding ways to ensure that an expensive piece of equipment is not left idle.

A resource is critical if:

- A process cannot operate without it.

- It is a high-cost item (especially one with a high fixed cost).

- It differentiates the company from its competitors and drives the firm's competitive advantage in the marketplace.

Companies need to have a clear understanding of which resources are most critical to a process so that they can then find ways to make the best use of these resources. For example, in delivering primary health care, the most scarce and costly resource is usually the doctor's time. Health care organizations should therefore seek to maximize the time that doctors spend with patients and to minimize the time they spend chasing misplaced charts, preparing examination rooms, or filling out insurance forms.

A good example of the way the answer to this question can lead to process improvement comes from those manufacturing companies that have learned not to send out delivery trucks full and to bring them back empty. These firms choose to earn money on the return leg by carrying cargo for others. In delivering excellent customer service, on the other hand, the most critical resource may be keeping a detailed customer database up to date and accurate.

Another example of a good answer to the question "How can critical resources be used more effectively?" is from a golf club that got around the problem of having too many players wanting to tee off at the same time by designing a double-tee process. One group starts off at the first hole while another group simultaneously tees off from the tenth.

How might less information or fewer controls simplify operations and improve efficiency?

One way of improving efficiency is to minimize the amount of information needed to perform the activity. The effort to capture, analyze, and process data can sometimes be overwhelming. It typically adds little value, and it can be a burden on customers who are required to provide this data. A previous client of mine manufactures, sells, and leases copying machines. As anyone who has a large copying machine knows, there is a little meter on the machine that is used to charge customers who lease machines. The way this process used to work was that each month a postcard would be sent to the person to whom the copying machine was registered. That person would go to the meter on the copying machine, write down the number, and mail the card back to the company where someone entered the details from the card into a computer.

Simple, right? Yes, but there were two recurrent problems. First, customers did not like getting the cards. (Some people were very negligent in filling them out.) And second, there was typically a high billing error rate due to unreturned cards, poor handwriting, and data-entry problems. So how should this problem be solved? I've asked this question of thousands of people and the first answer is almost always, "Use remote telemetry." Have the copying machine call up the company and send the information. I find it interesting that most people turn first to the technology-oriented solution.

Some people then suggest that the copying machine print out a bill at selected intervals. Other answers are more interesting, such as "Why use the meter? Bill on the basis of something else, like the toner or paper or some other consumable item." All excellent answers. The answer to this problem, however, lies in a best practice. Who is the expert at meter processing? Is it a copying machine company? No, of course not. It has to be a utility, such as gas, electric, or water. And what are some of the methods that utilities use? One is budget billing. Usage for the year is estimated up front and then that amount is averaged over the 12-month period. Thus customers receive a flat bill every month. Then, once a year, when the service representative goes to service the machine, the meter is read and a reconciled bill is issued. No new technology is required, and because meter reading is combined with an existing task (i.e., servicing the machine), no additional work is required. Innovation through simplicity.

How might more information enable greater effectiveness?
Sometimes increasing the amount of information captured can enable a business to be more effective in the delivery of its services. And it can also help the business to make more informed decisions. For example, insurance companies that gather more information about their customers are able to assess risk more effectively.

Another example of increasing information for greater effectiveness concerns a company that I will call Air Inc. Air Inc. is a manufacturer and distributor of gases, namely pure hydrogen, oxygen, nitrogen, and other derivatives needed for industrial manufacturing. In the past, a customer who owned an Air Inc. gas tank would call the company when supplies were running low. Air Inc., in turn, predicted needs based on previous usage. Their motto was, "You Call, We Haul." The only problem was that when a customer who was using more than the average amount forgot to call, supplies would run out. Lots of frantic calls at the last minute would ensue. The solution was to put remote telemetry devices on the tanks so that they would automatically notify Air Inc. sales when the levels were running low. You might say, "Hey, in the previous example of the copying machine, which is also about meter processing, you said to avoid technology and use estimated usage. Now, you are suggesting the opposite. What gives?" The main difference is that in the copying machine example, the meter is for a noncritical function of the business, namely billing. In this example, the technology is serving a more critical set of functions and providing more benefits. Customers benefit because they no longer need to worry about calling, and they never run out of air. And Air Inc. benefits because the advanced notice of air levels allows them to optimize the usage of their trucks so that they are always full. Their new motto is, "You Rely, We Supply."

R6: REASSIGN
The Reassign dimension is concerned with the question, "Who does the work?" Today, there is an enormous array of possible answers to this ques-

tion. In nearly every industry, organizations are turning to suppliers, customers, strategic partners, outsourcing partners, subsidiaries, temporary workers, and others to do work that was previously done in-house. And on occasion, companies provide more services to customers than have typically been provided. In my opinion, this is the most powerful of the Rs, as it has the potential to significantly alter a company's operating model. When work is reassigned, barriers between companies are broken down, work is carried out by those best equipped to perform the activity, customers often gain more control, and the company can focus on the core aspects of the business. Everyone wins.

The answer to the "Who?" question is no longer bounded by the historical constraints of geographical location, organizational payroll, or even the level of skill. Today's developments in IT and changes in the competitive landscape have thrown companies together in such a way that coworkers and organizational partners can come from the most unlikely places.

Even direct competitors are finding that it is better to be partners than to fight each other. This is particularly so when they are developing a capital-intensive new venture and the risk is high. But there are also plenty of more mundane examples. For instance, GE and News Corporation, the media group led by Rupert Murdoch, both have stakes in Madison Square Garden. Yet GE owns the NBC TV network, while News Corporation owns Fox, a rival network that competes with NBC to cover events at the Garden.

The wealth of options in this new business environment creates great opportunities for process innovation. In many cases, when the "Who?" dimension of a process is changed, the "What?" and the "How?" can be changed as well, and a whole new process can be created. With such a rich array of choices, how do companies decide when to move all or part of a process to a different group of people or to another organization?

Once the general questions have been answered, the organization is in a position to go on and consider more specific ways it might reassign specific processes and tasks.

Question Time

Again, a number of questions can help to spark bright ideas.

Can existing activities and decisions be moved to a different organization?
When United Airlines wanted to offer a lower-priced commuter service, it created United Shuttle, a separate organization with a culture

and processes suited to providing cheap flights. The company rethought everything, from boarding procedures to ticketing, and it asked the employees of the new organization to learn to perform several different tasks. The degree of culture change required (and the negative attitude to multi-skilling within the existing company) made it necessary to create an entirely new organization for the new operation.

Can the process be outsourced?

In the past, when the barriers to entry were high, companies could be good at a few things, and okay at everything else. Now, with increased competition, companies need to focus on their differentiators. In fact, this topic is so important that Chapter 7 is devoted entirely to targeting innovation.

Companies need to ask themselves, "What are my differentiating Capabilities and strategies?" Or, rather, they need to ask, "What do I want them to be?" Once the question is answered, the company should ruthlessly outsource all other activities. It may, for instance, make sense to outsource a noncritical process so that the company's management can focus on more important things. Sometimes noncritical activities can be outsourced to the customer; in effect, the company hires its customer. Customers are cheap labor, and they like having a higher level of autonomy. Alternatively, a company may want to invest in retraining people and changing its portfolio of skills so it can perform at a world-class level in a process the company considers to be strategically important. But be sure it is the right portfolio of skills.

A number of Capabilities can be outsourced. For a long time now, IT services have been outsourced to third parties. And many companies are turning to FedEx Logistics Services, SonicAir (a division of UPS), and similar companies for outsourced logistics, warehousing, and even customer service. And now with the Internet, nearly every process can be outsourced, from human resources and purchasing to complex program management and design. The extensive use of outsourcing is leading to the creation of more and more "virtual" companies, organizations that carry out only a very small number of core processes and hand everything else over to others. In Chapter 5, on technology, I introduce a fascinating virtual company, Universal Leven. And in Chapter 7, I discuss sourcing strategies that help a company to be more competitive.

Can things be arranged somehow so that the customer performs the activity?

One form of outsourcing is to hire your customer and have them perform a particular activity. Sometimes it can be something as mundane as having your customers filling their own cups (with free refills) in fast-food restaurants. Let's face it, the cost of an employee filling the cup is probably more than the cost of the syrup and carbonated water. But often the change is much more sophisticated than that. When technology transforms a process, it often transforms the behavior of customers as well—witness the growth in catalog shopping and the shift from the use of physical bank branches to other channels such as ATMs, telephone banking, and electronic banking. For too many customers, however, this has had the unfortunate effect of merely "relocating" the position of their queues. What used to be inside an air-conditioned branch is now outside the branch in the wind and the rain. The next step was to bring the queue back indoors again—not into the bank branch, but into the customer's home. The queuing then took the form of a wait—sometimes extended—on a telephone line listening to Muzak and a voice telling you how many people there are ahead of you in the queue. Electronic banking does, for the most part, offer the same set of activities that a physical bank offers, but has eliminated some of the bottlenecks.

Regardless of its flaws, technology-assisted self-service is perceived as a valuable convenience rather than a burden. Customers often prefer DIY (do-it-yourself), be it tracking their own packages, looking up their own loan rates, or using pay-at-the-pump technology when refueling their cars. FedEx has had great success with a piece of software that it developed which allows its customers to schedule pick-ups, track and confirm deliveries, and print routing bar-code labels themselves, without having to make use of a single FedEx employee. This form of self-service has reduced FedEx's customer-service calls and costs by some 60 percent.

Can the organization perform an activity that is currently being performed by the customer?

If we consider electronic banking once again, we see that, as in most businesses, e-commerce has done nothing more than automate the existing processes. In the past, billing statements were mailed to customers. The customers would then open the envelopes, confirm they had enough money in their account balances, write a check, and mail the check. Home banking did little to change that other than replace an envelope with an electronic check. But recently a number of companies, such as paymybills.com and Paytrust, have done things for their customers that the customers formerly had to do on their own. The bill statements are sent to the service providers who use high-speed scanners. Customers then log on to one site, view all bills, and approve them for automatic transfer from their accounts.

Could suppliers or partners perform the activity?
In a number of cases, producers and retailers have come together to coordinate their stock plans. In such cases, the producers track retail inventories, initiate replenishments, and, in some cases, also manage the merchandising of the items on the selling floor. One of the first instances of this type of collaboration was when Procter & Gamble managed Wal-Mart's inventory of P&G's disposable diapers; this was an early example of vendor-managed inventory (VMI). Another example is Dell; nearly all of Dell's strategic commodities are currently handled through a VMI program. Under VMI, Dell's suppliers oversee and take responsibility for device procurement, inventory holding, and delivery logistics. One reason that VMI works is that it drives a move away from company-dictated initiatives, where costs are pushed downstream to the suppliers, to an environment in which all supply chain parties share responsibility and absorb the risk of inventory control. This helps drives efficiencies throughout the entire supply chain.

Can a consortium help gain economies of scale?
Companies can often gain economies of scale by banding together and sharing resources. Manufacturers of noncompeting consumer goods, for example, can solve the problem of how to deal with small, infrequent shipments by cooperating and shipping their products together. This situation is win-win-win. The two manufacturers lower their per-unit delivery costs, and customers benefit from receiving more up-to-date stock and more rapid order fulfillment.

Even competing firms can gain economies of scale in this way. The phenomenon of "clustering," the gathering together of many firms from a single industry in close proximity to each other—for example, the bankers of the City of London, the computer firms in Silicon Valley, and the tulip growers of Holland—is partly explained by the ability of such firms to gain from the formation of loose-knit consortiums among themselves. Such consortiums are often set up for joint training purposes, for example, or for shared research facilities. And in today's electronic environment, competitors are collaborating in business-to-business (B2B) exchanges. These sites allow companies, even competitors, to pool their purchasing resources, either through a shared infrastructure or through combined purchasing power. Business-to-business exchanges are further discussed in Chapter 5.

How can supply chain partnerships reduce costs?
By forming partnerships up and down the supply chain, participants can reduce the total cost of a process while maintaining service levels and rates of return. Such partnerships have tended to focus on a few specific aims, such as:

- *Dedicated Capacity.* Suppliers agree to reserve some prearranged quantity of production capacity for a particular customer.

- *Shared Cost Information.* Supply chain participants share both their cost- and process-flow information in order to help them identify win-win opportunities and to help eliminate non-value-adding activities.

- *Coordinated Production Planning.* Production planning is coordinated right across the supply chain by sharing both forecasts and production schedules.

- *Partnering in New Product Development.* Involving suppliers in the design of new products makes it easier to smooth out supplier-related lags and errors later in the process.

With such partnerships, processes may not only cross the boundaries between an organization's immediate suppliers and customers, they may also cover the entire extended enterprise, encompassing everything from the suppliers' suppliers to the customers' customers. When trying to develop innovative designs, it is always wise to have in mind this broad extended enterprise, to see, as it were, the big picture.

R7: RETOOL
The final R, Retool, is about how work is accomplished—about the technologies, the human capital, and the competencies that enable organizations

to achieve their aims. Few truly innovative processes are created today without the extensive introduction of new technology and new skills and without creating new sources of revenue. Retooling is a particularly effective agent for change for a number of reasons.

First, technology has the power to transform processes, not just to change them. Organizations need to think beyond mere automation when it comes to using technology. Automation may be a sensible move, but it is unlikely to create sustained competitive advantage. The real payoff from using new technology lies in its power to transform.

Not long ago, the use of hand-held computers on the lots for returning rented cars was a novelty. Now the speed, convenience, and accuracy that this technology brings to the job have created a new standard for the industry and wrought the kind of technology-related transformation that process designers should be seeking. The role of technology in innovation is discussed in Chapter 5.

Second, retooled (or "reskilled") human resources are in any circumstances hard to beat. Designers should think beyond the capabilities of an organization's current human capital. Depending on the desired outcome of the process, employees may need more skills, fewer skills, or just different skills in order to be more effective.

It is foolish to insist that a new process must match the current skill levels of an organization. The costs of reskilling should be balanced against the expected benefits of the new process. However, companies must expect some employees to thrive on new processes and others to shy away from them. Chapter 3 discusses how employees and culture play a critical role in innovation. Chapter 5 covers how technology can enable reskilling through e-learning and other approaches.

Finally, only when a company understands its existing competencies can it start to think about how these competencies might be used in new ways. For any company with a world-class process (or underutilized resource), the best opportunity may lie in extending the process (or assets or capabilities) into new areas. This is the path followed by virtual organizations such as the Virgin Group. They know their core competencies and assets and they extend them all the time into new markets. For example, Virgin's primary asset is its brand strength, which includes Richard Branson himself, and Virgin has used this brand strength to partner with other companies—train services, insurance, banking, mobile phones, and soft drinks—all with a limited number of Virgin employees. In Chapter 4, I talk about how companies are expanding into new businesses by extending their core Capabilities.

Question Time

Following are some questions that might help tease out ways of being innovative in the area of retooling.

How can technology transform the process?
New technology can inspire ideas for processes that will lift them onto an entirely new level of excellence. New technology increasingly means the Internet. Now that the first flush of excitement over the early dot-com companies is over, the more interesting things on the Internet are being done by mature organizations that are using it to transform their traditional processes and business models. A major European telecommunications operator began to take an interest in the Internet in the early 1990s, but, as in many other companies, its facilities grew without proper coordination. By the end of 1997 the company had a mess of sites with limited interactive potential, all set up in isolation by its various business units. So it decided to undertake a major review of its Internet involvement, as a result of which it created standard content, design, and technical infrastructure for all its sites. It then set out to use these sites as a platform to deliver revolutionary standards of service to its customers. Customers were able to pay invoices online, for example, to send e-mails, and to search yellow pages. But at the same time the company was capturing key information and building up its customer profiles so that it could in the future meet their needs almost on a one-to-one basis.

Since the project began, the average length of time that customers spend on a visit to the company's site has increased tenfold. The project has also helped to reduce the company's operating costs by over $3 million, and it has put this company at the forefront of e-commerce.

How can assets or competencies be leveraged in a way that creates competitive advantage?
One company that came up with an innovative answer to this question was the Williams Companies, a natural gas business that was facing increasing competition due to deregulation. The company's executives had come to realize that the rights-of-way used for their pipelines could be a tremendous asset—but in a completely different industry, namely telecommunications. The Williams Companies used these rights-of-way to lay fiber-optic cables through decommissioned pipelines. This was the groundwork for the creation of WilTel, which

was to become the nation's fourth-largest long-distance network. When Williams sold most of the fiber network to what is now World-Com, they retained a single fiber on all routes, as well as the established infrastructure that became the foundation for the Williams network, which is now known as Williams Communications.[6]

How can up-skilling, down-skilling, or multi-skilling of process performers improve the process?
One answer to this is that the enhancement of an employee's skills can enable that individual to handle a wider range of tasks, thereby reducing the need for hand-offs. For example, a leading health management organization (HMO) in the United States asked its registered nurses to work on the telephones in place of less skilled health professionals. This enabled the HMO to handle a wider range of patient queries over the phone—rather than (more expensively) in the doctor's office.

There are, of course, times when lower levels of skill may be more cost-effective. When widely dispersed customer-service specialists are replaced by centralized call centers, for example, the call-center employees do not normally need as wide a range of skills as their predecessors. They are able to provide a more consistent and cost-effective service with lower skills because they are backed up by all the relevant customer and product information via computer links.

PUTTING IT TOGETHER AT INVENSYS
Invensys, the global electronics and engineering business mentioned in Chapter 1, was created by the merger of BTR plc. and Siebe plc. in 1999. At that time it was headquartered in London and had annual revenues of about $10 billion with over 90,000 employees. It operated globally through four divisions—Software Services, Controls, Power Systems, and Intelligent Automation. Within those divisions there were approximately 30 product groups, each of which operated in the countries of its choosing. Profit and loss accountability was at the product group level, giving a fair amount of autonomy and supporting the company's decentralized philosophy.

Invensys is particularly relevant for this book because of its six core competencies. Four are process- or innovation-related—*rapid innovation, Six Sigma, quality management*, and *stretch performance*—and the other two—*bias for action* and *highest integrity*—are cultural.

When the companies merged, they looked for opportunities for integration and improved effectiveness. Of course in a decentralized company such as Invensys, any attempt to coordinate efforts is bound to present a challenge. But everyone agreed that procurement should be one of the first areas to be tackled. In the past, most purchasing decisions had been conducted at a business unit level and as a result, Invensys was going to market in a piecemeal way and fail to realize its full potential.

In the past, all procurement decisions had been left to the lowest levels of the organizations. In the new world, the goal was to create an integrated sourcing and purchasing model that coordinated efforts across the company and around the globe. The target was $500 million in cost reductions over three years. To do this, 44 global commodity teams were put in place, each led by an experienced commodity manager. Introducing these teams did *not* mean that the purchasing function was being centralized. Rather, the intent was to "stay with the end user," but with effective coordination.

The challenge for Invensys is to balance the need for flexibility at the divisional level with the desire to optimize activity across the business. The global purchasing area is measured on contract value signed per year, but it is not responsible for delivery of savings to the bottom line. These savings are the responsibility of the four division heads, the divisions being responsible for implementing the contracts that global purchasing signs. The division heads, however, are not always in 100 percent agreement with these contracts, because the goal is to optimize across all the divisions rather than focus on the needs of an individual business unit.

Given that the divisions in Invensys have largely been free to operate their businesses in the way they want to, tensions inevitably arise in any effort to coordinate procurement across the groups. But tension is a part of the innovation process. It brings to the surface the types of issues that need to be addressed. This is a positive factor as long as there is a structured vehicle for addressing the issues.

During the reviews with the divisional chief executives, one of the questions that is addressed is, "How is localized innovation working to the detriment of the organization as a whole?" Of course, local innovations are hard to control, especially since the incentive system doesn't always encourage people to think about the best interests of the organization as a whole. Instead, they tend to be looking after their own profit-and-loss account. But as discussed in the previous chapter, this Darwinian view of business is healthy: it promotes competition and ensures that resources are being put where they will create the most value.

Invensys has learned to place more emphasis on the interrelationships between the pieces of their business. As stated previously, it's not the boxes (the processes or activities themselves) that matter so much as the lines that connect them—the interrelationships between people working in completely different areas.

MAN FROM MARS AND THE SEVEN Rs

Procedures in all companies take root over time, and often prove resistant to any attempt at transformation. Because in mature companies a given set of procedures may have been in place for a long time, the roots can be very deep indeed. Managers at such companies might ask, Why fix something that has worked for many years? If you accept that the business environment is in a state of flux as never before in history, the answer is clear: Because the world is moving on. Sometimes it takes a fresh pair of eyes—the proverbial visit by a man from Mars—to spot irrelevant or inefficient processes immediately. I have found that applying the Seven Rs can accomplish the same goal by bringing intellectual discipline and a tried-and-true framework to each of the steps in the analysis.

CREATING A CULTURE OF INNOVATION

"The only one who likes change is a wet baby."

RAY BLITZER

A *culture of innovation can be a company's primary source of competitive advantage, and it can pay off steadily over the years. Any high-performance culture is difficult to replicate, but innovation is in a class by itself. Once embraced by employees, innovation becomes a way of life. It ensures that all the human capital is in step and striving to produce outcomes of value for the organization. Most importantly, competitors cannot copy an innovative culture. In this chapter I look at ways to stimulate innovation in people, ways to build up an exciting culture around them, and how to put the two together. I also debunk the myth that creativity and innovation are talents of a few gifted people. In fact we all can release our innovative potential if our work environment allows it. Many companies around the world have successfully planned and implemented this kind of deep cultural change—not always with-*

out trauma. But the results in growth, profitability, and industry lead-ership have been worth the cost. Leadership and unflagging commit-ment of top management will always be key ingredients for success. It is the bias for innovation that must become a core competency if a com-pany is going to be an industry leader, not a follower.

In a client meeting not long ago, I asked the question, "What is most important to your company—products and services, people, or processes?" The group was divided. The smallest vote was for prod-ucts and services. Its supporters felt that without good products or services there wouldn't be a business for very long. The next most common answer was "processes." This group believed that good products have increasingly short life cycles and that a good product development process is required to bring new products to market. And while people come and go, the processes stay put. But the largest and most vocal group believed that the most important thing was people. Let's face it, they said, it's people who execute and improve processes. And people are the source of innovation. Of course, there is no single "right" answer to this question. It's like asking, "Which is more important, the brain, the heart, or the lungs?" They are all vital to our survival.

But I would like to suggest that in fact there is a fourth aspect that is critical to a company, one that affects every person and is extremely diffi-cult to replicate. That is a company's culture. And not only is it difficult to replicate, it is also extremely difficult to change. The ability to bring about culture change is precisely what is required for companies to become per-petually innovative.

When I give presentations, I often ask the audience, "How many of you are or have tried to lose weight?" A large number of hands go up. I then ask those people with their hands up, "And how many of you know what to do in order to lose weight, such as eat right and exercise?" Most of the hands stay up. Finally I ask, "Okay, so how many of you are losing the weight you want to lose?" Usually this gets a large laugh from the audience when most of the hands go down. The reason people aren't losing the weight they want to lose is not because of a lack of knowledge, a lack of processes, or a lack of tools. It is a lack of the right behaviors and discipline. Similarly, for a shift in culture to be achievable and sustainable, it has to be more than a series of actions; it must be something that becomes core to the way busi-ness is done. This reminds me of a quote from Aristotle: "We are what we repeatedly do. Excellence then is not an act but a habit."

In this chapter, I will lay out some ideas and examples of where cultures have been shifted, even if only subtly, to move them toward 24/7 innovation.

Companies almost always underestimate the innovative potential of their people. A study carried out at Eckerd College in Florida presents a clear example of the hidden creativity within us that yearns to be released. It also shows the most effective way to use creative types within the organization.[1]

Managers who came to the Eckerd leadership course over a four-year period were given a problem to solve. The problem was called The Hollow Square. For this they were divided into teams of eight, and each team was then subdivided into two groups of four. One of the groups was designated as planners, and its task was to work out a solution to the problem. The second subgroup consisted of implementers. The implementers were to be told by the planners what to do in order to form a hollow square with the tools that had been made available to them.

Before being allocated to their teams, however, the managers were assessed as to whether they were "innovators" or "adapters." The measure used was a scale developed by M. J. Kirton that rates how people perceive and solve problems and how they communicate with others. In general, innovators score highly on the scale. They tend to "do things differently" and are prepared to break with rules or past traditions. Adapters, on the other hand, score lower on the Kirton scale. They are focused on "doing things better," but they tend to work within the rules as they are and to accept the status quo.

The study had several different combinations of innovative and adaptive people. But three groups in particular interested me. In the first, the team of planners was made up of innovative people and the team of implementers consisted of adapters. In the second group they were all mixed up together. The planning team had both innovators and adapters, and so did the team of implementers. In the third group, however, the teams were turned upside down. The planning team contained only adapters and the implementing team contained only innovators. Now, which of these three combinations would you expect to be the most effective?

I've asked this question of many different audiences around the world and, surprisingly, not one of them has opted for the first combination. I say "surprisingly," because this is how most companies implement change. They take the most innovative, creative people and lock them in a room while they develop a new process. Then they expect the people who have executed company processes for dozens of years to implement the change.

Around 90 percent of the people I put this question to vote for option two—the cross-functional approach. I suppose it sounds like the safe answer:

hedge your bets on both sides of the job, design and construction. But in reality, the third option—the one where the adapters do the design and the innovative types implement it—is the one that is the most effective. The adapters are able to come up with a design very quickly, albeit an imperfect one. And the creative types are then able to take that design and to build something from it, correcting and improving as they go along. When a problem arises, they are able to solve it then and there without referring back to someone else. This is just as well because in the real world the "someone else" is usually by then doing a completely different task and has forgotten at least half of the reasons why the elements of the design are as they are.

The important point is that innovative ability is much more pervasive and ubiquitous than most of us imagine. Innovation is not invention, something to be fostered in a carefully controlled atmosphere. Invention is the process of discovering things that have never been discovered before. Innovation is the discovery of new ways of creating value. Not everyone can be an inventor, but everyone can be innovative.

CREATING A WORLD-CLASS TEAM: WILLIAMSF1

In the real world, an innovative culture operates like a finely tuned, high-performance sports car—fast, competitive, sophisticated, and smooth-running. So who better to model your company after than a leading race team? The team I have had the pleasure of working with for the past two years is WilliamsF1, a Formula One racing car manufacturer. In terms of percentage wins, they are the most successful Formula One team in the history of the class. Even though Formula One racing is watched worldwide by over 350 million people, I admit I knew little about WilliamsF1 or Formula One when I started there. But I quickly became a big fan of this sport and its incredible technical innovations. Each car costs nearly $1.5 million to make, and can go from 0 to 100 miles per hour and back to 0 in less than six seconds. These cars are tested using a 170-ton 50 percent scale wind tunnel. Each WilliamsF1 car has a 3-liter, 800-horsepower V10 engine that is provided by the German company BMW. Anyone who knows anything about cars would be impressed by these figures.

But someone in business would be even more impressed by other figures. In fact, each car, which is made up of over 3500 parts, is completely redesigned and rebuilt every year. Very little is carried forward from year to year. Compare this to a product development life cycle of nearly two years for most car manufacturers, with a large amount of reuse from the previous model, and you get a sense of the degree of innovation this team has developed. At WilliamsF1, six cars are typically built each year—two for the race team (one for each driver), a spare for the race team, two for the test team, and one fully built car that sits in manufacturing in the WilliamsF1 plant at Grove, England. And every two weeks, each car is reconfigured to meet the specific aerodynamic needs of the track on which it will be competing. This requires replacing major components such as the front and rear fenders. Each year, when they build the new car in January, they are able to assemble the 3500 pieces, plus the BMW engine, in just four days. That's four 24-hour days—the 24/7 concept pushed to the max.

When I asked Alan Challis, the coordinator between the factory and the race test teams, and the former chief mechanic for 10 years, how they do it, he said, "It's the norm." He finds it hard to articulate what they to do to be innovative because it is just the way the business operates. This response is a clue that WilliamsF1 has a true culture of innovation. Similarly, some of the best jazz sax players have been unable to give me tips for improvisation, stating that they are just able to do it. But when taking a critical look at the success of WilliamsF1, we were able to identify five factors that contribute to their success.

1. *Leadership.* First and foremost is the leadership of Sir Frank Williams, the owner and founder, and Patrick Head, co-owner and technical director. They are icons in the industry, they have a clear focus on what they want, and their vision for creating a winning team is understood by every one of the 370 employees of WilliamsF1. They put nearly all of their money into the car, recognizing that a winning team gets more sponsors, which in turn generates more revenue, which can be put back into the car.

2. *Forethought.* Everyone is focused on the end game, which is a winning race team. This requires that a winning car be delivered on time. Working back from there, they know when manufacturing needs to be completed, which drives development timelines. The race season starts in March, and the car has to be ready.

3. *People.* WilliamsF1 has a culture of enthusiasm, hard work, and dedication. Consider how avid dedicated sports fans can get, then imagine these enthusiasts working for their sports team. And they are not fair-weather fans. Quite the opposite. Adversity, major changes, and poor performance get the WilliamsF1 people even more excited. There is an energy that anyone who visits the plant can feel. And wandering around as a new guy at a staff party, I realized it was hard to tell which people worked for which department. They truly operate as one team.

4. *Contingency.* Considering the unpredictability of racing, you need to
    be ready for anything. The WilliamsF1 trucks that go to each race
    contain a minimum of seven to eight sets of every part needed for a
    car. This means that the trucks are filled with nearly 50,000 parts for
    each race. That's 25 tons of equipment!

5. *Practice.* Pit crews have long been admired for their ability to change
    the tires, fuel a car, and do required maintenance in minimum time.
    The WilliamsF1 team does it in 7 seconds. When asked how they did
    it, the answer was "practice." There are 19 people in a pit crew. And
    during practice, they move each of the crew members around until
    they get the best combination. And then they practice more. Yes, there
    are "processes" that each of the pit members uses, but in reality, they
    also need to think on their feet and deal with every situation they are
    handed.

Although not a large organization by international business standards,
WilliamsF1 demonstrates clearly how the concepts of 24/7 innovation can
be brought to any company.

Most companies cannot claim that they operate like a WilliamsF1. In
fact, most companies I have worked with are several laps behind. But
WilliamsF1's secret is not so complicated. As we saw, some key points are
leadership and having the right people with the right skills and behaviors.
Much of this chapter is dedicated to an examination of these elements. This
chapter also makes clear how important having a process for innovation is
in helping companies achieve their goals.

LEADING FROM THE TOP

It is almost never a straightforward task to install a new culture—innovation or any other kind. Companies with change programs going at full bore
almost invariably have to play doctor to their employees' "change neu-
roses." Typically, everyone is wrought up to some degree over losing the
comfortable work patterns of the past and heading into the unknown.
Employees ask their managers, "When will we have the final version of this
thing so we can settle down?" The answer to that question today has to be
"Never," and nobody wants to hear that. Yes indeed, the wet baby is the only
one who likes change.

The most effective way to modify a company culture is to gradually bring
about a modified behavior of employees—leading the change from the top.
A program for change can cover dozens of things ranging from dress code
and office design to technology and working hours. And seemingly small

things can mean a lot. One international communications company in London that fell into the hands of a U.S. West Coast firm was virtually reborn the day a new CEO came in—neckties came off and the culture was irrevocably set on a steady course of change. Dressed-down men on staff were giddy for weeks in their pastels and earth tones.

Culture also embraces symbols, from exclusive parking spaces, for instance, to the way senior managers are addressed—by their first name, family name, or just their initials. "Had a good meeting with A.J. this morning. J.R. was there too." Change these and the culture changes too. "Met Bob this morning, and Harry popped in at the end." Mirage Resorts, third in *Fortune* magazine's list of the most innovative U.S. companies, is attentive to creature comforts, among other things. It spends generously on its staff canteens, a visible demonstration of its priorities and a powerful determinant of staff behavior.

The behavior of employees is also heavily influenced by stories and by myths, many of which record the exploits of legendary leaders of the past. At 3M, the company is still influenced by a statement attributed to a chief executive almost a quarter of a century ago. He said: "I don't want 3M ever to get to be just a place for people to come to work. I want it to be a place where people have joy in coming to work."

To some extent, any program of culture change has to go with the flow. Many industries have a strong traditional culture of their own—banking, for instance, or the movie business. New high-technology industries also tend to foster their own (frequently California) culture. Hewlett-Packard was highly influential in defining the culture for its industry, and it has worked hard (through extensive training) to maintain what it calls the HP Way, which includes respect for others, a sense of community, and plain old hard work. Management by walking around (MBWA) came out of Hewlett-Packard.

I have, in my travels, noted two extremes in culture. One I call "the right of infinite appeal." This is a culture where anyone, anytime, has the right to veto any suggestions, thereby bringing the process back to the starting point. However, in this environment, very little gets done. Innovation is completely stifled, as everything is reduced to the lowest common denominator. The good news with right of infinite appeal is that there is broad buy-in, and the big picture is considered. The other extreme is "run and gun." These are companies with lots of people with lots of ideas, all of which seem to be getting implemented simultaneously. The good news here is that there is in fact quite a bit of action. The bad news is that no one is talking to anyone else, and everyone is doing work in his or her little corner of the universe. A run-and-gun culture creates more anarchy than progress. It is a perfect example of box thinking. A company needs to strive for a combination of these two: well-thought-out ideas that get incubated and propagated rapidly through an organization.

EFFECTIVE LEADERSHIP

As indicated in the WilliamsF1 example, leadership is one of the keys to an innovative culture. In fact, as you will see later in this chapter, leadership-driven change is typically the first step in changing a culture. A senior executive, preferably the CEO, carries the torch for innovation up and down the company. Truly effective leaders have to be able to do a number of things:

- They have to be able to create a sense of urgency throughout the organization, artificially if necessary. Field Marshal Montgomery, one of Britain's top military leaders in World War II, once said that a leader "must have infectious optimism, and the determination to persevere in the face of difficulties. He must also radiate confidence, even when he himself is not too certain of the outcome." Leaders often drive change by exaggerating a "burning platform"—a competitive threat from online suppliers, for instance, or a crisis such as sharply falling profits—that can be used to drive people out of their comfort zones, to shift them away from their complacent belief that the way things are is the best possible way that things can be.

- Leaders also have to be able to identify and align the best resources for the job. They have to be able to pull resources together from across the organization and to gain support from executives and managers for the change effort and for innovative thinking. They have to gain support for the disruption that it inevitably causes to all their working lives. Any basic shift in culture can be painful.

- Leaders have to create and communicate the vision of what they are about. This involves painting a picture of, or finding some other way to communicate, the better world that is to come from the changes that are being undertaken. Only with such a picture can individuals see how the changes are going to fit together to produce the desired outcomes. Without it, employees are left to live with the infinite number of possible outcomes that their imaginations are able to create. Like good military leaders, business leaders must lead by doing, not by telling. An executive who expects his company's employees to work in teams, for example, cannot rule his or her domain in an old-fashioned autocratic way. He has to "walk his talk." Teamwork, like most other things, must be led by example.

- Leaders have to believe—to the depth of their being—that innovation is what will drive business improvement. Seniority and authority are not enough. The leader has to be evangelical about change. This is particularly important when there is no obviously compelling need for it. Companies that find themselves on the burning platform and are forced by circumstance to reassess their whole way of doing things are, in a sense, the lucky ones. When there is no compelling need for change, it is hard to make change happen.

- Leaders must have the ability to overcome adversity. They must keep their ears close to the ground for signs of any resistance. And if they hear rumblings they must immediately reinforce the commitment to the vision and defuse any doubts that stakeholders might have about what is taking place. In practice, it is more likely to be a case of *when* they hear rumblings rather than *if* they hear rumblings, for no move toward an innovative, entrepreneurial culture occurs without someone at some stage having serious doubts about the company's ability to achieve its aims. A true leader needs to prevent the right-of-infinite-appeal culture from derailing efforts.

- Finally, leaders must have the necessary clout to be able to reallocate the firm's best people, resources, and knowledge in a way that will support pervasive innovation throughout the company. They need to challenge and break down functional and organizational barriers. Leaders must be sufficiently well respected throughout the company to be able to navigate stormy political waters and overcome interdepartmental bickering.

Strong leadership is essential for any significant move toward an innovative culture to take place. We shall see in Chapter 9 the way Lever Brothers organized itself into a number of teams to switch from functional orientation to process orientation aimed at fostering innovation. But guiding the whole operation from the top was a team made up of the executive members of the company's board. And driving them was a new chief executive eager to shift from what he saw as a dangerously old-fashioned way of doing things.

However, the organization that is switching from a traditional management style to a more entrepreneurial culture faces a longer-term issue about leadership, an issue that is quite separate from the need for leadership to drive through the change itself. This arises from the fact that the style of leadership needed by an organization that is focused on innovation is essentially different from the style that is effective in a more traditionally structured company. Leaders who decide to bring about such change almost necessarily bring about their own demise. The person who has become well suited to a command-and-control linear power structure is unlikely to be the best person to head a team of teams with lines of authority that are blurred by intersecting vertical and horizontal layers. In this more fluid environment, simply ordering people to get on with it will not get the job done. Good leaders here must inspire people first and try to win an authority that has not been formally assigned to them.

A company must first change the corporate culture before any major changes can hope to be made. Otherwise, as my former boss Bill Stoddard puts it, changing systems and structure will be like "trying to push your way through a 50-ton marshmallow."

A PROCESS FOR INNOVATION

If leadership sets the tone for the culture of innovation, what are some tools that can help shape it? One is instituting a *process* for innovation. And although many people feel that a process for innovation is counterintuitive, I contend that it is an essential tool for creating an innovative culture. Otherwise, innovation will be random and subject to divine intervention. Whereas the previous chapter was specifically about business processes and how they enable innovation, this section is on the innovative process and how can it be a tool to help shift an organization's culture. This process facilitates diversity of thinking, and by robust refining and selection of ideas (the raw materials), it turns out workable high-value solutions that can be reproduced and turned into practice. The aim is to use a systematic approach to identifying opportunities and to generating ideas and refining them into high-value solutions.

Basically, to be innovative, we need to approach businesses from a new angle. We need to optimize patterns and look for relationships that are often not obvious. As Steve Jobs once said, "Creativity is just having enough dots to connect." The value, once again, is in the lines (connections) not the boxes (the dots). A simple example of "dot thinking" versus "line thinking" can be found in the way books are bought. In the past we used the library model—we had a title in mind and the clerk guided us to it, eliminating all the other books in the bookstore. The focus was on one answer. Now, if we go to Amazon.com, we can see "Customers who bought this book also bought...," enabling us to connect the dots. Our range of possibilities is considerably broadened.

The ability of people to focus on any relationships, not just process relationships, is an important cultural aspect of the innovation organization. This requires a shift in the way people think. When trying to make sense of a new situation, they need to move from asking, "What is this about?" (a dot question) to "What is this like?" (a line question). This helps lead to innovation as it forces the individual to think about each situation in terms of other situations.

This brings us to another critical aspect of the innovation process: the distinction between divergence and convergence, as shown in Figure 3-1. My experience has shown that a key to innovation is to generate many ideas (divergence) before evaluating their viability (convergence). And although this may be conventional wisdom these days, it is not always practiced. And this divergence/convergence model does not happen just once. In the four-step model described in the next paragraph, the key is that you generate a bunch of ideas and zoom in on one. From there, you generate more ideas at a more specific level, and then zoom back in. Using this approach, many ideas are left on the floor that can be used later or recombined as the context changes.

FOUR EASY STEPS TO INNOVATION

Below, I describe a four-step process for moving toward innovation designed to encourage innovation to spread throughout an organization.[2]

FIGURE 3-1.   Diverge, then converge.

1. *Envision.* In this step the purpose is to learn how to use data more flexibly. It sets out to create new perspectives on everyday facts and figures, and to explore relationships and patterns between them that might (just possibly) open the door to truly revolutionary insights.

2. *Enable.* Here the firm builds on the output of the first step, aiming to bring its insights sufficiently down to earth so that it becomes possible to see the first glimmer of a solution to whatever the issue at hand is—how to improve customer relationship management, for example.

3. *Explosion.* This step is where traditional brainstorming approaches to innovation begin. Here the possibilities that have been identified earlier are mined for ideas that might stand some chance of being effective. The first two steps have made sure that what is being panned for gold at this step is not just raw dirt. By now it is carefully selected soil where the gleam of precious metal has already been detected.

4. *EmpowerTool.* This final step is where the really good ideas are equipped with the Capability that they need in order to make them actually work in practice.

Envision

The principle underlying the first step, Envision, is much the same as one of the fundamental principles of brainstorming: in the early stages of problem solving, proliferation of choice, rather than an attempt to narrow the range of options, should be the order of the day.

An example of the power of this process is provided by a large telecommunications company where a team had spent many months benchmarking, studying best practices, and visiting companies. They felt that they had seen everything out there that was to be seen. But after using the innovation process for just three days, the client felt that more and better ideas were generated during that time than were discovered during the previous six months. Getting them to this point had been a challenge. Throughout the innovation process, the company's executives kept trying to reduce their options by continually diverting attention to a set of 16 large notebooks that were full of data they had collected over the previous months (interviews, status reports, etc.). "When are we going to go through that," they kept asking, "and incorporate it into the process?" The notebooks provided them with a foundation, something to build on, but also reduced their options. The notebooks focused them on the tree across the field at a time when they should still have been looking at the wide blue sky. If anything, the notebooks should have been a springboard for coming up with other ideas, not a funnel for reducing their number.

People naturally tend to converge onto a smaller picture when they should be diverging onto a bigger one. Analysis and dot elimination (eliminating ideas and connect points) are "converge" activities. Envision has to be a pure unadulterated "diverge" activity. But it takes a different mind-set to diverge. There is not a pill that you can take in order to be good at it. Nor are there "seven steps to divergence" that are sure to work every time.

Probably the best way to learn is by example. One famous soap company, for instance, has a strategic planning session every couple of years where it looks at its market share figures and thinks about strategy and innovation (not easy in the slow-to-change soap business). One year the company discovered that it had a 30 percent share of the market for deodorant soap. In a fractured industry like that, 30 percent seemed pretty good, and the company might have been expected to plump for a strategy that involved trying to increase that share gradually. But that is not what they actually did. Instead, they asked themselves, "How can we reinvent ourselves to capture one-twentieth of a large market instead of one-third of a small market?" In effect, they were asking, "How can we reduce our market share to 5 percent?" Such a strategy might not involve the company in selling one more bar of soap. Instead, it would direct it toward getting a smaller share of the (much bigger) toiletries market.

Enable

The image underlying this step is that of a filter. When you put a filter on a camera lens, it highlights certain hues and diminishes others. You see things in a new light. Here the aim is to create a set of filters with which to view the vision that has come from the first step.

The filters should enable the organization to see things that were previously blended into the background—ideas, patterns, relationships. It's a bit like being late for work when you see every single clock on the route, including several that you could swear had not been there the day before. (Chances are, of course, that they're all 10 minutes fast!) Your lateness acts like a filter, highlighting some things and obscuring others that are less relevant to your current situation. Or, when I bought a new car, all of a sudden it seemed that everyone was driving the same car. Before that, I had rarely noticed that particular make and model on the road. As J. Mitchell Perry, noted author and motivational speaker, once said, "What you focus on expands." And expansion is the key to innovation.

During the Enable step the aim is merely to figure out what is possible, not what would be the "right" solution. To illustrate this point, imagine that you have been asked to design a two-day tour of Paris and have been given a list of attractions.

When a number of people were given these directions, the first thing they did was eliminate certain attractions (dots) and come up with a list of priorities (i.e., they attempted to converge). Then they designed an itinerary (i.e., they found the right answer). But they had not considered many different facets of Paris. They had not allowed themselves enough time to diverge.

So they were encouraged to look at the problem in another way. In step one (Envision), they were asked to picture a tour of Paris, and among the ideas that emerged was a tour of the city that used all the senses, one which touched on its history and culture but which also allowed the visitor to come in contact with the families and children of Paris.

In step two (Enable), they were asked, "How do you think Mozart would design a tour of Paris?" And the Mozart filter suggested more filters, for example:

- What if the tour were to be organized around the sounds of the city?

- Or the smells?

- How might you organize a tour that had the flow and feel of an opera?

- Or the thematic development of a symphony?

Each one of these filters, or approaches, provided a route to a singular, distinctive, and memorable tour of Paris.

Of course there are an infinite number of filters that a business can choose from. One could be, "How are the competitors within our industry handling this situation?" But that is dot thinking and limits your options. Another filter could be, "How would a company in a completely different, unrelated industry handle this situation?" That is line thinking—making connections where they have typically not existed in the past. Remember, though, that none of the details are worked out during the Enable step. You still do not know exactly where you are going to go or what you are going to see (or hear or smell). For that you have to wait until the next step.

Explode

This is the step that is probably the most fun. By now you have a vision, you have looked at that vision through a number of different filters, and you have chosen the one you want to play with. Now you can explode with ideas. As stated previously, this is where traditional brainstorming often begins.

The step involves more, however, than just listing as many ideas as possible. The key is to focus on relationships instead of activities. Ideas that are rich in relationships are particularly valuable.

There are two criteria of success in the Explode step: the quantity of answers and what we call the "quantumness" of answers. Most approaches consider quantity only. The quantumness notion is more abstract, but just as important. In quantum physics, you cannot define one object in isolation—an atom can only be defined by its relationship to other particles. So it is with the ideas that come from this step—the greater their connection with other ideas, the more successful you have been in generating them.

EmpowerTool

In this, the final step, you begin to make your ideas happen by defining the Capabilities that are needed to make them succeed. What people do too often when they come up with an idea is to rush to implement it within their comfort zone, with structures and people that are familiar to them and with whom they feel comfortable. But, as Theodore Levitt, professor emeritus at the Harvard Business School, once said, "Nothing characterizes the successful organization so much as its willingness to abandon what has been long successful."

We tend to compartmentalize ideas into boxes. We tend to believe that there are either technology solutions or training solutions or process solutions, things that are familiar to us, when in fact there may simply be "solutions." The key to success lies in understanding the lines between the boxes, not so much the boxes themselves. Another attribute of an innovative organization is that they innovate on the means of getting to the end, not just the end. The most sophisticated, radical, innovative idea is worth nothing unless it is implemented.

THE INNOVATION HEARTBEAT
The company's culture has to place innovation at its heart. Innovation has to become something that employees take on board almost as naturally as they breathe. At 3M, innovation is the predominant element in the corporation's culture. The company purposely recruits people from diverse backgrounds in order to avoid homogeneous thinking habits. Risk taking is encouraged and employees are not punished for failure.

In too many companies, the fear of failure still discourages the innovative spirit. Try to eliminate the damage that failure can cause, but don't try to eliminate failure itself. Fred Reichheld, a consultant with Bain & Co. and an acknowledged expert on consumer behavior, once wrote: "The key to customer loyalty is the creation of value. The key to value creation is organizational learning. And the key to organizational learning is grasping the value of failure."

This requires free thinking and new sources of ideas that can be tried out. Kellogg's, the well-known food company, promotes divergent thinking by employing people from a wide variety of backgrounds. And they encourage these researchers to spend 15 percent of their time on their own ideas. As a result, according to a recent *Fortune* magazine article, in one month "researchers generated 65 new product concepts and 94 new packaging ideas."[3] One example that illustrates line thinking was when researchers who had noticed the popularity of products like bath oils with botanical and aromatic properties began to research the sensory appeal of foods. Another was when they came up with the idea for selling Special K Plus, which has extra calcium and iron, in a half-gallon milk carton to remind consumers of the nutritional value. In both cases, they connected dots. Aromatic oils to food, and milk to cereal.

INDIVIDUAL TALENTS

One of the encouraging aspects that will emerge as innovation is put on the agenda is the hidden potential that we all have within us. The popular myth is that some people are born creative, and some are not. There is, in this view of the world, a creative type of personality—Michaelangelo, Mozart, or Tolstoy, for example—and then there are the rest of us. But again this is totally wrong. It's all a matter of degree. We all have the potential to be innovative—perhaps not quite as much as Mozart, but innovative nonetheless.

This premise has been tested out many times over the years. For example, George Land and Beth Jarman, founders of Leadership 2000, gave 1600 5-year-olds a creativity test used by NASA to select innovative engineers and scientists, and 98 percent of the children scored in the "highly creative" range. When these same children were retested five years later, only 30 percent of the 10-year-olds were still rated "highly creative." By the age of 15, just 12 percent of them were ranked in this category, and a mere 2 percent of 200,000 adults over age 25 who had taken the same tests were rated at this level. It seems that creativity is not learned, but rather unlearned.[4]

And yet the business world has traditionally favored analytical thinking over the capacity to innovate and has seen to it that business schools produce highly trained young men and women to think along strict parameters. But times have changed, and now the mission has to change—to help people unlearn their uncreative habits.

CHANGING THE CULTURE

Unfortunately, organizations are not made up of five-year-olds with an infinite supply of creativity, energy, and flexibility. They are typically made up of adults with long histories, territories to protect, and boxed-in thinking. This makes any kind of change difficult, and culture change particularly difficult. Therefore, central to moving any company toward 24/7 innovation is understanding the company's capacity for change.

Structural changes alone are not sufficient for an organization to become innovative throughout. Changes must be made in virtually all parts of the organization, from the management style to the measurement systems. For example, ramming a new change program through a company without preparation would be a bit like dropping a high-powered engine into a Volkswagen Beetle without altering the transmission, the drive train, the suspension, and so forth. It can be done, but chances are the finished product won't work very well.

Admittedly, it is difficult to be precise about something as vague as an organization's capacity or willingness to change—some people may be enthusiastic about it while close colleagues are not. It is somewhat less difficult, however, to say whether an organization's capacity for change is in general high or low. And if a company has a low capacity, it may be easier to start afresh—to create an entirely new business unit or division—than to attempt to change the existing culture. Of course, this is not always a viable option.

It is also important to recognize that even the greatest enthusiast has finite limits to the amount of change that he or she can tolerate. And while you can reengineer processes, you cannot reengineer people. Since each company is made up of a unique bunch of individuals, each company's capacity for change is also unique, and any company's plans have to take this into account. The timing of the change, the approach to it, and the people to be involved in leading it will all vary depending on a company's particular circumstances. There are no templates here.

Before pushing enthusiastically for big changes, companies should assess how much change has occurred in the organization already, how recent it was, and how successful it has been. Is there change fatigue? Are people just unable to handle any more? Or, as is the case with a recent client of mine, are they enthusiastic about change but have little capacity to make it happen? In fact, a company's capacity for change is heavily influenced by its track record and history. If it has experienced a successful change program in the recent past, then it is likely to be receptive to plans for further change. If, on the other hand, it has just been through a traumatic and unsuccessful effort to bring about change, then management (and consultants) might be well advised to let sleeping dogs lie for a little while.

In either case, major change should be complemented with some quick wins, some small but very visible successes that don't require a lot of time or resources. For example, software, such as Plumbtree, enables companies to create fantastic intranets in only a few weeks. A couple of high-profile successes of that kind can build up momentum and enthusiasm and help make the culture more ready for change.

From my experience, culture change goes through three waves of S curves as it moves toward a culture of innovation (see Figure 3-2). Each wave starts at a modest level, then builds until it reaches a plateau. You then rest there for a while (as if to take a breath) before gathering enough momentum to go to the next level. Successful companies move through all three waves, each of which increases the company's capacity for change: leadership-driven capacity, structural-driven capacity, and organic capacity.

- *Leadership-Driven Capacity*. At this early stage, progress is invariably based on the tenacity and leadership of a single individual, someone who gets the bit between his or her teeth and runs with a particular opportunity for improvement. By taking responsibility for it, the individual drives the change. This top-down approach requires the individual to create such a sense of urgency about the initiative

FIGURE 3-2.   Three waves of organizational change.

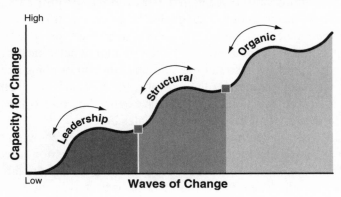

that he or she prevents it from falling into what is all too common—a debilitating series of fits and starts. If there is no compelling need to change, change is unlikely to happen. Earlier in this chapter, the attributes of these leaders were discussed.

- *Structural-Driven Capacity*. At this stage the responsibility for change no longer rests with an individual. To some extent, it has been taken over by the organization. Mechanisms have been put in place to enable employees across the business both to implement change and to drive it. Typically, such mechanisms include various performance measures, organizational structures, and lines of communication. This stage often includes a move toward a process orientation. Process improvements in one area eventually help to build up the organization's general ability to improve. The better a company becomes in one area, the more skilled it becomes at getting better in other areas. In other words, the experience curve applies to process innovation.

- *Organic Capacity*. By this stage, the capacity for change has become built into the organization, and it is often being driven from the bottom, with employees seeing it as an integral part of their jobs. This comes about partly because companies that reach this level have focused specifically on developing change competencies in their employees. They have reached the idyllic stage where innovation has become an integral part of the organization's culture.

IDENTIFYING AND TRAINING THE TALENT

The newfound mobility that employees enjoy in the current market for talent has complicated our lives significantly. The much discussed "war for talent"—a battle in which top employers compete ever more fiercely for skilled employees—is heating up. Even Accenture has joined the fray by offering certain high-caliber new recruits a signing-on fee designed largely to help graduates clear their student loans. Other companies do the same or more, and as a result, talented people are increasingly subject to tempting outside offers.

Once upon a time, a reputable firm could reliably expect that most of its workforce would remain loyal for years. People were known to be "an IBMer" or "a P&G person," or "the man from the Pru." But that world is fast disappearing. Job turnover rates today are higher than they have ever been. People are less loyal as customers, and they are less loyal as employees. The average manager now works for about twice as many employers

during his lifetime as did his counterpart 30 years ago. The man from the
Pru may have been the man from Chase last year, and might be the man
from Salomon Smith Barney next year.

There are three key skills that employees need in order to be productive
innovators in an organization. When looking at these categories, it becomes
clear why the war over finding and keeping good people has reached such
a pitch. The skills required today are atypical and are in scarce supply. They
are rarely taught in schools and are hard to learn.

Macro-Thinking

This first category gets at the breadth of thinking, not just depth. It's about
mind-set rather than technical expertise.

- Employees need to focus on outcomes and results rather than on the
  specific activities they are performing. This is a big change for someone who has spent all his working life in a function. They need to
  have a better understanding of how their work contributes to the
  whole, and they must feel responsible for the results and be willing to
  step aside from their assigned tasks in order to make sure that the
  overall objectives of the business are achieved. This is, in my opinion,
  the crux of the cultural shift, as it gets people to focus on what adds
  value rather than ticking things off a checklist.

- Macro-thinking is a kind of cross-functional thinking; it requires
  cooperation. Employees must understand how one worker's role
  relates to the work of others on the team, and beyond. They must be
  able to see the lines connecting different capabilities as well as the
  boxes (the Capabilities themselves).

- Macro-thinkers must be happy working in teams, and they must think
  of themselves as part of a team and not (as has tended to happen in
  the past) as individuals undertaking a task in isolation. They are members of a band, not soloists. To encourage team spirit, some element of
  an employee's pay should be related to the performance of the team to
  which he or she belongs.

- Employees also need to be willing to learn new jobs and new skills so
  that they can perform different tasks when needed; multi-skilling,
  however, can sometimes can seen as a threat. New technology, for
  example, tends to bring out the latent Luddite in all of us. Human

beings are essentially conservative, and probably for good reason. But anybody who chose to ignore the computer and/or the Internet over the past few years ("Oh no, dear, I think we should keep using that nice old typewriter.") is unlikely to be doing very rewarding work. High performance requires continual learning, at all levels. For example, a number of companies, including GE and Asea Brown Boveri (ABB), have implemented reverse mentoring programs. The younger, more technically adept employees mentor the senior executives on the impact that e-commerce is having on the business.

At Koch Industries, their MBM philosophy facilitates this breadth of thinking and cross-functional cooperation. For example, driven by a desire to move from commodity sales to ventures with higher returns, many of Koch's businesses began in 1996 to search for opportunities to use their unique capabilities and knowledge to develop unique products and services. With this end in mind, Koch's Chemicals business put together a small diverse team consisting of Koch experts in chemicals, operations, trading, accounting, and law to explore possible ventures. After working through several potential deals, the team discovered the possibility of a much larger deal. This opportunity was a joint venture with the Isaac Saba family of Mexico City to purchase the Hoechst-Trevira Polyester unit (soon to be renamed KoSa), which became the largest deal in Koch's history.

The authority on this team was not apportioned based on tenure, but on performance. For example, a controller with only one and a half years of experience with Koch did so well during due diligence that he became one of the team's lead negotiators. Because this team was motivated by a clear vision to maximize the value for Koch Industries as a whole, rather than in silos, diversity that might have led to cross-functional battles in other companies led to valuable synergies and cooperation. The operations representatives, for example, made several concessions in the operational setup after they were convinced that doing so would minimize Koch's risk in the venture. Leaders at Koch Chemicals believe their focus on providing incentives to improve the whole business rather than its parts is one competitive advantage they have in the marketplace.

Entrepreneurial Mind-Set

This category focuses on employees who work well in environments of ambiguity, flexibility, and risk taking.

- Employees have to be able to make critical decisions and take the initiative. This is essential if organizations are going to foster improvisation and an ability to bend with the wind, to adjust rapidly to changes in the environment around them. They have to be able to see decision making (and the identification of opportunities and problems) as an integral part of their jobs. In an innovative environment, the rule book, the policy guidelines, and the directions of supervisors become much less important. As difficult as it is for leaders to shift from the more traditional command-and-control style, it is just as difficult for employees to deal with the newfound freedoms they are given in their new environment.

- In a team-based, flexible environment, members must learn to value contention, and they must be able to handle other people disagreeing with ideas that they put forward. Competing ideas spark off innovation, and good performers should be happy when such sparks fly, from whatever source. But of course they also need to know how to evaluate these ideas. Not every idea that ends up in a suggestion box has the potential to create value.

- Employees need to act, behave, and feel like owners. They need to go beyond what is expected of them in order to generate new ideas for generating profits for the business.

Koch Industries has created this feeling of ownership through performance-based incentives. One example can be found in their Minnesota refinery, where in late 1993 an operator who is a big auto racing fan brought in a sample of racing fuel and analyzed it with some help from his colleagues. After that he developed a way for the refinery to make high-quality racing fuel at a lower cost than competitors. In order to make his case stronger, he developed a list of industry contacts and did market research to convince managers his idea would be profitable. One year later the refinery was in the racing fuel business. The operator got a considerable bonus for his initiative, but the rest of the story reveals the power of incentives other than money. One of the operator's colleagues, also a racing fan, worked in Koch's asphalt business, which provides high-performance pavement design for auto racing tracks. He was so enthusiastic about Koch's entry into the racing fuel business that he asked for the opportunity to market the new fuel using his racing industry contacts. He was allowed to make that change, and the business doubled its sales each of its first three years.

Making Use of Knowledge

Employees must be able to use knowledge, as opposed to being passive recipients of information. Today's employees should not be like the message pushers of old who took information in, spun it around, and sent it out again, sometimes in a different direction but with no value added. They must have and use the tools and the skills to manipulate information, to analyze it, and to use it in order to add value—by helping customers, by improving operations, and/or by exploiting new opportunities.

Koch Industries recognizes that knowledge is the key capital in organization and finds ways to leverage it. Many of Koch's business operations require stringent safety precautions to avoid injuries. Not satisfied with industry-average accident and injury rates, a number of years ago Koch set a goal of moving to the top tier in its industry. Because Koch's philosophy is that employees have much more knowledge dispersed among them than any small group of corporate planners can have, Koch went about pursuing world-class safety by building this goal into the responsibilities and authorities of employees throughout the company. Rather than have a few safety engineers scour the company for unsafe conditions, Koch gave this responsibility to all employees, with rewards both for uncovering unsafe conditions and for discovering new ways to conduct business more safely. This initiative resulted in 35 to 50 percent improvements each year in the number and severity of accidents across Koch Industries. Within one year the company had moved from being in the middle of the pack to having one of the best safety records in its industries. Now Koch's goal is to use the same process of dispersed decision making and incentives to achieve equal success on its goals for environmental excellence.

THE TRAUMAS OF CULTURAL TRANSFORMATION: MÖLNLYCKE HEALTH CARE

Mölnlycke Health Care (MHC), the Swedish medical manufacturer referred to in Chapter 2, was formed in 1998 through a merger between the former SCA Mölnlycke Clinical Division and the corresponding division, Kolmi-Set, in the Finnish Tamro group. And although the main shareholders are Nordic Capital (one of the leading private investment firms in the Nordic region) and Tamro, the plan is to go public. After the merger, the CEO, Finn Johnson, was given three years to turn the company around and prepare it for float.

Mölnlycke Health Care is a good example of a company that has moved toward a culture of innovation. They made this change because of a desire to float the company, and they see innovation as one way of boosting its value. This started with culture change led from the top, then moved to process-led culture change, and is now seeing the emergence of organic change. This case study illustrates the traumas a company can go through as it shifts to becoming more innovative. It also highlights the different roles of leaders, managers, and employees in making this happen.

As I've said throughout the book, a change of this nature is a major cultural shift for companies, one requiring strong and dedicated leadership. In the case of MHC, Johnson, the CEO, made a huge difference in shaping this culture. He is a large-framed person who is well respected and confident. Although he is a tough decision maker, he also gives a fair amount of autonomy to the other leaders in the business without meddling too much in the details. But he also holds them accountable for delivering results. Much of the initial wave of cultural change can be attributed to Johnson's leadership.

The Struggle of Management

As part of Johnson's move toward creating an innovative organization, the business identified six processes.

- Plan and Manage Operation

- Develop Customer Solutions

- Customer Management

- Supply Customer Solutions

- Manage Human Capital

- Provide Supporting Infrastructure

Each of these processes was assigned an owner. Initially, the Plan and Manage Operations process was owned by the CEO himself. After a year, he handed it over to the division head, to help build more leadership within the organization. The Develop Customer Solutions process was assigned to the development director. The Customer Management process had the sales director as its owner. For these three processes, each owner maintained line responsibilities in addition to process ownership responsibilities.

The interesting case here was the Supply Customer Solutions process. The assigned owner, the former deputy director of the company, gave up those responsibilities to become the process owner. In his ownership role, he had responsibility for both the design and execution of the process. Although Supply Customer Solutions included manufacturing and the factories, this part of the process was not part of his execution responsibilities. However, procurement was part of his execution responsibilities. And since the products of the Wound Management Division deal extensively with suppliers of patented products, procurement/supplier management is technically the responsibility of the Develop Customer Solutions process, and not Supply Customer Solutions. This meant that the process owner of Supply Customer Solutions had execution responsibility outside of his process.

The story of the Supply Customer Solutions process would be interesting if it ended there. But there is another lesson to be learned. We know that being a process owner is very different from having line responsibilities. Functional heads, given the fact that they own all of the resources, have typically operated in a command-and-control manner. Communication skills have been less important than management and technical skills. In the process-focused world however, communication, facilitation, and people skills are critical; without them, a process owner can not succeed. The owner of the Supply Customer Solutions process was a very strong organizational and technical person. He was also a strong decision maker and good at getting people to do things he wanted. However, it was recognized that he had poor communications skills and inadequate leadership attributes and that he did not inspire the employees. This proved to be his downfall, and he was ultimately sacked.

This highlights the need to have the right people in your organization—people who have not only the technical skills of old, but also the communications, coordination, and innovation skills needed to be competitive and flexible in the new economy. At MHC, the original procurement manager in the company after the merger had to be sacked after six months. The original director/CEO was replaced after the merger. And the Quality director was let go a year into the process because he was stuck on the old, rigid ISO model, needing the i's dotted and the t's crossed rather than developing the business. As I said in Chapter 2, a key way to foster innovation within the organization is to get the right people. Some people can be reshaped. Others just need to be replaced.

The Struggle of Employees

The people challenge is not limited to the leaders and owners of a business. There are issues with employees at all levels when they discover this new freedom in how they do their work. For example, in the Develop Customer Solutions process at MHC, it was discovered that none of the product managers were initially able to function effectively in the new world, because all of them were used to more prescriptive instructions. They had needed only to operate their bit of the process. They were experts in their piece in the sequence, but they did not have, for example, the necessary clinical, manufacturing, and sales background. Mölnlycke struggled to find the right people, and in the end, they relied heavily on training, education, and some new hires.

In another example, when one of the factories was sold, the logistics manager was let go. However, since he was deemed to have excellent logistics skills, he was salvaged during the divestiture of the factories and was put into procurement. After a few months it became obvious that although he was exceptional at logistics, he did not have the breadth of skills to be good in procurement, and he soon left the company. Nimble companies require nimble people who are good at multiple tasks. Depth in one area is insufficient.

Finally, people can burn out due to the new stresses involved. One of the procurement leads, a very capable person, needed to take a leave of absence after a few months in the new environment. The new freedom and flexibility unleashed within the organization was so big and powerful that many people felt insecure about their ability to meet the challenge. The move from a detailed model to a more output/results-oriented culture meant that people were told what to achieve, but not what to do. This forced people to ask the question, "How should I do this?" And when this question was posed to managers within the company, they often did not answer the question, but rather forced employees to solve the problem for themselves. This helped reinforce the new culture. Although there was some turnover in the workforce, the good news is that once people became better educated and gained more confidence, they were able to perform more effectively than ever before.

Tension and Creativity

The focus on both processes and line responsibilities turned MHC into a highly matrixed organization. Process owners were responsible for identifying improvement opportunities, while line managers were trying to run the business. As you can imagine, this caused a great deal of tension within the organization. And although tension is often thought of as undesirable, at MHC the debate and discussion unleashed creativity in the organization. Issues, and hence opportunities, surfaced much more quickly. However, if there are deadlocks in these debates, creativity is stifled and progress cannot be made.

Although the CEO often played a Solomon-like role in resolving disputes, it was not practical for him to do this all the time. So he assigned a program manager to become the judge, negotiator, and umpire in these disputes. And the key tool the negotiator used in solving disputes was cash flow. Since Nordic Capital, the owner of the business, manages its holdings primarily based on cash flow, the goal within MHC has been to optimize around this measure. A blend of cash flow and Economic Value Added (EVA) (a value-based management system developed by Stern Stewart & Co.) was used, and when disputes could not be resolved, the negotiator made decisions based on which solutions would maximize value creation for the business as a whole.

This focus on value became the rallying cry. Not only did it help resolve disputes, but it also aided in the identification of new opportunities. One example was production: after the merger in 1998 there were 13 factories; now there are 4. Some factories were sold to materials producers who are now suppliers. A focus on value also helped drive the decision to move all transaction management activities (e.g., invoicing, order management, customer and supplier account management) into a separate entity.

Connecting the Dots

Although the business was committed to moving away from the old function silos to a process-driven organization, the company needed to be careful to not start creating process tunnels. It was a struggle for MHC to get the process owners together since they were so busy. This posed a potential risk because the owners were not taking the time to deal with the interfaces and interdependencies between processes. Fortunately, they recognized the need for better communication, so a team of people worked behind the scenes to identify these dependencies to ensure that nothing fell through the cracks.

Another form of tension emerged as a new intranet was rolled out. In the old world, people had very little awareness of what the rest of the organization was doing. In the best case, they might have known what the people immediately before them and immediately after them were doing. In the new world, every role description and process segment is available to everyone. Everyone now knows what everyone else is supposed to be doing, and therefore anyone can challenge what anyone else is doing. This creates more tension. But again, this tension—the ability to bring problems and opportunities to the surface—has become a new form of innovation. For now they are able to see dependencies that were previously hidden.

One connection that was identified as being particularly important was the relationship between procurement and the Develop Customer Solutions process. In the past, R&D did its piece of the process and handed the specification to procurement, which negotiated with a predetermined supplier who handed that over to manufacturing, and so on. When the development team looked at the interdependencies and the process that it was responsible for, the team determined that procurement had to get involved in the actual product development. This made for some heated discussions because in the past, product development was used to designing a product and handing it over. No complications. No hassle. And no arguing. And no real opportunity for true innovation. When procurement got involved, they suggested contacting suppliers earlier in the process, getting materials from suppliers for testing, and getting suppliers involved in product development. And since the supply managers were the ones who had the strong relationships with suppliers, they became a more powerful voice in the product-development process.

Although MHC is still in the midst of their cultural change, they are right on track for quadrupling their shareholder value over the next two years.

CONTINUOUS INNOVATION
A culture of innovation is vital to a company, and very difficult to replicate. But there are some keys that can help move a company in the right direction. First and foremost, the company needs an impassioned leader who will be an advocate for innovative thinking and who does not tolerate cynics. The company needs the right people with the right skills—skills that are difficult to find and that are also difficult to build. A company needs practice and patience. It needs to move at a pace that is in lockstep sync with its ability to absorb the change. Moving at a snail's pace may only perpetuate the status quo. Bold change, mandated change from the top, can help drive the new culture and let people know that the old ways of working are no longer acceptable. The key is to drive innovation.

Innovation—a talent we all had when we were young—can be relearned and pooled in a culture of innovation to confront and overcome competitive threats. The combined creative power of all employees pulling in cross-functional teams can provide the spark to produce winning performance in the marketplace.

C H A P T E R

4

CUSTOMER
STRATEGIES

*"Businesses realize that public opinion is important and
should not be left to the public."*

UNKNOWN

*T**his chapter brings us to a critical stakeholder, and the third of the
blueprint elements: the customer and associated customer strategies. After decades of efficient mass production, consumer individualism is back with a vengeance, prompting manufacturers and service
companies to listen much more closely than they ever did to the
demands of the marketplace. The task now is to find ways to bring the
consumer inside the tent. Acknowledging the codependence between
producer and consumer will help companies satisfy market demands in
a way that can surpass competitors and also produce profit. Some
activities long performed by the producer are being reassigned to the
consumer, with companies in effect "hiring the customer" as an extension of the business. And in some cases this can lead to more knowledge*

95

of consumer preferences, new sources of revenue, and differentiation in the market. Meeting this challenge cannot be done without innovative thinking that intimately involves the consumer.

When I recently surveyed a number of European companies, asking them to rank the importance of their various stakeholders, "customers" were always listed on top. Their reason, as though they had all been listening to the same motivational tapes, was that customers are the only stakeholders that directly create revenue. "Employees" were almost universally listed as second most important stakeholder, since they are the ones who make it all happen—the all-important culture of innovation that I described in the previous chapter. Interestingly, "shareholders" were typically ranked down the list in the third position. These results imply that most companies consider themselves to be customer-centric, putting the customer in the forefront of their thinking and making them the center of attention. How do most companies become customer-centric? Some companies try and understand their customers using customer satisfaction surveys and customer-insight and data warehousing tools. Although useful, these alone will not do the trick, as they still propagate an "us" versus "them" mentality. Know your enemy, set your sights on the target, and take aim. This assumes that businesses are in charge and that their purpose is to satisfy customers. The truth is that customers are now in the driver's seat. Customers determine how they want to do business, when they want to do business, and even the price they are willing to pay (through Internet auctions, for example, or Web sites letting customers specify the price they will pay).

We have moved from a customer-centric world to a buyer-driven world. Customers are now in charge. We need to know the customer's needs, hopes, and dreams even better than the customer does. And often this requires not just satisfying customers, but deeply involving them in the business. Companies need to *hire the customer* and accept the reality of mutual reliance. Hire them as part of your business redesign efforts, hire them as extensions to your sales force, and hire them as participants in your product-development process. If you don't hire your customers, they may just fire you. As Sam Walton of Wal-Mart used to say, "There is only one boss. The customer. And he can fire everybody in the company, from the chairman on down, simply by spending his money somewhere else." In this chapter, after some discussion of consumer power, I talk about ways of adding value to your customers, hearing your customers, serving your customers, and hiring your customers. This includes ways of adapting your business strategy to further build relationships with your customers.

Regardless of what they say, many companies are, organizationally speaking, still focused on products, not on the customer or the marketplace. Production departments count and record the number of goods that are produced, in what color, and at what price. When these goods roll off the line, they are like orphans waiting to be adopted. It's up to somebody else—a separate department with different aims—to get them moving out of the warehouse, to persuade some consumer somewhere to take them in—and at a good price.

Organizations in which the production mentality dominates don't concern themselves much with *who* buys their goods—are they old people or young people, single or married, car owners or boat owners? And, more importantly, they don't concern themselves with *why* they buy the goods—how will my products help them live their lives or run their businesses more successfully? Because of this, they fail to find the answer to a key question: "What else can I provide my customers that goes beyond what they are getting today?" These companies often make the mistake of hunting down new customers for each of their products or services as they become available. Obviously it costs several times as much to find a new customer as it does to sell to an existing one.

My message here is that the cost of finding new customers can and must be reined in. It will always be cheaper to sell a range of different products to the same customer than it is to sell a string of similar things to different customers. And often this requires offering customers something they didn't know they wanted, even perhaps moving from products to services and solutions. Or it may involve identifying new sources of revenue that are extensions of the existing business. Innovative thinking is obviously the basis for this kind of development.

The key here, as I have stated throughout the book, is focusing on the lines, not the boxes—in this case, the line between the business and the customer. And there is a continuing shift in where the boxes are drawn. In this chapter, I focus on rethinking the way organizations engage their customers in what they are trying to accomplish. I've always said that to be truly successful, a company should redesign the customer's processes as the starting point. You must understand how your customers (as well as your suppliers, intermediaries, and other stakeholders) think and do business, and then design your business from the outside in. Involve your customers in your innovations and then figure out how to differentiate yourself in the marketplace. This leads to new products, new services, and new ways of delivering those products and services.

CONSUMER POWER

The origins of the power consumers are now wielding are related to the prosperity boom in the Western world since World War II. Better-heeled consumers have turned the tables. They are gaining so much power that mighty corporations are now restructuring themselves to please them. The general public tends to be better educated, and that has made a difference in consumers' ability to judge the quality of products and whether they represent value for money. In the developed world, as consumers have become much more wealthy, products have become much less expensive. In real terms, for example, products such as white goods, wine, and winter over-coats cost far less today than they did just 25 years ago. As a result, many more people own cars, televisions, and other consumer durables, and the sheer force of their numbers gives consumer groups a degree of power that they lacked when they were fewer and poorer.

But numbers and wealth are not enough to account for the exuberant enthusiasm of companies for today's consumers. The attentions of mar-keters are inescapable as never before. Sheaves of paper now drop daily through the letterbox of any half decent address in Europe and the United States inviting the occupants to take advantage of insurance offers or spe-cial car deals or credit-card facilities, deals whose seeming generosity is often suspect. And the number of telemarketing phone calls received at din-ner time is high enough to have aroused serious social comment. And, although some find such calls intensely aggravating, enough find what's on offer sufficiently enticing for the practice to continue.

What, other than changes in consumers themselves, has made produc-ers suddenly so solicitous? I suggest that three changes in the environment around consumers have been, and will be, prime movers.

Government Concern.   Governments have increasingly come over to the side of consumers, having for many decades favored business in part because of the political contributions companies have traditionally made. When the old established tire maker Firestone, now part of the Japanese Bridgestone Corporation, was forced to recall 6.5 million tires in 2000 (after analysis had indicated that 1 in every 4000 was liable to split apart suddenly and lose its tread), *The Economist* commented: "America's Senate and House committees, scenting blood from a consumer-versus-big busi-ness issue in an election year, will move in for the kill." They came down on the side of the consumer, of course, and there was to be no mercy, no cover-up. In the United States at least, politicians have come to value consumers' votes more highly than the campaign contributions of their corporate backers.

Economic Change.   Along with the political environment, economic conditions have also improved for the consumer. In the industrialized nations, the virtual disappearance of that old bogey inflation has removed the urgency behind many shopping trips. No longer is there the feeling that what you don't buy today is sure to be more expensive tomorrow—an important psychological factor in retailing. With a growing number of products, the reverse is now true. Consumers hold off buying things such as personal computers because they believe that the price will be lower tomorrow than it is today. Nowadays sellers have to be far more persuasive to convince consumers that they do really need or want it, and that they really must buy it now.

Technological Advance.   The most powerful influence on consumers has been the remarkable technological developments that make goods longer-lasting. Cars have more life in them, and so do appliances, electronic goods, and men's clothing. This means that the manufacturers of these products are involved in a continual struggle to persuade people to change their existing model for a new one when there is no real need for a new one. Manufacturers have to add something extra, something innovative, that makes the replacement purchase more than a straight replacement.

Thus, vinyl LP records were replaced by tape cassettes, which in turn were replaced by the compact disc, which now is being replaced by MP3, DVD, mini-discs, and other products. All do exactly the same thing: provide the consumer with high-fidelity recorded music. But each new product, by promising such things as ever-greater clarity or convenience, persuades the consumer that it is worth making a new purchase.

The most revolutionary progress in recent years has undoubtedly been in IT, which has transformed virtually any business that depends on information. Industries such as financial services and tourism have had layers of intermediation ripped out by IT's ability to put data directly into the hands of the consumer.

Consumers now have access to more information than ever before. Information is now so quickly and widely disseminated in the financial services industry that the playing field can be called relatively level. A striking example is the practice at CNBC financial television news of

interviewing CEOs while displaying on screen the real-time tape of their
stock price running along the bottom of the picture. Investors can see the
share price jump (or drop) as the CEO makes revelations in response to the
interviewer's questions.

Investors are also able to make real-time online price comparisons in
electronic marketplaces such as E-Loan and Annuity.net. Via electronic
transfer systems like NextCard and OneSource, they can then switch
rapidly and painlessly to the cheapest provider. In this environment, the
Citicorps, Barclays, and Deutsche Banks of the world are finding it
increasingly hard to compete. They are burdened with a legacy of expensive branch networks whose reorganization is proving to be one of their
biggest challenges, a challenge that they get no thanks for taking up. Barclays was subject to fierce criticism when it began a radical program of
branch closure in the United Kingdom—an initiative that was forced upon
it by the changing economics of its business. These shifts in customer
power and knowledge are affecting all industries. Nearly everyone who
buys a car or a computer system, for example, gets information through the
Internet. Independent marketplaces are forcing sellers to compete more
aggressively for business through participation in auctions.

ON THE MOVE: THE IMPACT OF MOBILE COMMERCE

Another technology that will continue to empower the consumer is mobile
telephony and m-commerce. In Scandinavia, where large, remote expanses
of countryside make it difficult and uneconomical to lay copper wire,
nearly two-thirds of the population has a mobile phone.

For many developing countries, the technology of the mobile phone
has already enabled the mobile handset to be substituted for fixed-line telephony. Forecasters predict that in the first decade of this century, mobile
phones will outnumber fixed-line phones worldwide. In places as far apart
as Cambodia, Lebanon, and Brazil, almost half of all telephone subscribers
are now using mobile services. The impact of mobile phones on the
economies of these countries promises to be far greater (and certainly far
quicker) than the impact of the automobile. Vast areas of previously
neglected territory will attract outside investment because it is now possible to communicate with people and companies all over the world from
those areas. The future is clearly wireless.

The rapid spread of the mobile phone is being matched by the increase in
Internet access. The next level (the third generation) of technological advance-
ment in telephony will link up the Internet with mobile communications,

giving consumers Web access while on the move. Wide-area protocol (WAP) services are bringing these two technologies together today, albeit on a limited basis.

The Norwegians are not yet using their phones to go shopping while they flit from fjord to fjord, but that time is not far off. Business-to-consumer (B2C) e-commerce is taking off faster than most people could have predicted. Several billion dollars worth of computer hardware and software is being sold over the Internet today, as well as several billion dollars worth of travel and financial brokerage services. The linkup of the mobile phone with online vendors will soon take all the current capability of the Internet (and more) out of the home and onto the streets.

Satellite communications will enable customers to reach producers wherever they are and whenever they want—be it at the South Pole at midnight or on the slopes of Everest at dawn. Traditional business models required the customer to go to wherever the business was. In the future business will come to wherever the customer is. In this new environment the consumer becomes a distinctly different animal from what he was 30 years ago (or, more likely, what *she* was—recalling the advertising pioneer David Ogilvie's 1963 reminder: "The consumer is not a moron; she is your wife"). Consumption is rapidly becoming independent of gender, time, and place.

The implications for the way companies organize themselves around the consumer are enormous. Above all, there is an urgent need for firms to stop being inwardly focused, to stop being—as outgoing General Electric CEO Jack Welch has put it—an organization "with its face toward the CEO and its ass toward the customer." To be truly outward looking, firms need to move beyond a customer focus. They need to recognize the great shift of power between producers and consumers that has already occurred, and they need to structure themselves so that they will be sensitive to further shifts in the future.

With that context of consumer power in mind, I'd like to focus the remainder of this chapter on four ways in which you can get closer to your customers by rethinking your customer strategies:

- Adding value to your customers

- Hearing your customers

- Serving your customers

- Hiring your customers

ADDING VALUE TO YOUR CUSTOMERS

As I said in the beginning of this chapter, most companies are conscious of the need to become customer-centric and to take a fresh look at customer relationship management (CRM). Customer relationship management looks to be a key concept for the first decade of the twenty-first century, as business process reengineering (BPR) was in the 1990s. But doing CRM now and doing it right is another matter. Many managers are simply uncertain of how to go about it.

While looking at your capabilities, identify opportunities for changing the business and creating new products and services. As you seek innovative ways to design from the outside in, it becomes apparent that there is an inextricable link between your operations and your go-to-market strategy.

The key to retaining customers in this new environment is for companies to be creative in the ways they add value to things that consumers are prepared to pay for. Finding the way forward is not as obvious as it sounds, but some industries have made a good start. Food manufacturers, for example, have discovered that shoppers will pay extraordinary premiums to have someone peel their fruit and wash their lettuce for them. Whereas their grannies bought lettuce and tomatoes from a traditional greengrocer and they had to spend time scrubbing off the soil, slugs, and fertilizer, their children can now buy their produce washed and ready for the plate—but at a price that would give granny heartburn.

Given the need to satisfy increasingly fickle customers, I suggest focusing on three main ways of adding value: offering convenience, making customers feel good about their purchases, and decommoditizing products.

Convenience.   Offering convenience, as the food companies are doing, is a great way of adding value. And more and more firms are looking to provide it—convenience in the home, convenience when shopping, and convenience at work. The supermarket now puts the chutney next to the rice and the lemons next to the fish. The travel agent sells insurance and maps at the same time that it sells packaged tours. The movie video/DVD rental giant Blockbuster has expanded into snack foods, so you can munch while you watch, just like at the cinema. As a result, Blockbuster has become one of the world's largest retailers of popcorn.

Convenience also helps producers differentiate their products in a world where everything is becoming increasingly standardized and commoditized. One PC is now very much like another—with the possible (and still marginal) exception of Apple. They've all got Intel chips and Windows software and—except for Apple—they've all got the same beige plastic on the outside.

So what makes a consumer buy one manufacturer's machine rather than another's? The answer has largely to do with convenience—the convenience of ordering the thing in the first place, of having it delivered to the right location, and of having somewhere to turn if it breaks down. The top computer companies are not tops at manufacturing—in many cases they leave that to others. The computer companies are increasingly those that have the best generate-demand Capability, the best order-fulfillment Capability, and the best CRM Capability. In other words, it's not so much what they do, but how they do it.

Smart appliances are already out there in small quantities testing consumer appetites for the next level of superconvenience. ICL, a U.K.-based technology company, and Frigidaire have teamed up to create an online refrigerator that allows customers—from their kitchens—to access selected retailers; order, scan, and purchase goods; pay their bills; even watch television and send e-mail messages. NCR has unveiled a prototype of its Microwave Bank that allows users to cook dinner in a microwave oven while accessing online banking, shopping, e-mail, and a television using an LCD touch screen in the door of the oven. In addition, it has the capability to read bar codes, allowing users to scan in the codes on household and food items to generate a shopping list and send the list to an online shop for home delivery. When a user consults a recipe list, the machine has the ability to point out unused foods in the refrigerator that are near their expiration according to their use-by date and in turn recommend a recipe using the items. Now if it could just prepare and cook the food for us, we'd be all set.

Feel-Good Factor.   Another way for producers to differentiate their products (i.e., to add value) in a commoditized world is by making consumers feel good about their purchases. This tactic was pioneered by The Body Shop, the cosmetics retailer that trades on an image of caring about the environment. Now organic foods are providing retailers with another way to add value by making their customers feel good about what they are buying. Organic foods are not only kinder to the consumer's environment, they are kinder to the consumer's health.

Other possibilities are emerging. Consumers in the developed world would like to think that the clothes they wear have not been manufactured by a 12-year-old Asian girl in a crowded, windowless room. Of course, most consumers' self-righteousness may be outweighed by their not wanting to pay full price and an unwillingness to bring back the world's textile manufacturing to the developed countries and the high labor costs that would come with such a shift.

Decommoditization.   Creating product lines in which one size does not suit all—the exact opposite of what most markets have been trying to do for the past 80 years—involves customizing goods and services, making them uniquely suited to an individual's needs. At first sight, such "mass customization" may suggest the end of economies of scale. For if no two things that are sold are ever the same, where's the scope for scale? And where is the chance to hone processes and to improve them along the way? But this view involves a misunderstanding of what mass customization is about. For it does not mark a return to the nineteenth century. It's not like *haute couture,* where, literally, no two dresses are the same. It is "bespoke" tailoring within limits. It is individualism built on the top of certain basic platforms. It may be true that no two BMWs are the same, but all of them are based on a very small number of basic models, on top of which are built opportunities for customization. It is with these platforms that companies are able to gain economies of scale.

The Dell Computer Corporation, for example, is known for its ability to configure products to meet individual needs, but the configuration takes place within defined limits. Dell goes only so far in giving customers what they want. For the Ford Motor Company, Dell has set up several different product configurations based on the needs of various groups of employees. When an order comes from Ford it comes with a job description of the person that the computer is intended for. Dell then knows which bits of hardware and software to package together for that person.

In the past tailor-made clothing relied on a relatively low-paid workforce of seamstresses and pattern cutters. Today's tailoring is different. For example, with Levi Strauss's Personal Pair jeans for women, there were 5000 different sizes for about $15 per pair more than the standard off-the-shelf jeans. This kind of choice is only made possible by intensive use of information and other technology.

The moral for companies is that they should not try to address absolutely every case that might crop up, which in turn means that they should not build in the capability of handling the most complicated cases. When managers try to design processes that can handle every situation, no matter how rare, the result is usually greatly increased complexity and rapidly diminishing returns. As a boss of mine said many years ago, "Design to handle the exception, not for the exception."

A good example of how to handle the dichotomy between customization and value is to be found in the medical profession. Every patient could be said to be unique. No two sets of symptoms are identical. Hence health care products, one might think, need to be designed to handle exceptions since every patient *is* an exception. In practice, however, the medical profession narrows the field somewhat by using a small number of different processes to handle different kinds of cases. It uses outpatient care for minor complaints such as flu, for example; hospitalization for major medical problems; and emergency care for urgent, life-threatening cases. Thus not every patient has a solution individually tailored for him or her, nor is there a one-cure-cures-all type of solution. The process that adds value for both parties is somewhere in between these two extremes.

ADDING VALUE: NEW BUSINESS STRATEGIES

Adding value to customers can come in the form of new products or services. Opening up development strategies to innovative thinking can lead to expansion into new businesses under a company's established brand. Customers will respond to a wider range of products and services once companies understand themselves and their markets better. Credit card companies, for example, have access to a gold mine of information about their customers—what restaurants they like to visit, where they take their holidays, and what books they buy. They are in a powerful position from which to set up competing providers to meet their customers' needs, should they have a mind to. We have not yet seen an AmEx singles bar in downtown Seattle, a MasterCard book and coffee shop just off London's Piccadilly, or a Visa/Kuoni online joint venture tour operator. But they (or their like) may not be too far off.

As I said previously, some of these innovative companies may be entering into your industry. New entrants are changing the rules of the game. In financial services, for instance, insurance companies are finding themselves competing not only with other financial institutions such as banks, but also with complete outsiders like retailers and supermarkets.

Here, deregulation is giving the whole change process an extra boost. Deregulated utilities, for example, are finding that they can do each other's businesses just as well as they can do their own. We can get electricity now from a gas company and water from an electricity company, and the electricity company can easily be of a different country to the customer who is buying its water—which might be confusing enough to deter the customer were the price reductions not irresistible.

Some established companies, to be sure, are already learning to use the knowledge they gather about their customers in the normal course of their traditional business in order to change the rules of the game and enter new businesses. Centrica, for example, which grew out of the once state-owned monopoly British Gas, decided that it knew its customers well enough (and had sufficiently excellent billing and marketing processes) to sell not only electricity to them (a competing source of energy) but other services. In one year they added 1 million customers by providing new services such as a cobranded credit card and home security products and services. And between 2000 and 2002, Centrica is spending £150 million (approximately $214 million) to build up a telephone business to offer cut-rate calls and compete with British Telecom (BT) and other established names in the market.

Conversely, BT is entering the financial services market with a range of mortgages and home insurance deals. It has even discussed creating an online real estate agency. Although the schemes will be primarily offered over the Internet, phone backup service will also be provided. British Telecom will serve as a broker to help find the best deals in the market. Customers using this service will not only potentially save money on their financial needs, but will also get 10 percent of their premiums cut from their phone bills. British Telecom is hoping to replicate the success of supermarkets that have moved into the financial products.

Financial companies are not content with sitting still and letting others take their turf without returning the favor. Barclays has created a new venture called B2B, the goal of which is to connect companies that are already customers of Barclays to each other. They hook up those middle market companies that are already buying products and services from each other. Barclays is leveraging its brand name, its client lists, and its electronic settlement features. This helps reduce costs significantly for customers who are selling products and helps the buyers more easily find what they are looking for.

Inevitably, marketing and innovation are the driving forces behind the customer-focused organization. As Peter Drucker once insightfully put it: "Because its purpose is to create a customer, the business enterprise has two—and only two—basic functions: marketing and innovation. Marketing and innovation produce results; all the rest are costs."[1] Production nowadays has to take a back seat, doing what it is told (and when) by these two new drivers. This is in stark contrast to the traditional organization where the production department sits at the steering wheel and keeps marketing and R&D firmly behind it, more or less at its beck and call. This model has been typical of engineering companies, which often have great products but little understanding of customers or the marketplace.

One engineering company that has certainly gone against that trend is Caterpillar. Well known for its bright-yellow earthmovers and backhoes, Caterpillar has moved into the electricity-generating equipment business and found a source of great new revenues and profits. They have taken engine-driven generators, which until recently were primarily a source of emergency backup power, and turned these units into a major source of power and revenue. Due to deregulation, the growth of energy-hungry Internet equipment, and power needs in developing countries, power-generation equipment accounted for 10 percent of Caterpillar's 1999 sales. Caterpillar is merely extending a product line to meet new demands.

Caterpillar also recognizes that "customers want holes, not drills." That is, they don't value a product or service per se; they value what it does for them. So Caterpillar, in addition to selling and leasing heavy equipment, now offers a service that helps customers to do the excavation they want the company's equipment to perform. The company has shifted from selling a product to selling a result that its customers value.

But adding value is often much more than extending a product to a service. Intel, the manufacturer of computer chips, has successfully moved into the computer hosting business, creating Intel Online Services. Yes, they were able to leverage their product and dominant position in the industry. But more importantly, they also leveraged Capabilities that they excel in. The manufacture of those chips requires production facilities with high levels of performance, predictability, and reliability. These are Capabilities that are also required for the running of a good hosting facility. Here was an opportunity to extend a Capability to create customer value.

HEARING YOUR CUSTOMERS

The innovative company of the future will, at a minimum, have the customer always in the front of its mind. The key is to link the business outcomes to what the customers value. Those outcomes in turn define the business Capabilities that the organization needs to develop (or outsource to others) in order to create value for its customers and, ultimately, for itself. As I have said, this design has to start from the outside—from the customer's perspective—before it can be adapted to fit within the organization itself. This is a fundamental rule. And the only way to understand what it is that customers value is to listen carefully—and often—to what they say and to watch carefully what they do. If a customer likes something and is prepared to pay for it, then it has value.

Deutsche Telekom (DT) introduced a new smart billing system—the electronic invoice service—that is highly valued by its 2 million business customers. This innovation demonstrates how a carrier can take advantage of new opportunities created by Internet technologies to build a better relationship with customers and at the same time measurably increase the business that they do. The electronic bill presentment and payment product was designed from scratch with 20 of DT's customers (including Procter & Gamble, Kodak, Lufthansa, and Deutsche Bank) in joint application development sessions using rapid prototyping.

Another company, Multibras S.A. Appliances, is the leading manufacturer of home appliances operating in South America, supplying 70 countries on five continents. To be competitive and sustain market leadership in a changing Brazilian marketplace, Multibras embarked on an ambitious change program that ultimately generated $50 million in cost reduction benefits for the company, reduced time to market by 35 percent, and cut development costs by 15 percent. This was achieved by focusing the business imperatives at three levels: industry, customers, and competencies.

Multibras first looked at future discontinuities in the *industry* by mapping potential future transformations and expected changes. They did this through the creation of scenarios and business imperatives. The changes were then fed into a view on what customers would want in the future. What are customer (current and potential future) expectations, needs, and wants? This was done using current customer knowledge, involving customers (e.g., Whirlpool) directly, and leveraging marketing expertise. This exercise made extensive use of quality function deployment, mapping what customers want against ways of delivering to those expectations. This helped drive the definition of the distinctive Capabilities required in the future. And to deliver the results, management allocated the best team possible for this effort and challenged the team to change the current status by establishing stretch goals.

In both examples above, the companies engaged their customers directly in identifying opportunities for improving the company's products and services. But don't fall into the trap of thinking that such initiatives can come out of brainstorming sessions with flip-charts and Post-it Notes. Groupware tools, such as Group System's Ventana or Comshare's DecisionWeb, enable data gathering and decision making in a much more sophisticated way. These types of tools facilitate innovation by mitigating communication barriers associated with organizational, personality, job-level, gender, and cultural differences, ensuring anonymity, supporting quality decision making, facilitating idea generation, resolving issues, building consensus, and promoting synergy across organizations. And because many of these tools are Web-based, interactions can take place virtually. Go beyond data warehousing and find more innovative ways of tapping into a customer's latent wants and needs.

HEARING CUSTOMERS: CUSTOMER COLLABORATION

Here are two examples of customer collaborations that led to interesting solutions to problems.[2] The first involves a hard drive manufacturer whose reputation for producing quality products landed them a long-standing relationship with several large computer manufacturers. However, despite its reputation as a technology leader, the company stood to lose its largest account. The reasons for the impending loss were threefold: (1) the company could not build hard drives fast enough to meet the demand of the computer manufacturer; (2) competitors were offering to deliver drives more quickly and at a cheaper price; and (3) in an attempt to meet increased demand, the company had acquired several smaller hard drive companies in a short period of time, creating a mishmash of corporate cultures with little or no customer-driven attitude.

In an effort to overcome these challenges and retain its largest account, the hard drive company collaborated with its most valued customer and learned several important things. The computer manufacturer's increase in demand was largely due to a new program whereby customers could return their old equipment for upgrade and refurbishment. The program was a tremendous success, and the computer manufacturer's need for hard drives increased dramatically. In an effort to increase its quality image, the computer manufacturer decided to offer quality brands only in the upgrade package. Additionally, the hard drive company discovered that the computer manufacturer was challenged by a shortage of warehouse space needed to store incoming components.

As a result, the hard drive company created a manufacturing line to refurbish returned disk drives. The company discovered that by refurbishing old drives, it could meet the increased demands of the computer manufacturer, shorten the delivery time, reduce the cost of the drives so they were in line with competitor's prices, and maintain the quality for which the company was noted. In addition, the hard drive company partnered with the computer manufacturer to more closely link their supply chains and to share warehouse space, saving both companies time and money. The hard drive company also partnered with the computer manufacturer to offer special prices for customers who chose their brand of hard drive as part of the upgrade package. The specials generated an 8 percent increase in upgrade sales and in hard disk demand for the computer manufacturer.

By partnering with the computer manufacturer, the hard drive company not only retained its most valuable customer and created new manufacturing capacity, but also increased the profit of hard drive sales to the computer manufacturer by over 18 percent.

Another example of customer collaboration leading to mutually beneficial solutions is from a major manufacturer of home improvement and repair products. By partnering with one of their major accounts, a large retailer of their products, they discovered a creative solution to a growing problem. The manufacturer invested heavily in developing a how-to education program designed to create new opportunities for product sales by educating consumers. The basic idea was, "If they know how to use our products and understand the benefits of repair and improvement, they'll buy more of the products." The educational program was supported by a customer support center with a toll-free phone number. Shortly after the educational marketing campaign was launched, the support center began receiving an unmanageable number of calls.

The manufacturer learned that its education program was, in fact, frustrating consumers. The basic problem was that the how-to instructions were too complicated for the average do-it-yourselfer. Confused by the instructions, customers were calling the support center to request help, complain, and ask for material refunds and replacements. Most of the calls were for help or further instructions, and many callers expected the support representative to stay on the line and actually talk them through a project. A few callers even asked for first aid instructions. The sales staff of the major account retailer was also plagued with support requests for the manufacturer's products. The educational marketing campaign had generated a tremendous amount of interest in products sold through the retailer's stores, but it would not have been cost-effective to walk each customer through a project. As a result, the sales staff avoided selling the manufacturer's products, and sales began to drop at an alarming rate. The retailer threatened not only to withdraw the educational campaign, but also to transfer the manufacturer's preferred status to a competitor.

Despite its frustration, the retailer wanted to find a solution and maintain its stock of quality products provided by the manufacturer. Through collaboration sessions, the companies agreed to develop and offer hands-on educational classes at the retail stores. As a result of the new education program, consumers gained valuable knowledge about home remodeling and repair. The manufacturer increased product sales across the product line an average of 25 percent in the first year. The calls to the manufacturer's support center dropped by 65 percent, and the majority of calls the center receives now are questions about when a class will be held. The retailer has experienced significant increases in store activity and retail sales. Partnering with the retailer allowed the manufacturer to retain one of its most important accounts and maintain its preferred status with that account.

The president of the manufacturing company has stated, "The relationship that we have established with this account and the creative potential that we have discovered will increase the value of both of our companies for a long time to come. Understand that we are not resting on our laurels. We will give the same attention to all our most valuable accounts."

HEARING CUSTOMERS: PREDICTING THE FUTURE

As Mark Twain once said, "The art of prophecy is very difficult—especially with respect to the future." Although this may be true, companies cannot afford to sit idly and wait for everything to change around them. Many companies lose sight of the fundamental requirement to focus on shifting market conditions and customer needs because they become blinded by their own success. "We know what our customers want," they say. And they believe what they say. But companies that sustain a successful position typically have excellent ways of scanning their environment, of resetting strategy in response to changing conditions, and of adapting quickly to support that new strategy. This requires an additional set of Capabilities that serve as a "radar system" for detecting environmental changes and guiding the company. Some companies refer to these as governance or strategic management Capabilities. This type of sensing Capability helps detect shifts in the marketplace and enables a company to rapidly respond with new strategies. It is important to recognize that this is quite different from strategic planning, which, according to Brian Quinn from Dartmouth University, "is like a ritual rain dance. It has no effect on the weather that follows, but those who engage in it think it does. Moreover, much of the advice related to corporate planning is directed at improving the dancing, not the weather."[3]

Strategic management Capabilities must identify shifts in market conditions, new entrants, changes in customer demographics, discontinuous innovations, and other factors that could directly impact a company's direction. Addressing these issues cannot be an annual event. It must be pervasive and ongoing. And, as with any Capability, it is important to make sure that the monitoring process not be confined to a small inner circle of executives. As many eyes and ears as possible should be involved. Feedback from front-line employees who deal with customers can be particularly helpful in providing early warning signals of changes in a company's markets.

The needs of customers change, and the things to which they attach value change. For a start, their expectations of speed, quality, cost, and convenience—the four dimensions of value—are constantly rising. Traditionally, successful companies excelled in one of these four dimensions. They were either the lowest-cost provider or the leader in customer service, for example. Nowadays, however, consumers are coming to demand higher levels of performance across all four dimensions. They are saying, "It's not cheaper things that we want, but expensive things that cost a lot less."

When mobile phones first came on the market, they had the shape and weight of a brick. Customers at the time did not mind because they had not seen any alternatives. But 10 years later, when a company called Iridium launched the first satellite-based phone on the consumer market, it flopped, in part because it also had the shape and weight of a brick. The market research was there to indicate future success, and the complex satellite system worked reasonably well. But mobile phone users had moved on. By then they wanted cheap handsets, and the smaller the better. The mobile phone will evolve steadily because manufacturers will forever be scratching their heads to figure out new things that they can add on to persuade consumers to discard their "old" phones and buy new ones. The key to keeping ahead of rapidly changing tastes is to make regular assessments of what your customers value.

HEARING CUSTOMERS: WHO TO LISTEN TO

How do you go about finding out what it is that customers value? To some, it is simply a matter of increasing the amount of market research that you do. But to others, including Anita Roddick, founder of The Body Shop, market research is "like driving along looking in the rearview mirror. You are studying what has gone." And there is some truth to what she says. Market research tells you what was the case, not what will be the case. Nevertheless, companies do still need that information. They need to know what has just happened in their markets. Nobody drives without a rearview mirror unless they have a powerful death wish. Admittedly, the information that a driver gets from a rearview mirror has a limited shelf life, but in that short time it is absolutely vital to life and limb.

But it is not enough. To have any hope of anticipating future markets and market trends, companies have to become much more innovative in the way they listen to their customers. Each time an answer comes back, they need to ask themselves, "Does this suggest ways that we can change and deliver more value in the future?" And they need to ask this question about all the four dimensions of value—speed, quality, price, and convenience.

Competition often comes from behind, catching companies off guard. In the 1980s, Xerox knew that competition was coming from the lower-priced Japanese products. And Xerox successfully fought back to take on that competition. But what they hadn't expected was competition from manufacturers of other products, namely laser printers. Hewlett-Packard and others have eroded Xerox's market share because customers have found that it is more convenient to print directly to a local laser printer than to go to the central copying machine, regardless of the fact that a photocopy is many times less expensive than a laser-printed page.

When trying to pick up signals from customers, it is vital that companies listen to the right ones (Figure 4-1). Customer satisfaction surveys tend to poll only those who come from the middle of the range—the typical, or average, customer. But the greatest insight often comes from a small number of "leading customers," the influencers, those who are more sophisticated than the norm and ahead of the trends. These are the early adopters—those whose tastes will be imitated by others. They are the people that others are going to follow, and their views are particularly valuable.

Former customers can also be a useful source of information. If possible—and this is not easy—ask questions of those who have been lost to the competition. Information from defectors can be particularly helpful in flagging changes in consumer tastes and the competitive environment. Why is last year's Adidas customer this year buying Reebok? Why does everyone suddenly want a particular type of Nokia mobile phone and not the Motorola models that were all the rage last April?

Defectors can also indicate when there is a slippage along one of the four dimensions of value—in the quality of service, for example, or in the price of a product or service relative to competitors' prices. When BT lost hordes of customers to cut-price competitors after the U.K. telecom market was opened up, it did not need to talk to many of those defectors to find out that its pricing structure was out of line. When it revamped its charges, it

FIGURE 4-1. Listen to the right customers.

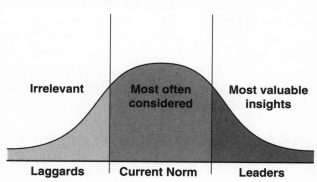

made a virtue of inviting people to "rejoin" BT and aggressively advertised that thousands were "coming back."

It is also good to talk to potential customers, people who are thinking for the first time of buying a mobile phone, say, or a DVD player. Potential customers are often able to suggest new sources of value because they are looking at the product afresh and, as it were, from the outside.

SERVING YOUR CUSTOMERS

In general, there are two types of customers: product-oriented customers who will buy individual products and service at the best price, and service-oriented customers who often want convenience and one-stop shopping. Product-oriented customers often have a better understanding of the products and services they are buying, and so they hunt for bargains. They are willing to invest the extra energy to get exactly what they want at exactly the price they want. Service-oriented customers go for convenience, focusing on bundled solutions that deliver a specific outcome. They tend to focus on the linkages between products and services rather than on individual offerings.

Product-oriented customers use various bargain-finding engines to get the best deals on loans, insurance, a Palm Pilot, or any other product or service. They tend to be sophisticated buyers who know just what they are looking for. They tend to go the low-cost route and will often choose, for example, Internet banking services, with their higher yields, and online stock trading, with its low commissions. Service-oriented customers demand service. They would rather pay a little more for convenience than hunt for a true best-of-breed solution themselves. They will pay for advisors and use portfolio managers and full-service functions. Service-oriented customers are often dealing with more complex issues or with one-off issues (e.g., moving, wills) that they don't face regularly.

An example of a company that targets product-oriented customers is LendingTree.[4] This online service provides customers with easy access to over 100 providers of mortgages, home equity loans, automobile loans, credit cards, and personal loans and small business loans. They target customers who are technically literate; Internet users with a wide range of credit histories. The key is that they force competitive bidding from providers. The consumer gets a choice of up to four proposals from a nationwide network of lenders on all loan types with approval within two days and mostly within minutes or hours of application. You can then compare and select the loan that is best for you. The service is free for buyers, and there are no broker charges. In a three-month period, they processed nearly 70,000 applications, worth nearly $5 billion, of which nearly $500 million resulted in closed deals. Companies like LendingTree are designed for customers who want to get the best deal possible for a specific product.

SERVING CUSTOMERS: DIVINING INTENTIONS

Service-oriented customers are looking for more than a particular product or even a particular solution. They want to satisfy what can be called "life-intentions," the broad personal goals that all consumers have and that to a large extent determine many of the things that they do and buy. These include things like "a healthy old age," "a secure future for the children," or "a desire to see the world."

To some extent, of course, intentions are no more than a bundle of solutions. And solutions, in turn, are no more than a bundle of goods and services. These goods and services can be provided by a number of companies, and aggregating is often the role of an intermediary. The Internet is full of intention-based sites. Microsoft's HomeAdvisor allows a consumer to do practically anything he or she wants relating to a house move, including finding a house, getting financing and insurance, making the move, turning on utilities, and obtaining guides to various locations. Follow this line, and it's clear that the firm that can be trusted to meet a consumer's intentions is going to have a great deal of diverse business coming its way. No firm can hope to get itself into that position, though, unless it first becomes intimately acquainted with its customers' lifestyles, desires, and preferences. And for that to happen there has to be an almost continuous two-way learning process between the organization and its customers, something that goes well beyond customer relationship management.

There needs to be an almost infinite flexibility in many of the business operations that are traditionally at the core of a company. Fulfilling demand becomes a matter of having the right product ready at the right time, of being able to arrange the extravagant cruise just after the insurance policies have matured or just after the wealthy aunt has died.

SERVING CUSTOMERS: CUSTOMERS' PROCESSES

At the same time a company thinks about ways to improve its own processes, it can also be thinking about how it might improve those of its customers and those of the interface between them. Any search for process improvement should not stop at an organization's own factory gates. In B2B dealings, processes increasingly transcend boundaries between organizations as well as boundaries between functions. The growth of networks of strategic alliances and outsourcers has forced process design to embrace not just individual customers but whole communities.

Every company should try "walking in its customers' shoes," especially when those customers are themselves other businesses. The customers' markets are probably changing at least as fast as yours are. Look at the gas and electric utilities, where deregulation stretched and squeezed the organizational boundaries in almost every direction, causing significant change almost weekly. Dozens of utilities created whole new "energy services" companies that offered everything from facilities management to environmental consulting, activities that their customers used to have to do for themselves. And companies like paymybills.com and StatusFactory.com created their businesses around removing the non-value-adding activities of the customers—all of the manual processes around receiving, opening, reading, and processing invoices. These activities are now all outsourced to companies like paymybills.com and StatusFactory.com.

HIRING THE CUSTOMER

When companies look at ways of increasing their innovative potential, a simple question should spring to mind: "Who is in a position to produce the best outcome for the customer?" And they should consider both the internal possibilities and the external possibilities—people inside and outside the organization. They should also think well beyond the boundaries of the team, department, division, or company that is performing a given task at present. Who has the best skills and assets for serving the customer? Sometimes the answer is (not so surprisingly) the customer.

Customers can participate in a number of a company's Capabilities, from product development to order acquisition and service. The Internet is making all of this possible. *Collaborative product commerce* tools, as they are being called, enable customers and suppliers to collaborate, on a real-time and virtual basis, with a manufacturer's product-development Capability. This is especially applicable in the business-to-business environment, where manufacturers need to know the specific needs of their customers, whether they are a computer manufacturer or a hospital. Web-based collaboration tools, such as Parametric Technology Corporation's (PTC) Windchill and Agile software, enable customers, partners, suppliers, and members of the extended organization to collaborate with manufacturers throughout a product's life cycle. These tools collect information from diverse sources, including proprietary and legacy systems, enabling the creation of a "product specification." This ensures that all members of the value chain, including customers, have easy access to timely and accurate product information, enabling the sharing and visualization of valuable product and process knowledge. For example, important legacy information, once locked away on mainframe systems, can now be accessed through a Web browser and used to make mission-critical decisions. Purchasing agents, who might be unfamiliar with computer-aided design (CAD) tools, can use their Web browser to identify, visualize, and mark up models, providing engineers fast and accurate responses to inquiries. These tools enable companies to deliver more innovative, customer-driven products to market faster.

Other Capabilities where customers can be hired are sales and service. When Lloyd 1885, the innovative Italian insurer and a sister company of the giant Riunione Adriatica di Sicurta (RAS) insurance group, set up an online insurance service, it had to come up with innovative and original processes for what was an almost entirely new business. In redesigning the selling process, it decided to reassign a number of steps to the customer. Through the company's Web site, customers are now able to peruse existing offerings and to create proposals that meet their needs without using an intermediary. They can obtain quotes, discounts, and special rates, and they can obtain information on the physical delivery of the policy they have bought—all online and without the intervention of a third party.

E-commerce enables customers to serve themselves. This tends to lead to greater satisfaction, and it reduces the costs to the company. But it also enables the business to focus on activities that add even greater value to customers. By having customers do the more mundane and administrative tasks (e.g., order management and order tracking) sales reps (for example) can spend time providing services of high value, such as relationship management, complex problem resolutions, and face-to-face sales time.

The scope of many processes extends naturally into a customer's organization. So when drawing the boundaries, let them stretch to their full extent. Doing so may open up new opportunities, such as the following:

- Enabling customers to serve themselves (for example, by paying for their own gas by credit card while at the pump).

- Allowing the sharing of information on supply with customers (for example, by providing available stock levels and shipment dates).

- Allowing the sharing of information on demand with customers (for example, ranking products in terms of popularity and customer-written reviews).

- Allowing you take over the running of a nonessential part of a customer's operations (for example, managing their inventory).

- Setting up a partnership to develop products and services jointly (for example, via preferred supplier agreements).

Another example of hiring the customer might involve peer-to-peer computing, where (roughly speaking) the customer's computers provide the processing power and storage capacity. An interesting example of this can be found in the Search for Extraterrestrial Intelligence (SETI). The SETI@home project[5] uses thousands of Internet-connected PCs to help in the search for ET. The idea behind SETI@home is to take advantage of the unused processing cycles on personal computers. Interested computer owners download free software from SETI@home. Periodically, data that has been collected from giant radio dishes searching the skies is downloaded to their computers. The computers process this data during idle time (when the users are not at their workstations). After processing, the results of the analysis are sent back to the research team. This research combines the processing power of legions of Internet users in order to carry out research that would otherwise be impossible (or prohibitively expensive). As of February 2000, SETI@home had 1.6 million participants in 224 countries. The amount of computing time contributed in the first year was equal to 165,000 years, averaging 10 teraflops (about 10 times more than the largest supercomputer on the planet). It is the largest computation ever done, and this is the ultimate in hiring the customer.

SERVING AND HIRING THE CUSTOMER: SUN MICROSYSTEMS
Like most companies, Sun Microsystems has been plagued by an explosion of phone numbers (over 60 numbers in the United States alone) for its call centers, back office contact centers, sales support facilities, and numerous other customer touchpoints. If a customer wanted to buy a server, some software, and professional services, they had to deal with three different organizations. Of course, this caused numerous frustrations for the customers as well as the sales reps. In fact, it was estimated that 50 percent of calls to call centers were not resolved during one interaction, certainly not in line with Sun's goal of "all done in one."

In one case, which I suspect many other companies can relate to, a government customer trying to place an order was bounced around for several days as he hunted for a way in. One call center had to acknowledge that it did not deal with government contracts and could not help him because the customer service rep had no history of the caller to refer to and so did not know where to forward the inquiry. Eventually, thanks to dogged determination, the customer found the Sun team dealing with government contracts and placed the order.

Since Sun had no specific system in place for tracking customer satisfaction, no one had overall accountability for this kind of multiple hand-off.

It was, therefore, even difficult to assess how extensive the problem was. To resolve it, Sun embarked on what it called the Sun Centers program, a plan aimed at creating an improved and unified customer experience. This required aligning the many independent call centers worldwide, integrating Web support capabilities into these centers and finding ways of "hiring the customer" through their Web presence. The goal was to have customers solve most of their own problems and inquiries, liberating the sales force to build relationships with customers.

The focus was more on improved customer experience, improved e-rep experience, and improved economics, to be accomplished through better coordination across centers, improved and streamlined business processes, improved knowledge management, and increased customer self-service.

Sun identified several key opportunities for self-service/self-management. One is customer involvement. By providing common information about orders, ship dates, configurations, and other key information, Sun made it possible for customers to answer their own status questions. To increase user friendliness, natural language query tools were put in place to help customers get quick answers to their questions. Plans for the future include providing wireless access to some of this data. Sun also enables self-service by deflecting request to knowledge tools. For example, EDI links are now being used for standard orders, bypassing even the Web and speeding transactions.

All of this is good from a customer-support perspective, and it also reduces costs. Both gains are clearly important to the success of any business. But there is another important benefit of these changes. Administrative work can now be shifted away from highly trained field sales reps to the clerical customer service reps who are capable of handling most routine order management items. This frees up significant time for sales reps to spend with their most important target customers.

One of the keys to success is to understand all of the customer touch points. Most of the Web e-commerce activities were initially done by the marketing staff. Then sales got involved, and then service, and so on. And each of these departments had developed in silo fashion. The key to a successful redesign was to identify *all* customer touch points, not just the historical ones. Sun also found that by involving key accounts such as Cisco in the redesign, they could more effectively reshape the customer experience. Now Sun can be confident when they say, "done in one."

CREATING THE FUTURE

Since predicting the future is difficult, perhaps the best way to control your destiny is to create your own future. In the end, listening to customers alone is not enough, for they do not always know what they want. Consumers didn't know they wanted the Chrysler mini-van or the CNN 24-hour news service, for example. And the Sony Walkman was not invented because customers were clamoring for it. Three new markets were thus created out of pure innovation. The need didn't exist; it was created.

Just as the Walkman revolutionized the music world back in the 1980s, MP3 and Napster are now leading another revolution: MP3 is a computer-based format for recording, distributing, and listening to music, and Napster's first incarnation was as a peer-to-peer network where people could freely post or download music, even copyrighted materials. Of course lawsuits began to fly as the music companies tried to stop Napster from posting their music, and in February 2001, Napster was forced to change its business model to avoid copyright infringement. Even with Napster's early model effectively shut down, numerous other sites have cropped up that offer free music. And Napster's success has forced many recording labels to offer a similar service, albeit at some cost. Although the future of free music on the Internet is up in the air, the complaints about Napster are somewhat reminiscent of the days when radio was introduced. Record companies are now doing their best to keep their artists from working with Napster for fear of losing sales. The same thing happened when the popularity of radio took off in the 1920s. The record companies attempted to boycott radio because they didn't want to give their product away for free. Of course radio increased sales, and it is common for record companies to pay radio stations to get their artists on the air.

Another way to connect the dots by focusing on the lines involves realizing that new technology sometimes brings old issues to the surface: the true innovators exploit the lessons of the past and don't get distracted by the technology.

Using the survival-of-the-fittest concept as described in Chapter 1, some companies have been able to hedge their bets a little. Capital One, a global financial services company, offers 300 different "products," most of which vary only slightly from one another. But for Capital One, the cost of offering these products through the mail or the Internet is quite low. And by offering so many, they are able to identify which are successful and then rally to heavily promote those products. Seiko claims that they developed 100 variations of their watches, knowing that only 2 would survive—but also knowing those two would be big winners, and they could reconfigure manufacturing to rapidly produce more of them.

Many firms have made clever use of branded items to create new revenue streams while also getting their name into the marketplace—in effect creating thousands of walking advertisements on the streets, and, in effect, hiring the customer. In the case of Caterpillar, mentioned earlier in this chapter, the "Cat" brand has become ubiquitous on construction sites. More controversially, branded clothing for Camel, Marlboro, and other tobacco brands has replaced some of their advertising that was banned by health authorities. Not only do they save money on advertising, they make money on the clothing.

I have tried to show in this chapter how the power in the marketplace has shifted from producer to consumer. Understanding a customer's needs, desires, and intentions—and taking the initiative to satisfy them—holds far more value-creating potential than simply focusing on internal operations. Information technology is providing the tools to enable this new symbiosis, this new codependence. Look for ways to serve your customers better by creating more value for them. Identify ways of getting closer to your customers, collaborating with your customers, and hiring your customers. This approach to embracing the customer is the only way to stay ahead in today's customer-driven marketplace.

5

C H A P T E R

TECHNOLOGY
AND INNOVATION

*"Applying computer technology is simply finding the right
wrench to pound in the correct screw."*

*I'm not prepared to declare yet that technology will solve all the
problems of global business, but the potential for it to improve and
transform performance is clearly enormous. Companies need to think
about how to Retool—how to put technologies to work in innovative
ways and how to take advantage of sophisticated new technologies to
drive new business models. There can be few firms that have not been
affected by the combination of telecommunications and computers.
Information technology has revolutionized production processes,
turned supply chain management upside down, and created completely
new distribution channels. Collaboration with partners worldwide is
now a possibility—at minimal cost. The biggest challenge today is to
think creatively about how the potential of e-commerce can be used to*

123

improve the ways in which organizations operate. Innovative compa-nies are finding their way forward through technology every day.

Today as I sat down to write this chapter on technology (the fourth element of the Capability blueprint) and its role in orga-nizations, I got a rude reminder that technology is no panacea for business. In fact, it can be a creator of new headaches. I wanted to go from London to Paris for the weekend, so I decided to do something really simple—buy a couple of airline tickets. Before the availability of e-commerce, I would have picked up the phone, called a travel agent, and booked my tickets within minutes. But now we've got this new wonder called the Internet, giving us more autonomy and choices than ever for booking our tickets. And it is all done from our com-puter. Simple.

The theory is, you log on, book your flight, then either have your tick-ets delivered or you can pick them up at the company's office or at the air-port. If only it *were* that simple. I logged on to one of the well-known travel sites, and after quite a bit of searching I was able to find flights at the right price on the right dates. Excellent. I entered in all of my information. When I tried to confirm, the system kept giving me a cryptic error message. I tried again. This time it said my password was wrong, which it wasn't. I reen-tered it several times and kept getting the same error message. Finally, I thought it was going to work, because it was "thinking" a lot longer than usual. But no, my computer was crashing and I lost everything. Panic set in. Did my reservation get confirmed or not? There was no way to tell from the site, so I resorted to the phone. The man who answered could not tell me right then and there, but said he would call me back. A half hour later he did call back saying that the ticket was booked and confirmed. Okay, good.

I asked him to send me a confirmation via e-mail or something just so I could have a record. He said okay again. An hour went by and no word and no confirmation. So I called the main number again and got a different person. I asked again for confirmation, and again this person could not answer and said he would have to call back. Thirty minutes later he called and said my flights were *not* booked. I asked him to make certain because I did not want to be charged twice. He said he would send this to the "home office" for verifica-tion. Two and a half hours later, no word back. Did I have tickets or not? Should I book elsewhere, or had I already paid for my flight? I was now five hours into the process. It would have been faster for me to take a taxi to Heathrow Airport, 45 minutes away, book a ticket in person, and travel back.

But I like technology, so I decided to have faith. To be patient. I also wanted to see how far this was going to go. Eventually I called back. Obviously, I was not the only one with a problem because I had to wait 20 minutes on the phone line, then I was asked to leave a voice mail. My voice mail was an urgent plea to "call me back." An hour later, I still had not received a callback. So, being a technophile, I decided to go back to the high-tech route. Since I did not know whether my order had been processed, I was hesitant to book elsewhere. I logged back on to the site and selected the "chat" option, where I was supposed to be able to have a real-time dialogue with a real person.

Finally I got someone who was able to answer my questions. No, my tickets were *not* booked, she cheerily confirmed, but she promised to check it out further. She called me a few minutes later to take the rest of the details by old-fashioned telephone and book the ticket. And she was so helpful that she reserved a seat for me while we were on the telephone. She even arranged it so that the tickets would be processed quickly because I needed to pick them up that evening. (Fortunately, the ticketing place is only a 10-minute walk away.) Soon the ordeal would be over. Or would it?

I walked there and gave them my name. They had the tickets. Finally! Then I looked at the price. The price I had been quoted was £99.50 ($142). The tickets said £107.60 ($154). When I pointed this out to the man who had handed me the tickets, he asked whether I had booked online. I said I had tried but in the end a real person had processed the tickets for me. Hmmm ... an offline sale. And obviously offline sales are processed in a completely different way because he could not look up my ticket status on his computer. So he had to check with another call center. After 10 minutes of back and forth, the person on the other end of the phone said that the tickets should have been priced at £99.50. (Houston, we have a problem, I thought to myself.) So I had a ticket that I tried to book online, that was booked offline, and that was mispriced and no one can figure out why. After about another 15 minutes, the gentleman returned with a smile on his face and said, "Oh, this price is not what you are being charged. This is the price that everyone else is paying."

As it turned out, there was an obscure code somewhere on my ticket that indicated to someone (I'm not sure who) that this ticket would not be charged at face value. But the existence of such a code seemed to be a little-known fact among the company's employees. Even the customer-facing staff didn't know about it. The good news was that after eight hours of worry and hard work, I had my tickets in hand. And I had saved £8 ($11) off the regular price. Or had I? In fact, two weeks later when my credit card invoice arrived, I discovered that I had been charged fives times for the tickets. What a bargain.

And my Internet experience is not unique. According to a recent Accenture e-fulfillment study, 67 percent of deliveries that were placed during the 2000 holiday season were not received as ordered and 12 percent were not received in time for Christmas. The same report also noted that 7 percent more Web sites operated by traditional retailers and mail-order catalogers delivered orders in time for Christmas than did pure-play e-tailers—and the e-tailers also did a poorer job of simplifying the return process.

NOT THE SILVER BULLET—YET

Clearly technology has its limitations, and at the beginning of this discussion it is important to be aware of them. But first, it is useful for us to be using the same definition of the word *technology*. I think of technology in the broadest sense as including:

- Application suites (SAP, Oracle, or Baan), focused applications (e.g., Internet Explorer), and Net-sourced applications running through the Internet
- Information and data used to run a business and gathered about customers to help target offerings
- Equipment such as computers, personal digital assistants, and mobile phones
- Technical infrastructure such as networks, Web servers, routers, and operating systems
- The Internet itself, including the World Wide Web

Given the wide range of sophisticated tools available at our fingertips, it is easy to understand why many companies—and individuals, including myself—sometimes expect too much too soon. They would like to see technology become their silver bullet, waiting to be fired into the flabby flanks of the organization and transform it into the sleek nimble beast that they know it has to become to survive in the current business climate. But technology injected in isolation from other aspects of an organization cannot be expected to work miracles.

Technology must always be considered in conjunction with the organization and its processes. What I want to discuss in this chapter is how technology can enable and facilitate innovation. When we introduced Capabilities, we discussed the need to focus on the lines that connected the various elements of the business and the need to avoid focusing on any one component in isolation. It is the relationship among processes, people, and technology that counts. But most companies still like to focus on technology as the answer, in isolation from these other components. And too often, enterprise resource planning (ERP) systems are forced in without consideration of the impact on the rest of the business—an approach I call "package-ectomy." (Although package-ectomy is not semantically correct, since an "ectomy" is the removal of something, I think you get the point.) But as we discussed in Chapter 1, best practices give you par. And ERP systems are just that, par golf in a world of world-class players.

Technology is to an organization as musical instruments are to a jazz band—great when there's somebody there who knows how to play them but pretty useless when there isn't. So although technology is a necessary part of revitalizing virtually any company today, it is by no means sufficient by itself. Technology is only a tool, and it has to be appropriate to the processes and the organization to which it is being applied. We've all seen small fortunes spent on new hardware and software that have actually ended up raising costs, not reducing them. And there are numerous examples of doomed dot-coms with great Web sites but poor business models. A case in point was Boo.com, the heavily promoted pan-European Internet retailer that went under in mid-2000 after just a few months of operation. Or the fulfillment and financial woes of eToys.

It may seem obvious but I think it is worth restating that in order to produce results, the technology being contemplated has to be absolutely right for the organization and its strategy. It has to fit. In this context I like the story told by Professor Chris Parker of the University of Lucerne about a tribesman from a remote part of Malaysia who was taken to Singapore for the weekend as part of an anthropological study. It was his first exposure to the outside world. After a tour of the bustling city, his guides asked him what had struck him most about this place, one of the great high-tech centers of the world. The tribesman said without hesitation that the biggest surprise was a wheelbarrow that he had noticed being used to haul a large quantity of bananas, more bananas being hauled by one conveyance than he had ever seen before.

All the computers and all the mobile phones on the technology-mad island meant nothing to him. He was most impressed by nothing more sophisticated than the big wheelbarrow because in his organization (the tribal community) the processes that matter still focus on basic gathering and distribution of food and water. The digital world has yet to have any bearing on their lives. The technology of choice for this tribe would be a consignment of new wheelbarrows. Of course, in the context of business, technology is more sophisticated than the wheelbarrow, but no more important to its success.

AUTOMATING PROCESSES

Technology has been and will continue to be an effective way of taking rules and parameters and imbedding them in software to reduce costs and error rates. Even the Internal Revenue Service (IRS) has found ways to improve itself through technology—electronic tax returns. It found that the error rate with the new system was only 1.3 percent, whereas the error rate with paper-based forms was approximately 15 percent. This of course saves the IRS significant rework and cost. And the electronic filers are also rewarded for using this channel. In general, they receive any refund due to them within two to three weeks. Taxpayers who insist on using paper still have to wait four to six weeks to get their money back. Through technology, the IRS has found a way to improve accuracy, reduce costs, and generally serve the public better.

Interestingly though, the technology was initially available only to tax preparation services, who chose to tack on an additional fee for filing electronically. As a result, there was a disincentive for people to use the innovation that would have been beneficial to the IRS. The IRS probably could have paid people to use electronic filing and still saved money overall due to the accuracy and productivity gains.

Another interesting innovation that sprang from electronic filing (although it probably would have come up anyway) was the "rapid return." (This is a good example of a Resequence move.) Traditionally, you would file your return and wait for your refund in the mail. This could take up to eight weeks. Then the tax preparation services developed the idea of offering a rapid refund. For a fee, taxpayer's owed a refund can get the refund as soon as they filed. In fact, what they are really getting is a loan for the refund amount, with the interest disguised as a service fee.

Another example is the price of an annual subscription to the daily newspaper *The Wall Street Journal*. Before the Internet, a paper-based subscription cost $329. Via the Internet, the electronic version costs a mere $49 a year. The information the reader receives is the same, but the producer of that information gets rid of the bother of printing it and delivering it physically to the subscriber's home or office.

In practice, the economics of publishing print products on the Web are still being worked out. Other major publishers such as *The New York Times*, *The Washington Post*, and *The Economist* give away the full content of their publications—plus background links—on the Internet at great cost to themselves while simultaneously selling the printed version the old-fashioned way. And in some ways, the Web sites are superior to the printed product. The electronic newspapers are updated at regular intervals so the person who logs onto the papers' Web sites always gets the latest edition, unlike the person who buys the paper from a vendor on the street or the subscriber who has it delivered at home.

Over time, the processes that *The Wall Street Journal* so efficiently performs to print and distribute its papers speedily will become less and less central to the company's strategy. Indeed, the more the paper is read electronically, the more those processes become secondary to its core business. In the end, the company may decide that the printing and distribution functions have become sufficiently peripheral for them to be outsourced to others.

The processes the *Journal* needs to improve in order to fend off competition from other news providers on the Web—and it doesn't take much to set up a good-looking competitor—are things like the accuracy, originality, and timeliness of its information. The processes that deliver those outcomes to customers are the ones that nowadays create most value for the company.

When we look to how technology can transform rather than just automate processes, we see some new Capabilities that the *Journal* needs to be good at. A key here is using technology to enable personalization, profiling, and filtering. They will remain ahead of their competitors if they can provide the most relevant information to their customers with the least effort on the customer's part. In the previous chapter we talked about convenience for the customer, that is, making the company easy to do business with. The more you learn about your customer over time, the less your customers should have to sacrifice, and technology plays a major role in enabling this.

CONNECTING THE DOTS THROUGH TECHNOLOGY

When addressing the role of technology and innovation, the benefits go far beyond cost reduction through automation. As I discussed earlier, innovation is about connecting the dots. Lines, not boxes. And technology's greatest power in driving innovation is connecting the various dots and boxes that exist in the business landscape, such as customers, employees, suppliers, and intermediaries.

When talking about technology, first, and most obviously, comes the Internet and its main vehicle the World Wide Web. These provide a kind of universal connectivity that has led to new marketing approaches, new delivery channels, disintermediation, hyperintermediation, direct interactive links between manufacturers and consumers, collaboration across distances, and (of course) e-commerce. And this list will only grow longer with time.

Universal connectivity has been a major driver of globalization in recent years. It has enabled companies to integrate subsidiaries and suppliers into their main businesses, no matter how remote they are. New developments such as the integration of mobile phone networks with the Internet have opened up opportunities to bring even more remote stakeholders (and stakeholders that won't stay still) into an organization's network. The traveling executive can call in from her car and receive last minute e-mails or spreadsheet details just before she goes in to see a customer or a supplier. We have moved from home telecommuting to mobile telecommuting; cars (and a lot of other unlikely places) can become complete mobile offices.

Although there are many ways that technology and innovation are related, I am going to focus my discussion on five ways that technology is either facilitating innovation or creating innovative business models. Technology enables innovation when it is used to:

- Create a virtual enterprise
- Change the rules of the game
- Collaborate throughout the value chain
- Increase knowledge of employees
- Launch new businesses

Of course these are not mutually exclusive. Collaboration can help create a virtual enterprise, which focuses employees on sources of competitive differentiation, which in turn increases their knowledge and makes them more effective.

CREATING VIRTUAL ENTERPRISES

The Internet has been able to give new companies low entry costs, economies of scale, and the reach of a global giant almost overnight. This has enabled small, unknown companies to take on incumbent market leaders in several industries in a way that was inconceivable just a few years ago.

The influence of the Internet upstarts has been particularly strong in those industries with a high information content, such as financial services and publishing. A 1999 report from the Forrester Research group cited a number of specific cases. Before the Internet era, it cost $100 to place an order in the equity markets. Using the Web, an order can be placed for $15. Such a dramatic economy had never before been seen in the history of the stock market.

Barriers to entry have dropped so low that anyone can set up a business overnight for under $100 and an investment of time. But of course that doesn't mean it will be a successful business. Having a presence on the Web is a small part of what it takes to be successful.

Going Virtual at Universal Leven

Technology is helping all kinds of companies, not just start-ups, create virtual enterprises. The Internet, combined with massive outsourcing, gave rise to one particularly remarkable spin-off in Europe. Imagine an insurance company established only two years ago that has already contracted 15,000 policies and is issuing 200 new policies every week. Now imagine that the company has only two employees. This is Universal Leven, a Netherlands-based subsidiary of Allianz, focused on large, professional broker organizations. The two employees are in charge of corporate strategy, network expansion, and product development. Everything else, including product branding, product design, marketing, and all back-office operations (e.g., policy administration and financial administration) has been outsourced to strategic partners. Web-based product information and contract status help make the rest possible. Universal Leven is setting a new standard for the innovative use of technology in the insurance industry.

Outsourcing nearly all of the nonstrategic functions was the only way to rapidly increase scale and grow the business. All back-office operations (outsourced to Accenture) were up and running within six months, and within one year the company was fully functional. Universal Leven is in business with seven broker organizations and three banks. Core products are savings, mortgages, pensions, and annuities, all on a unit-linked basis. This means that instead of a fixed amount of money being put in, you put money in an investment fund and the units within that fund determine your returns.

The operating model allows brokers to deal with Universal Leven through multiple channels: Web pages (for product information), mail and telephone (personal support by account managers), and application software such as "Central Information Application" (online policy status and information) and "Policy Express" (which digitally sends applications). These interactions then feed through the rest of Universal Leven and the strategic partners.

The role of Universal Leven's partners is different from traditional outsourcing roles. Outsourcing has grown from its application maintenance roots, to IT outsourcing, to business process outsourcing, to highly evolved new business models known as *enablement* models. These revolutionary new strategic partnering relationships allow companies to concentrate on their core competencies; less strategic activities are performed outside by best-in-class companies. A new core competency has thereby emerged for all companies operating in this manner: alliance management. The goal is to string together the various companies in such a way that customers feel they are dealing with one company. All functions must be coordinated and seamless. As I have said throughout this book, the focus is on the lines rather than the boxes.

Although not directly related to outsourcing, it is important to note that this type of relationship requires rigorous service level agreements (SLAs). New management processes are also required. For example, partners can enter change requests that benefit the business or reduce the cost level, regardless of where the changes take place. The intent is to optimize the whole.

These changes are agreed upon on a quarterly basis and are used to update the SLAs with strategic partners and the operational level agreements (OLAs) (activities to be developed by Universal Leven). Strategic partners are paid by transaction (e.g., new policies, changed policies, terminated policies, claims) and are also given premiums for exceeding agreed-upon service levels. An operating committee, comprised of Universal Leven and partners, is responsible for evaluation of SLAs and OLAs, monitoring and driving developments within the insurance industry, and arbitration of disputes.

Although the processes are highly automated, the key has been in determining where decision-making authority starts and ends. Putting all of this together, Universal Leven has been able to create the first truly virtual enterprise that is becoming a major player in the insurance industry.

Brokers, banks, and investment brokers such as Fidelity agree that Universal Leven provides exceptionally strong customer service, and greater flexibility and more favorable pricing than competitors. This flexibility was achieved by having different parties focus on their core capability.

CHANGE THE RULES OF THE GAME

E-commerce has spawned more start-ups in a short period than ever before in the history of business. As Michael Porter of Harvard Business School put it: "New entrants, unencumbered by a long history in the industry, can often more easily perceive the potential for a new way of competing. Unlike incumbents, newcomers can be more flexible because they face no trade-offs with their existing activities."[1]

But don't count out the big companies of yore. There is a change afoot, and the giants are fighting back. The disadvantages that the incumbents suffer are often more than offset by the advantages of having a well-funded organization with a respected brand and large numbers of loyal customers. And large companies are taking advantage of new technologies not just to automate existing ways of doing business but to create new businesses.

New Business Models at Fiat Barchetta

A key to being successful in this environment is to rethink your business model and change the rules of the game. In the automotive industry, companies that have used technology have, for the most part, automated the existing processes. They still use the dealer network that has been long established. But several companies are using e-commerce to go straight to the customer. A pioneering use of technology came out of Italy's Fiat, which decided to turn the traditional model of car marketing on its head. Fiat created a direct OEM-to-customer sales channel, and made the first sale of a car by an OEM organization entirely through the Web, including payment by credit card and home delivery. One key challenge was avoiding conflict with the existing dealer network. This was accomplished by using car models not available through the dealers. A special convertible version of the Barchetta was created specifically for this new market. The site, www.barchettaweb.com, was launched in 1999 to an enthusiastic reception.

The Web site allows customers to configure their car, select from additional services, conduct test drives at rental car locations, and work out economic and finance simulations. The customer has three payment options:

1. Cash, with an online credit card prepayment and final payment via bank transfer
2. Used car trade-in, with preliminary evaluation on the Web and final promises to purchase from Fiat Auto at the customer's home after a proper technical assessment
3. Financing through an online application

Trade-ins and financing activities use the same business model because of the complexities of these transactions. A different business model was used for cash purchases because of their relative simplicity, and the cash model was implemented first.

The key capabilities of the Barchetta Web site are:

- *Test Drive.* The customer can get a test drive at a National Car Rental agency, booking it on the BarchettaWeb site.
- *Car Configuration.* The customer can select the trim and colors of the exterior and interior and can choose from a variety of options.

- *Trade-In.* A first evaluation of the used car is made through the Web site. Then, if the customer desires, he can request its real value to be determined by a professional. Fiat buys the used car at the price set by the appraisers.
- *Financing.* The financing application is submitted online, with preapproval given through e-mail. Supporting documentation is sent via express courier. Final approval is communicated via e-mail, and the client receives the financing contract at home.
- *Home Delivery.* The car is then transferred from the nearest branch to the customer's home, pulled by another Fiat car.

The future for the Barchetta Web site is in the area of e-service, offering the customer an integrated maintenance and repair service leveraging Web technology in partnership with the dealer network. All of these initiatives are viewed as a proof of concept to drive future investments and help create a new market image for Fiat.

Replay TV is using technology to change customer television viewing habits. It is the first company to offer viewers the ultimate convenience of watching whatever they want and whenever they want, regardless of broadcast schedules. They use intelligent recording devices that can freeze-frame live television broadcasts as well as do sophisticated recording that has until now been unavailable to the nonprofessional. To achieve all of this, the box only needs to be connected to a phone line that allows for television schedules to be downloaded to the machine. New software can be downloaded along with the new schedules, increasing the functionality of the device. Although it looks like hardware sitting there on the television, the major components of it are in fact software. This means that products that appear to be physical can in fact be reinvented without anyone ever touching the box. One of the capabilities they are now able to deliver is to send an advertisement to the screen during freeze-frame time. Another capability recently downloaded to machines is the ability to program the device through the Internet. Technology is truly changing the rules of the game and the way people live their lives.

COLLABORATE THROUGHOUT THE VALUE CHAIN

Collaboration is about bringing people, departments, companies, and communities together. Once interlocked, this collaboration can make possible the seamless processing that global organizations—and less ambitious ones—need in order to stay in the game.

A key in collaboration is data handling and distribution. There are only three things to remember about retooling: data, data, and data. And retooling is not about gathering gigabytes of data, but rather about enabling the sharing of information inside and outside the company. As the flow of information becomes seamless and transparent, the place where work is done is no longer important, who does it is flexible, and even when it is done becomes more transparent. Collaboration can now take place with suppliers and customers up and down the value chain.

Even collaboration with competitors becomes possible. Consider the rapid emergence of B2B exchanges, such as Exostar (Aerospace), ApplianceZone (home appliance and consumer electronics industries), and ChemConnect. Business-to-business exchanges bring together a number of companies and allow them to use a common technological platform for buying products and services through the Internet. For example, ChemConnect, founded in 1995, is currently the largest global Internet exchange for chemicals and plastics. John Beasley, CEO of ChemConnect, had a vision for the exchange to be the Nasdaq of the chemicals industry. Its first offering was an online suppliers' directory, and in 1997 services were expanded to include online transactions between buyers and sellers. Two years later, the company established an online bulletin board where users placed ads to buy and sell chemicals. In 1999, World Chemical Exchange was launched. Membership is free, but ChemConnect collects a percentage for transactions. Trading for both buyers and sellers is anonymous until the transaction is complete. Through the exchange, manufacturers and producers have the means to instantly identify and convert chemical needs, surpluses, and shortages into trading offers. It is estimated that up to 15 to 25 percent of the $1.6 trillion chemical industry will be moving through Internet exchanges within the next three to five years. Other industries that have followed suit are reaping the benefits. Exostar, for example, has 37,000 suppliers, handling $120 billion in purchases a year, with savings of 30 percent for buyers.[2]

Collaboration also takes place within companies and across the value chain, and it helps create communities within the customer base. The goal is to go beyond typical repetitive transaction processes and move toward true collaboration. Programs such as Lotus Notes make previously restricted information potentially available to all the workers throughout an organization. And several Internet-based tools such as NetMeeting and AOL Instant Messaging allow people to collaborate on a real-time basis. This is particularly important in integrating the back-end worker with the front person who makes the sale and with the person or team who fulfills the order. And some newer tools and service providers are enabling collaboration across companies and customers more effectively. One such company is ClickCommerce, a provider of enterprise channel management solutions. It provides software that leverages the Internet so that companies can reach customers around the world, enabling suppliers and customers to access real-time information whenever they need it. This is, in effect, one-stop shopping for all of their needs.

At one company, ClickCommerce is used as a customized Web portal that allows customers, suppliers, and employees worldwide to obtain account status and product information via an illustrated product catalog. Customers can also receive targeted presales promotional information specific to their role, place orders online via the company's e-commerce system, and perform accounting and sales transactions with customers and suppliers on a real-time basis. In addition, the customer/supplier exchange provides a wide range of collaborative functionalities, including the ability to enter forecasts, review inventory usage and requirements, do requests for proposals for project-related business, view online inspection reports (including future material requirements), and gather feedback. The result is greater interaction between the company and its customers, increased efficiency throughout the extended value chain, and significant savings across the board.

Collaboration is also about overcoming some of the limitations of geography by allowing an organization to coordinate processes across regions and across borders. Small numbers of far-flung customers and suppliers can be aggregated into the company's network to create a large global market that can be serviced in a highly efficient manner.

Gathering data from remote locations and then spreading it out more widely was central to the multimillion-dollar savings that Caterpillar made when redesigning its engine production processes. As the world's largest manufacturer of construction and mining equipment, Caterpillar used a manual system of sequencing some of the production functions at the company's highly centralized production facility in Peoria. When orders did not match the assembly line's production rate, employees had to do some short-term forecasting of key variables in order to fill in the gaps. This inevitably resulted in new production sequences and a waste of the JIT materials that had already been delivered for assembly.

Data on the organization's shipment histories, actual orders, and projections of future sales was fed into the production planning process, together with the production constraints that were imposed internally on the assembly lines (for example, the fact that no more than two engines of the same type could be made in sequence). The improvement in forecasting and scheduling that resulted from this electronic collection and dissemination of data led to a 67 percent reduction in outsourcing costs for the physical resequencing of materials along the assembly line, a reduction that led to savings of some $1 million a year.

All this is made possible by collaboration. And one way the Internet is taking collaboration to the next level is by enabling (and in same cases, forcing) companies to move from being an international presence to being truly global. Making this happen requires that a company provide "one face," and speak a single "business language," to all its customers. Unfortunately, what seems like a simple idea of putting up a Web site is often a complex undertaking.

One client of mine has recognized this need to be truly global, to embrace e-commerce, and to make the company easier to do business with. It's an extremely successful, highly decentralized company, with several hundred business units and a similar number of ERP systems. And unfortunately for the company, each ERP system has different number schemes for customers, suppliers, parts, and products. This makes any type of collaboration difficult, as if each business were speaking a different language. Yet the goal must be to present one face to the customer. Customers who place an order don't care whether it will be processed by four different business units. As long as they believe they are dealing with one company—and get one invoice and one shipment, and have one point of contact—they will be happy.

Making this happen requires a translator that can convert the language of one business unit's ERP to that of another. And it needs to know how to route orders and queries to the appropriate company. To get there, companies are increasingly using enterprise application integration (EAI) software such as Vitria, STC, and Websphere. This works as a combination parser, translation, and work flow software. For example, suppose customer Smith places an order for four items and the four items are from different business units, with different ERP systems and hence different numbers for this customer. The EAI software needs to know that customer Smith is really customer J. Smith to business unit 1, and that orders for specific items get routed there.

In the context of innovation, EAI software creates a structural standard (as opposed to a specific process standard) to allow entities to share information. This structural standard allows the units that are conducting the processes to perform locally to adapt and improvise given whatever situation they find themselves in, and yet leverage centralized coordination to enable information sharing. This is a perfect example of focusing on the lines that connect the units and allowing the boxes (the units) to operate freely. Here, we are standardizing on the outcomes, whereas in the past we tried to standardize every process so it could accommodate every case and/or exception. Inevitably some were missed, which created bottlenecks when the situations arose.

This is what the "new" process design is all about. These structural or coordination standards are the key, rhythm, and tempo of the music that holds the organization together. Here we are standardizing to enable *heterogeneity* rather than standardizing to ensure homogeneity. We don't want every experience to be the same; we do, however, want every outcome to be. It is a means for marrying local autonomy and flexibility with centralized coordination.

INCREASE EMPLOYEES' KNOWLEDGE

Another form of collaboration is the sharing of knowledge. And knowledge (or at least the ability to convert knowledge into action) is at the heart of innovation. But knowledge is much more than sharing information. Yes, technology can be used to capture and disseminate the "learnings" of an organization. And much has been written over the past few years on knowledge management. What I want to focus on here is how technology can truly create knowledge, which in turn fosters innovation. One of the keys to doing this is off-loading repetitive, administrative tasks, whether to customers, clerks, computers, or other companies, so that knowledge workers can focus on the high-value jobs.

It is often assumed that e-commerce is only about cutting costs. But its greatest value comes from its ability to leverage an organization's assets (and in particular its people) to enable them to do more valuable work. True, the electronic version of *The Wall Street Journal* costs far less than the paper-based version to produce. But it also enables the paper's owners to concentrate resources on higher-value-adding activities—gathering news and writing and editing, for example, rather than the mere lifting and shifting of paper.

Most of the employees at the social services department in Merced County, California, are social workers. But in the past how much of their time was spent on social work? Almost none. They were mostly busy with administrative tasks such as entering claims forms and searching records manually. Now, new systems have helped to automate those tasks, freeing the social workers to do what they were hired to do. The quality of service has improved significantly.

I have noticed a similar challenge with sales reps in almost every company I have worked with. When we look at how much time these valuable workers spend face to face with customers, it is appalling—20 to 40 percent.

The rest is spent traveling, filling out forms, and attending meetings. One notably bad example I observed was a food company where brand managers, particularly important in the food business, were spending less than 30 percent of their time doing brand management; the rest was spent on administrative work.

The way forward is to get your knowledge workers doing knowledge work. Transactional work should be eliminated, simplified, automated, assigned to clerks, or, better yet, outsourced. One key to this, as discussed in Chapter 4, is to hire your customer. Once customers identify and personalize their requirements, they can be more efficiently targeted and thereby more self-sufficient. Sites should be designed in such a way that customers can review product catalogs and reviews, self-configure solutions, enter orders, process payments, track orders and shipments, upgrade their software packages by downloading the new versions, register products, resolve simple problems, and much more. This allows employees, whether they be sales reps, engineers, or customer service agents, to focus on adding more value. They can do more knowledge work such as marketing strategies, negotiations, face-to-face selling, and answering complex questions. The key is to focus on your core business and get people working on what matters most. In Chapter 7, I discuss strategies for achieving these objectives. But of course one way is to outsource less critical Capabilities. Companies like epeopleserve and ICGCommerce provide Net-sourced human resources and indirect material procurement.

Once your knowledge workers are focused on knowledge work, it's time to increase their capacity. The Internet has opened up many new e-learning opportunities. Accenture, for example, uses the Internet to conduct training programs. Participants receive presentation materials in advance through e-mail, and then they log on to a Webcast to see the presenter discuss the topic at hand. Chat-room technologies are then used to allow participants to ask questions.

An international mobile telephone company created a package with an outside supplier designed to train retail salespeople worldwide, via a dedicated intranet, on the selling points of this company's technology. Immediately the product's strengths were clarified to the sales force, making a direct impact on sales volumes. The intranet package can be updated at will, and salespeople can log on at no expense other than an investment of time. The alternative—bringing hundreds of people together for training sessions periodically—would have resulted in a big hit on the firm's bottom line.

As in e-commerce, the powerful values of e-learning lie not only in the operational gains it makes possible, but also in it its ability to enable anytime, anywhere learning and access to knowledge. It can lead to improved workforce productivity and, when linked to outside partners such as distributors, can boost sales quickly and efficiently. Learning is a means to an end, and that end is performance. E-learning provides a new learning environment that fundamentally changes the processes.

The major lesson we have learned from e-commerce is that success, and with it the greatest rewards, comes from fundamental and systemic change to an organization's business model. E-commerce is not about using technology to do the same things in different ways. It is about using technology to do things that are different from anything ever done before. Similarly, e-learning is about making fundamental changes in the learning process; it is about helping people learn in ways they have never learned before.

Several cognitive processes are involved—in learning—from simply paying attention to retrieving complex patterns of information from our long-term memory. For people to effectively construct new knowledge (built upon previous knowledge), they also rely on three important experiences, all of which can be delivered via e-learning:

1. Interactions with the content and context to be learned (discussions, activities, or problems in the context). Without experience with the content—playing, applying, or discussing—learning does not go very deep and is likely not to be retained.

2. Interactions with intentions or purposes, enigmas, mysteries, or problems to solve. These stimulate and organize learning. Wonder about answers to questions creates the mystery that stimulates further knowledge seeking, organizes the content, influences how it fits with other knowledge, and drives what else to know about the content.

3. Social negotiation or collaboration that evolves learning. Other people's alternative views challenge thinking and serve as a source of puzzlement. Equally important during learning are social negotiation and collaboration. Talking with our colleagues as we learn stimulates the highest form of motivation and enhances our ability to make sense of our surroundings.

New e-learning business models incur high initial costs followed by steeply rising ROI from the reduced cost of delivery and employee travel costs. But even more valuable, organizations will reap benefits when employees repeat their e-learning experience, returning again and again to access knowledge and easily accessible learning modules to improve their productivity. In short, companies that invest in e-learning are realizing improved employee performance.

Simulated Learning at BellSouth

BellSouth, the international communications company, has its own version of e-learning. BellSouth's consumers expect reliability and demand exceptional customer service. The key to the market is, increasingly, people. BellSouth must have customer service representatives who are more motivated and knowledgeable than ever before.

To achieve this new level of performance, BellSouth created a program called Business Excellence through Simulation Training (BEST). In the BEST program, customer service representatives learn by doing via simulated customer calls. Using best-practice examples, trainees experience 16 to 24 hours of simulation. They learn judgment and communications skills normally provided through months of practical experience. Customer service representatives even coach each other—teamwork at its BEST.

Confident and empowered customer service representatives are great for customer relations, but the benefits of BEST go straight to the bottom line—some BEST participants have increased their sales performance by as much as 200 percent. That's not all. Because of a 13 percent reduction in training time, improved time-to-proficiency, and fewer repeat calls, Bell-South expects as much as $52 million in cost savings over a five-year period. It's no wonder that BEST has been used for new hire and continuing education training by more than 2000 BellSouth customer service representatives so far.

Although these technologies are effective in the global distribution of traditional classroom learning models, they also offer powerful opportunities for almost instantly increasing the abilities of workers through a focus on virtual experience rather than just knowledge. These tools work like flight simulators that immerse the user in an environment very much like real life.

LAUNCH NEW BUSINESSES

A number of innovative new businesses have emerged that are specific to the e-commerce world. One such company is Qpass, which is a player in the new world of micropayments, small charges that are too expensive to process individually. Until Qpass was created, content providers who wished to use the Internet for distributing their digital content had experienced disappointing returns, due to high up-front costs and primitive business models. Qpass created new revenue opportunities for these content providers by providing an end-to-end business infrastructure for selling digital content over the Internet. Qpass content partners offload customer registration, authentication, billing, merchandising, promotions, and ongoing customer care. Selling more than 1.9 million digital products from such prestigious content providers' partners such as The New York Times on the Web and The Wall Street Journal Interactive Edition, Qpass supports the sale of virtually any digital product in a variety of packages. Qpass is making content commerce work by enabling content providers to reduce the costs and risk of digital publishing, while providing quick and easy purchasing for online consumers.

But technology can also enable the creation of new businesses in existing industries. Today, the problem is one of choice. There is such a wealth of technology available with the potential to revolutionize whole industries that evaluation and selection have become the first potential pitfall. No one person can be sufficiently expert to take advantage of all the opportunities that the new technologies present.

Launching Global Village Telecom

One company that has been successful in pulling together the capabilities and technologies to rapidly launch a new business from scratch is Brazil's Global Village Telecom (GVT). Recent deregulation has led to a boom of over 20 telecom start-ups there. Over a two-year period, GVT invested more than $1 billion, including $55 million in IT investments in the first year alone. Within the nine Brazilian states there are nearly 40 million people spread over 1671 cities. Global Village Telecom has combined the advantages of voice- and data-optimized networks with flexible billing systems. In the past, inflexible billing has been one of the biggest barriers to innovation within the telecommunications industry.

GVT cherry-picked its target market, concentrating on 12 million people in 24 of the largest cities. A key to success has been selecting the right partners for networking and IT to make the business run smoothly from the start. It became clear early on that no single vendor would have the capabilities required to support all of the company's needs, so they adopted a best-of-breed philosophy. Although this created more connection points and interdependencies, they were able to go from concept to a fully running business in just six months.

Integration became quite a challenge. The more boxes there are, the more connecting lines are needed. Although this gives flexibility and potentially more functionality, it does create an integration challenge. In total, there were 17 projects, many of which brought together vendors who had never worked together before.

To make this a success, a few key principles were established:

- Be sure there is a clear business strategy and use it as the guidepost for making all decisions, both technical and functional, and back them up with strong program management.
- Design all the business processes before going too far down the software selection path. They defined over 200 business processes which would help translate the business strategy into action, and these processes became the basis for the systems. Clearly we are not talking about detailed processes, since the entire business was launched in six months' time, less time than many businesses take just to map their processes.

In the beginning, it was not thought necessary to automate provisioning. When the process design was discussed, however, it became clear that software was in fact needed to meet the desired business requirements. So they looked for systems that could support the requirements, and this spawned new alliance partners in the areas of workforce management and Geographic Information Systems (GIS). In fact, this was the first implementation of this package in Brazil, and it is considered to be the most modern technological platform.

Some key areas of competitive advantage GVT focused on were in the area of customer service: all information covered on the first call, installation scheduled on the first call, and a standard approach through all sales channels.

After launch, there was follow-up on the business processes. Because it was known that the processes must drive the business, and that these must be inextricably linked to the systems to avoid tempting people to take short-cuts, they put in place a robust change management process. They set out first to create a culture of customer focus. Most companies preach this gospel, but in GVT's case it is reflected in the business strategy, the processes, and the systems. What if a customer calls asking for a line or service? If this is in an area where GVT has coverage, on the first call they set up the field service request, set a date and time, and reserve the customer's phone number. No other telecom in Brazil had done this. Under the old telecom's monopoly, there was a history of long waiting times for lines and service, often over two years.

Customer focus is a selection criterion for the people they hire for the business. Employees must have this mind-set. This is a key differentiator from the existing phone companies. And the people must be proactive. They have an anticipatory view of the business, looking for problems before they happen. One example occurred during the provisioning implementation, when the software package was implemented from scratch in 13 weeks. This is a world record, and was the first time the product had been implemented in Brazil. And one of the main reasons for success was that the program management anticipated problems before they happened.

Another critical success factor was the IT team. Some 250 people were involved during six months from 25 companies including Hewlett-Packard, Lucent, Vitria, Oracle, Siebel, Metasolv, and SAP. Many of these companies had potential conflicts of interest, but through a strong team spirit the differences were overcome. Heavy emphasis was placed on solutions and team building. Parties were an essential part of the team-building efforts, and board members were always invited. And guess what—they almost always showed up because the team environment was fun.

When I asked Ruy Shiozawa, CIO of GVT, how he might take the knowledge gained from GVT and apply it to the old-world telecommunications companies, he said that creating spin-offs would be better, especially for new services. "Many of the people in the older companies are dinosaurs," he said, "and the good people are being poached by the start-ups." Also, he said that the older companies need to introduce controls while maintaining flexibility. Any good practices were in the heads of the best people, and when they left, the knowledge left with them. The telecom scene in Brazil will be dynamic for years to come, and GVT is well positioned to be a strong player.

SOME GOLDEN RULES

When thinking about technology and the ways it can be used to retool and improve processes, it's worth keeping in mind these steps:

- In the first place, make absolutely sure that the use of technology improves the value that is being delivered to the customer. If it doesn't, then ask very seriously why it is there.

- Keep a careful eye on the original process vision, and use technology to help bring about that vision. Process design should be enabled by technology, not driven by it. Watch for any warning signs that suggest that technology is becoming too dominant.

- Make sure that new processes and new technology solutions are designed in tandem. Start exploring technology options early on in the process redesign stage. Don't make the mistake of spending lots of time redesigning a process, only to discover far down the road that there is no technology that can support that particular design.

- Recognize that there is an inhibiting side to technology. Just as it can inspire process designs, so it can also present barriers to change. To get an idea of some of these barriers, ask questions such as:

  √ Is the technology viable? Or is it just cleverness for the sake of it?
  √ Will extensive training be required for the users of the technology?[3]
  √ How much lead time is needed to develop the system?
  √ Does the organization have the IT skills necessary to create and maintain the system?
  √ If the platform is nonstandard, are the benefits worth the costs that nonstandard platforms inevitably entail?
  √ Is the system flexible enough to change as the process itself changes?

- Make sure that any initiative to make major changes is controlled by operations specialists and not by IT specialists. Also, combine process and technology design teams so that both disciplines are included.

- Finally, don't focus on one technology only. There is a tendency to devote too much energy and resources to the "latest and the greatest," whatever that may be at the moment. This inevitably excludes other potentially valuable technologies. Too strong an emphasis on the latest fad can blind a project team to its overall strategic business objectives.

The power of technology can be deceptive. It can hold you back as mightily as it can hurl you forward. In one of the stranger twists of high-tech irony, the Internet has been a key vehicle for bringing together the growing number of groups that oppose the process of globalization that is being accelerated by this very technology. Protests mounted by these organizations have become a regular feature of the annual meetings of bodies such as the World Trade Organization (WTO), the International Monetary Fund (IMF), and the World Bank. The Web site www.s26.org, for example, was the medium that disseminated information about the plans for WTO demonstrations in Seattle and the IMF and World Bank meetings in Prague.

But used judiciously, technology will help you stay on the edge of innovation and in touch with your customers. The Internet has brought revolution to the boardroom in the space of just a few years, and it is obvious that we are only just beginning to make use of this important aspect of technology. Those who master the power of technology and e-commerce will own the future.

6

INNOVATION
THROUGH
MEASUREMENT

"We use two percent of what we measure. The rest is CYA."

A CLIENT

*M**easures are often thought to be the antithesis of innovation because they fence in business activity. In fact, however, proper use of measures fosters innovation by focusing on the results rather than the means of getting there. This gives employees the freedom to improvise in order to achieve their objectives. Objectives should be based on "stretch" targets, requiring employees to push harder to achieve quantum leaps in performance. The fifth component of a Capability, as described in Chapter 1, is performance measurement. Although there is general agreement on the need for performance measures, many companies still live in the dark ages and badly need to upgrade their methods. What's needed is a "measurement architecture" to suit each business, a set of measures that tracks progress in different categories of operations and fosters entrepreneurial thinking.*

But still there is some confusion as to which model or framework orga-nizations should adopt—and hence which measures they should actu-ally apply. In this chapter I examine the smart way to decide what to measure and how to do it.

A s I put this chapter together, I had just finished watching an excellent television show on George Martin, the producer for most of the Beatles' albums. And now, in the twenty-first century, he is still at it. In 2000 he produced a new collection of the Beatles' songs with the involvement of a number of today's stars, including Robin Williams and Jim Carrey. When setting out to create an album, it is typical to have everything well scripted and planned. But in this case, instead of trying to re-create what the Beatles had done, which would be equivalent to measuring and managing the process, he invited these comedians to apply their creative genius. He knew that involving such individuals would be a discovery process—he could count on them to do something that even he could not conceive of. And he was right. Both comedians contributed moments of brilliance by trying out dif-ferent tempos and variations on the familiar melodies that no ordinary per-son could ever have predicted or scripted.

Innovation emerges when people are allowed to give free rein to their creative talents within a set of simple rules. In the case of the music, the "rules" were the tempo and melody and the deadline for completing the recording. Martin was focusing on the outcome, not on how to get there. Within business, it is also necessary to focus on outcomes. Giving people the creative freedom that fosters innovation requires that management give up some control and allow the individuals to run the business.

Unfortunately, most businesses today still operate without the free-style creativity that nurtures innovation. Still within the domain of the bean counters, measures are largely confined to numbers: the annual balance sheet and the profit and loss account, and the management accounts that companies maintain for internal purposes. These statements were designed to indicate how a company was performing financially, month to month, year to year. Although money still talks today, it is not the only outcome businesses need to consider. And more importantly, it is usually not the one that fosters innovation.

True, many companies do recognize the fact that their measurement systems are not up to snuff. A recent study by Accenture and the Center for Business Performance (formerly at Cambridge University and now at

Cranfield School of Management) found that 96 percent of bricks-and-mortar, 96 percent of clicks-and-mortar, and 100 percent of dot-com companies said they wanted to improve their measurement systems.[1.]

But if so many companies know that there is a need for better measures, and they know that they are not performing well, why are they still in such sad shape? I suggest that there are two reasons. First, it is often difficult to determine what are the right things to measure. Second, even when companies can decide what their strategy is, they don't know what priority to give each measure. One manufacturing company's mission statement, for example, says: "This organization provides products and services which consistently meet or exceed standards set by our customers, on time and at the lowest cost." An admirable sentiment. But when the chief executive was asked how he knew whether he was on target, he had to admit that he had no way of knowing how to rank his degree of success or even whether he was being successful.

THE PURPOSE OF MEASURES

Before I go into more detail on specific measures, and how to measure the right things the right way, it may be helpful to agree on why we need measures in the first place. After extensive investigation, Accenture and the Center for Business Performance have determined that there are seven basic uses of measures:

1.   To *communicate* a range of performance targets and to report on their achievement.

2.   To *compete* successfully by making strategic decisions on the basis of hard data.

3.   To *compare* the company's performance with that of others and to target where innovation and improvement should be initiated.

4.   To *compel* corrective action by identifying variances beyond acceptable limits and to innovative solutions.

5.   To *comply* with the law, with regulatory standards, and with risk-related internal policies.

6.   To *complete* projects within planned horizons, including delivering the anticipated benefits.

7.   To *commit* employees to the company's priorities through recognition and reward mechanisms.

Most managers agree that a good business measure must be both accurate and objective. Accuracy does not imply that it must be precisely right to four decimal places. It means that the data it provides must be trustworthy and not the subject of dispute. It must be good enough for managers to be able to form the best possible judgments and make good decisions with confidence.

Managers also must ensure that there are sufficient measures in place that look beyond the "walled garden" of the organization—for example, don't just measure the firm's performance at shipping on time from its warehouse, measure whether customers actually receive deliveries when they want them (and when the firm promised them). Wherever possible, work with factual data rather than opinion. Subjective measures are only helpful when objective measures are not available, and they should only be used only as a proxy for the unattainable. Nevertheless, remember that perceptions have a way of becoming reality and must be taken into account.

Measures of a particular outcome should assess more than one dimension. For example some of the dimensions of quality are consistency, reliability, conformance, durability, accuracy, and dependability; of quantity, volume, throughput, and completeness; of time, speed, delivery, availability, promptness, and timeliness; of ease of use, flexibility, convenience, accessibility, and clarity; of money, cost, price, and value. The success of every one of these dimensions will depend on perpetual innovation by the responsible employees.

Nearly everyone agrees that there is a need to focus on measures. But where do we begin? I love stories about Sherlock Holmes, Hercule Poirot, and other crime fiction featuring master detectives. And from these, I can tell you that when a good detective sets out to analyze a crime scene or investigate a case, he never starts by asking, "What evidence can I gather?" He's much smarter than that. His first question is, "What are the questions I need to answer in order to allow me to solve this case?" He will probably look for someone who had the opportunity to commit the crime, a motive for committing it, and the means to commit it. The key questions will, then, concern motive, opportunity, and means. So it should be with measurement data in business—without the crime, of course. What are the key questions? What do we need to know in order to understand how well the business is doing?

WAYS THAT MEASURE DRIVE INNOVATION

There are, in my opinion, three primary ways that measure drive innovation in a business.

1. Focusing on outcomes.
2. Shooting for stretch performance.

3. Measuring the right things.

The first two are principles that need to be fundamental philosophies of a company. The third addresses the complexities associated with developing a robust measurement architecture, such as measurement frameworks and how to get the measures right.

Point 1: Focusing on the Outcomes

I am often asked by clients, "How do we know if we are being innovative enough?" A straightforward response is, "A company is innovative enough when it hits its performance targets." Of course, this implies that you set your performance targets in advance of undertaking any major business change. And sadly, in my experience most companies are still defining their measures and targets after the process has been designed. To properly drive and measure innovation, you must start with the measures and design everything to reach your objectives. And true objectives focus on outcomes, not on the means of achieving them.

Last year I spent a day with my sister's company discussing a number of opportunities for her HR department colleagues. At one point, I asked them to list their performance measures, and one in particular that I remember was "the effectiveness of 360 feedback." But this is a measure focused on "how" rather than "what." So I asked, "What does an effective 360 feedback system make possible?" That led us to the answer: "effective management." From there, they devised new and creative ways of achieving effective management. Finally, they had focused on results.

Charles Koch, Chairman of Koch Industries, the company introduced in Chapter 1, tells the story of a refinery employee whose job was to turn a valve when the pressure reached a certain level. This was clearly a prescriptive approach to managing the work that was done and left little room for innovation. When an outcome-based approach was applied, the operator was told to use judgment and experience in controlling the process, so long as it was within the tolerances of the equipment and it met the needs of any dependent processes (again, focusing on the lines rather than the boxes). After this change, the performance of the refinery unit shot up 20 percent, which is considered a quantum leap in a commodity business in which 1 percent gains are joyously celebrated. It's a good demonstration of measures stimulating innovation.

Koch's incentive systems are designed to foster innovation by covering more than just employee contributions to current profits. They also cover contributions to long-term success, including contributions to culture and communities.

Many companies delay quantifying the results they wish to achieve because measures can be difficult to design and agree upon. But this is a mistake. The establishment of measures and targets cannot be done after the fact. They need to be established early on in the change effort in order to provide clear goals that people can aim for. In the first place, it is virtually impossible to design a process without the "specifications" of how it is intended to perform. And it is impossible for employees to be innovative when they either don't know what they are expected to achieve or are constrained by prescriptive measures.

Only by measuring outcomes is it possible to determine whether a Capability is achieving its goal, because excellence is focused on producing outcomes of real value to stakeholders. A major beverage company, for example, tracked the number of repair calls on its vending machines because it was concerned about the rising cost of maintaining the equipment. While its measurement produced some interesting numbers, it didn't help much because it failed to show whether the company was attaining the outcomes it wanted—such as increasing the overall time that the machines were functioning properly. When the measures were changed to focus on outcomes, the company's costs dropped and the satisfaction of its customers increased.

Of course the performance of operations must also be measured. Only then can an organization be sure that a procedure is operating within the expected parameters of time, cost, and quality while producing the required results. In other words, there's not much point in producing the planned number of widgets if they're overbudget, late, and shoddy.

At one major entertainment company, it was an unspoken rule that if a new television show turned out to be a hit in the ratings (the outcome), all was forgiven on cost overruns or late schedules (the performance). Over time, though, this lack of attention to performance led to the company's costs running dangerously out of control. It also meant that programming schedules had to be juggled because new shows were not ready by their expected release dates. Eventually, the company was forced to adopt a more balanced set of process measures that included performance as well as outcomes.

Amid all this measuring, it is important that companies make sure they avoid measuring things for the sake of it—especially if the measures do little to guide behavior. As the quote at the beginning of the chapter implies, companies can get by measuring much less. The key is to measure the things that matter most.

Of course, in order to set measures on results, it is critical for the overall company goals to be understood. If an organization's desired outcomes are unclear, it should stop and clarify them. Efforts to redesign businesses flounder sometimes because of a lack of understanding of (or lack of agreement on) what organizational outcomes are desired or what strategies should be used to achieve them.

There is no handy template for measures that would suit all situations. Each company will have its own objectives and therefore its own measurement requirements. Take British Airways (BA) and EasyJet. British Airways is a provider of full-service air travel targeting business customers as well as economy travelers. EasyJet, on the other hand, is a provider of low-cost air travel only. Both are in the business of transporting people from one place to another, and, of course, both are going to have measures around safety and timeliness. But BA also focuses its distinctive measures on comfort and convenience for business travelers, while EasyJet focuses primarily on price and convenience for holiday travelers. Nearly all of BA's business is booked through travel agents, while nearly all of EasyJet's business is booked through its Internet site. Different strategies demand different measures.

Innovation and measures go hand in hand. Measures should tell employees what they need to achieve, not how to do it. And they tell management how well the business is moving toward its objectives. But as we are reminded by Koch Industries, measures force management to give up some control. Even when Koch managers know where things stand today, because of the entrepreneurial nature of their measures, they have little idea of exactly where they will be tomorrow. Risky, yes. But it has enabled the company to grow 200-fold in less than three decades.

Point 2: Shooting for Stretch Performance

Stretch goals can have a powerful influence on the way businesses are designed and executed. If performance targets are left ill defined, the company sacrifices an important tool for motivating people to innovate.

Setting stretch goals is a key area for sparking innovative ideas. Jack Welch, the long-serving chief executive of General Electric who is now heading into retirement, once said: "The thing that is always wrong with measurements is that you set them to a place where you can meet them." Companies proclaim victoriously that they have met the targets that they set themselves the previous year. But if those targets were undemanding and easy to achieve, where's the victory? If ambitious targets are set, then measures can themselves drive innovation. Ambitious targets—stretch goals—can force people to think innovatively, to think out of the box, and literally force them to find new ways of doing things. Setting a stretch goal means calling for a 50 to 100 percent improvement in performance rather than an incremental 5 to 10 percent gain. Stretch goals are based on what should be attempted rather than on what can be accomplished.

When they set ambitious targets, companies should reward good performance, even if the targets are missed, because this is better than shooting low and rewarding only those who achieve relatively modest goals. The employee who aims for a 10 percent improvement and achieves 15 percent deserves only a bronze medal. A silver medal should go to the one who aims for 30 percent and hits 40 percent. The gold goes to the one who aims for 100 percent and achieves 50 percent.

Setting stretch goals is a driver of innovation. With incremental goals (5 to 10 percent), you tend to focus on small parts of your business. You can afford to change 1 to 2 percent of your business, and if you do it three or four times, you might hit your goal. With stretch goals (let's say greater than 50 percent), you can't do that. You can't look at the boxes, because you'll never get there. You have to focus on the lines of the organization as a whole and make radical change. That drives innovation.

Electrabel, the utility company referred to in Chapter 2, shows how stretch targets can help drive innovation and adaptability. Because of the uncertain future Electrabel was confronting, a great deal of flexibility had to be built into the design of their new logistics organization. The new processes needed to be flexible enough to accommodate future changes in customer expectations.

Electrabel knew that competition in the future liberalized European utilities market would be sure to increase the expectations of clients dramatically. So they chose to build processes that would be capable—before the fact—of meeting the highest expectations. In the short term, the goal was for Electrabel to be among the best in the utilities industry. To find out which targets to shoot for, the company's managers defined a set of key performance indicators that would help measure their current performance and compare that performance with what it needed to be in the future. They also looked at how other utilities performed on those indicators. They also looked beyond utilities, at companies that excel in the distribution of goods, an area where customers have much higher expectations. And they used these standards as inputs to the design of their own processes.

For example, the new distribution network and its logistics organization were designed to handle overnight delivery—customers would be able to order by 4 p.m. on one day and receive the goods by 7 a.m. the next day. Originally, the company had planned for five-business-day deliveries, but building to handle best-in-class performance proved to be the right decision in the end. For during the course of the project, it was decided that for some residential connections (e.g., connecting people on the gas network for heating purposes), the company should go from an average lead time of over a week to a guaranteed connection within 48 hours. It was an ambitious goal, and they very nearly managed it.

Another company that made the impossible happen was a greeting-card firm whose senior executives set a stretch goal of getting new cards from concept to market within a year. In the past, cards had taken from 18 to 24 months to move from their original conception to shop shelves. Individual departments within the firm—the designers, writers, artists, printers, shippers, and so on—were aghast at the idea. Surely the executives did not understand what it took to produce cards? But the target became a rallying cry, and so successful was it that in the end the company managed to get its cards to market in only four months. The "impossible" goal had forced people to abandon their conventional approaches and to try something completely new.

Point 3: Measuring the Right Thing

My advice to be sure to choose the right thing to measure may not seem very insightful as a condition for driving innovation, but actually these choices are not as obvious as you might think. Many who have tried to unlock the mystery of choice have failed. Indeed, interest in performance measurement and its management has skyrocketed over the past few years. Different frameworks and methodologies—for example, the balanced scorecard, the business excellence model, the shareholder-value-added model, activity-based costing (ABC), cost of quality, and competitive benchmarking—have all generated great interest and activity, not to mention consulting revenues. But they have not always generated the innovation needed for business success.

The best known of them all is probably the balanced scorecard, a framework that grew out of the widespread dissatisfaction in the late 1980s with the tight focus on the financial dimension. The idea was popularized by Robert Kaplan, a Harvard Business School professor of accounting, and David Norton, a management consultant, in the *Harvard Business Review* in the early 1990s.[2] Behind their concept was the recognition that only if you look beyond financial results, and measure things from other perspectives, will you be able to achieve other goals. Kaplan and Norton argued that there are four elements that should be included in measurement architecture. Companies that take into account all four types will have what they termed a *balanced scorecard* and, by implication, all-around well-balanced results.

The four measurement categories they identified are financial, customer, internal/operational, and innovation/learning. The popularity of the scorecard can be explained partly by its simplicity and partly by the fact that it can be applied to almost any business situation. A significant problem with it is that managers become obsessed with the wrong question, the same trap I mentioned earlier. They ask, "What can we or should we measure?" What they should be worrying about is the more fundamental question: "What questions do we want to be able to answer when we have access to our measurement data?" As a result, too many managers have focused primarily on what *can* be measured, instead of what *must* be measured. Of particular relevance is the fact that the innovation/learning dimension was typically reduced to measuring employee satisfaction. Data on employee satisfaction may be interesting, but as this chapter shows, it doesn't answer the right questions.

The balanced scorecard's shortcomings also include the fact that many stakeholders—suppliers, intermediaries, regulators—are not included. Hence it is not uncommon to end up with what has been dubbed a "biased scorecard"—that is, a scorecard biased towards only certain, often easy to measure, stakeholders.

Recognizing these shortcomings, some organizations (most of them European) have tried to adapt other frameworks. One of these is the business excellence model created by the European Foundation for Quality Management (EFQM), on the basis of which it gives out European Quality Awards. It was not designed primarily as a measurement framework as it combines some results that are readily measurable with "enablers," some of which are not. And in the United States, a number of organizations have struggled to adapt the criteria used for the Malcolm Baldrige Quality Award. But this is not a framework designed specifically for performance measurement purposes either.

Other companies have adopted shareholder-value-added frameworks that plug the cost of capital into their equation but ignore everything (and everyone) else. Both activity-based costing and the cost-of-quality frameworks are views that ignore other perspectives on performance—such as the interests of customers and employees. And none of them puts the emphasis on innovation as an *effect* of the measures.

The popular practice of benchmarking, on the other hand, takes a largely external perspective, often comparing the performance of business operations with that of competitors or best practitioners. However, this kind of activity is frequently pursued as a one-off exercise aimed at generating ideas for—or gaining commitment to—short-term innovation or improvement initiatives. It is not, by and large, used as part of the design of a formalized ongoing system for performance measurement.

These widely varying measurement frameworks can coexist in the business world because they all add some kind of value. They all provide their unique perspectives on performance, furnishing managers with a different set of lenses through which to assess their organizations.

In some circumstances, an explicit focus on shareholder value—at the expense of everything else—will be exactly the right thing for an organization to do. In other circumstances, or even in the same organization but at a different point in time, it would be suicide. At times, the balanced scorecard or the business excellence model (or some combination of the two) might be the answer. For example, the new CEO of a company that puts too much emphasis on paring down costs and the short-term interests of shareholders may find the balanced scorecard or business excellence framework a useful way to switch the company's attention toward the interests of customers, the improvement of operations, and the development of innovative products and services.

The key is to recognize that, despite the claims of some of the proponents of these various frameworks and methodologies, there is no single "best" way to view business performance measurement. And the reason is that business performance is itself a concept of many and varied dimensions. But all is not lost, as I would like to introduce a new framework, the Performance Prism.

THE PERFORMANCE PRISM

What is certain is that pent-up demand is building in well-managed companies for a multifaceted, adaptable new framework—a framework that combines the need for clarity of purpose with the need for comprehensive performance measurement in today's highly competitive, rapidly changing environment.

Such a framework has been developed by Accenture and the Center for Business Performance (Cranfield School of Management).[3] Called the Performance Prism, it attempts to move on from the balanced scorecard and to provide the next generation of measurement framework. It provides a more inclusive model, one that helps stimulate innovation and leads the way to appropriate performance measures for the organization as a whole. "Of course the adage that you get what you measure is true," says a colleague of mine, Chris Adams, "but you'll only get what you want if you measure the right things in the right way."

The Performance Prism sets out to find the right things. As shown in Figure 6-1, it has five facets: Stakeholder Satisfaction and Stakeholder Contribution form the two triangles at opposite ends of the prism, and Strategies, Processes, and Capabilities are the three rectangular faces joining them.

The Performance Prism forces an organization to address five fundamental questions:

1.   Who are the key stakeholders and what do they want and need?
2.   What Strategies are required to ensure that these wants and needs are satisfied?
3.   What Processes must be put in place to ensure that Strategies are delivered?
4.   What are the required Capabilities?
5.   What Stakeholder Contributions are required if a company is to maintain and develop those Capabilities?

The order of questions is deliberate. Stakeholders, the first (and last) facets of the prism, should be the focus before strategy. Stakeholders are becoming an increasingly important component of corporate performance as public companies realize that they cannot satisfy their shareholders for long if they exploit their customers, employees, suppliers, or the surrounding community. Moreover, the significance of different stakeholders is shifting

**FIGURE 6-1.   The five facets of the
                Performance Prism.**

Performance Prism

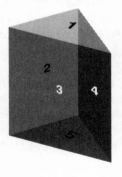

1 Stakeholder Satisfaction

2 Strategies

3 Processes

4 Capabilities

5 Stakeholder Contribution

FIGURE 6-2. The details of the Performance Prism.

over time. For example, as companies outsource ever-increasing numbers of noncore activities, they become more and more dependent upon their suppliers. Today, Boeing itself manufactures only three of the components on its 777 jetliner. Its reliance on suppliers for components and spares is immense, and its exposure, should its suppliers fail to perform, has grown proportionately.

One example of the dangers of this kind of exposure is provided by a start-up communications company that lost a $100 million satellite in a failed launch. Investigating experts had to uncover three levels of suppliers to get to the bottom of the responsibility question. At first the launch company was blamed; then responsibility was shifted to the rocket supplier; finally, it was determined that the software firm that built the electronics inside the rocket was to blame. Worried and confused investors relaxed only when the insurance company agreed to pay up.

Perhaps nowhere is the phenomenon of interdependency more pronounced than in e-commerce. Here intermediaries—quasi-customers or suppliers—are often intimately involved in the sales and logistics activities required to deliver the product or service that is being offered.

The e-commerce revolution has created yet another kind of stakeholder. The use of what are known as *complementors* is becoming common practice. Complementors are alliance partners that provide an enterprise with products and services that extend the value of that enterprise's own offering. This often involves cobranding or building complementary products. It can be found in the relationship that Yahoo! has with a number of other companies, where Yahoo! provides its brand name and distribution channels. Although not exclusive to dot-com industries, complementors are increasingly becoming a key component of an Internet company's armory. If these complementors' wants and needs are not catered to, they are likely to take their alliance elsewhere.

Regulators are also becoming increasingly important stakeholders. They are of course deeply involved in all the recently privatized industries around the world, but they also still have a significant impact on traditional private-sector firms. Microsoft's confrontation with the U.S. Justice Department over its commercial practices is just one example. National food and drug regulators, who often disagree with the decisions of their counterparts in neighboring countries, provide another example, making global strategies difficult to apply.

Less publicized is the $500 million fine imposed on a pharmaceuticals company in 1999 for its antitrust arrangements with firms in the vitamins sector—firms that were presumed to be its competitors. A former marketing manager of the company was jailed for four months and personally fined $100,000 for his role in the cartel. The company's top managers had failed to spot what was going on because they had no measures or mechanisms to monitor compliance in the regulatory area. And there is a long list of other companies that have been pursued in recent years for anticompetitive abuses or illegal practices that at first went undetected.

There is a final set of stakeholders that is in many ways more difficult to satisfy because of the potential diversity of their wants and needs. Pressure groups such as Greenpeace and Friends of the Earth have become enormously influential and have leveraged their results through their awesome communications skills.

Note that there is likely to be tension between what stakeholders want and need from their organizations and what the organizations want and need from the stakeholders—in other words, what stakeholders are required to contribute—and both need to be measured independently. The Performance Prism approach can take this dynamic tension into account because it emphasizes managing interrelationships (more lines) between stakeholders. It first involves making a list of stakeholders (each of whom may need to be further segmented), ordering them according to their relative importance, and then identifying each group's wants and needs. Customers, for instance, may well want "fast, right, cheap, and easy," while regulators want "legal, fair, safe, and true." How can these wants and needs best be quantified and the levels of satisfaction then measured?

Strategies and Processes, the next two facets of the prism, are familiar terms to most. The concept of "process quality," however, is difficult to define, because processes, unlike products, do not exhibit visible defects. In part, process quality can be judged by the quality of the goods or services that emerge from the processes—the outputs—and whether they achieve customer satisfaction—the outcome. Management can also measure some process-related attributes, such as volume, cycle times, costs, etc., directly.

The fourth facet of the prism is Capabilities, the concept we introduced in Chapter 1, which is less well known and has to date been used infrequently in the area of measurement. A Capability is the combination of elements that collectively create value for an organization's stakeholders through a distinct part of its operations—usually one or more of its business operations. Those elements can include the skills of the firm's employees, its business practices, its leading technologies, and its physical infrastructure. They are the fundamental building blocks of the company's ability to compete successfully today and in the future.

The fifth and final facet of the prism is the Stakeholder Contribution. Note that, in practice, though, the two stakeholder-specific questions (questions 1 and 5 on page 158) may need to be addressed simultaneously at an early stage in the design of the measurement architecture. This is to enable management teams to gain a better understanding of how critical stakeholder interrelationships can be. It is usually necessary to return to the contribution question again after the required Capabilities have been defined, in order to complete the cycle.

Few organizations go through this fundamental sequence when selecting their performance measures. Yet if they don't, they will fall short, for if no attempt is made to link the measures explicitly to the organization's strategy and stakeholder needs, and no attempt is made to identify the links between the different dimensions of performance, the result is an organization with only a marginally more comprehensive measurement system. Without a way of deciding what it needs to measure to help clarify its strategy, the organization will lack clarity about its future direction and (inevitably) there will be widespread disagreement about what its priorities should be. The organization will not be in a position to use the measurement system to communicate its strategy or to use the measures to check whether its strategy is being implemented. It certainly cannot use the measures to challenge the very basis of the strategy and to answer the question, "Are we, in fact, implementing the right strategy?"

It's one thing to define a set of measures. It's another to be able to communicate and report on these throughout the organization. Frequent sharing of performance data with employees at all levels is a crucial step in the process. At one U.S. utility, the chief executive held a meeting with his 50 top managers to say how unhappy he was about the fact that the company was tens of millions of dollars below its revenue target for the quarter. And he added that he was even more unhappy about the lack of urgency that his managers had demonstrated over that shortfall. The managers reacted with some surprise. Many were unaware of the revenue shortfall because the information was not generally shared outside the utility's inner circle of top executives. Their lack of urgency was essentially due to their lack of awareness of the situation. The CEO quickly understood that leaders must be consistent and active in communicating information. Measures send a powerful message about what is important "around here," and the message inevitably influences the behavior of a company's people. And this broader participation in the fate of the company is what creates a culture of innovation.

So far, I have discussed how measures play a role in innovation, including how to go about determining what the right measures are. Here are some additional suggestions for getting the measures right.

AVOID SQUEEZING THE BALLOON
Companies have to be careful to avoid "squeezing the balloon," where one part of the business is improved dramatically while other parts are allowed

to deteriorate. This can be a result of too much focus on financial measures to the detriment of process measures; a heavy emphasis on one dimension, quality, for example, that has a negative affect on another, such as time; or a focus on one process without considering its impact on other processes.

For example, in a move that improved the appearance of its books, a large beverage company kept fully depreciated vending machines in operation well beyond their normal useful life. The firm's customers suffered, however, because as the machines got older, they broke down more frequently. What looked good on the books was in fact evidence of a deteriorating business.

Or consider the manufacturer that found it was losing business and had an extremely low rate of customer retention (a nonfinancial measure) because of its poor service. That insight spurred the company to find innovative ways to improve its service, and as a result its sales (a financial measure) increased.

A misguided focus on any one measure is sure to distort behavior. A few years ago, for example, a well-known retailer measured the performance of its auto centers on volume alone. This led to massive fraud, as the centers started billing customers for repairs that weren't necessary and that sometimes were not even performed. The fraud eventually landed the company in court. While this is an extreme example, it does show how true it is that you get what you measure.

Another classic mistake is sales being measured on revenue rather than profit. A company that sells electronic goods, for example, that wanted to create an incentive system for its salespeople, decided to create a reward if the salespeople were able to get the customers to purchase five add-ons, like modems and mousepads. It was later realized that the incentive should have been based on the overall margin of the shopping cart, not the number of items it contained. It is tempting for the customer to fill a cart with a pile of low-margin, cheap products that bring nothing to your bottom line.

It is not always necessary to have a multitude of measures to achieve a balanced outcome. It is possible for a single measure to provide the necessary balance. For example, the purchasing department of one company used to measure its success in terms of how successful it was at buying the lowest-cost items available. Over time, however, the department found that low initial costs sometimes meant long lead times, less frequent deliveries, and large minimum orders—all of which contributed to increased inventory levels. So the department modified its measures in a way that allowed it to track costs over the entire life cycle of the items. This was a single measure, but one that encouraged people to balance low cost with quality.

A vivid example of the failure to balance costs with quality occurred at an American municipality that suddenly became painfully aware of the large sums of money it was spending every year on filling potholes. In order to control these expenditures, the municipality encouraged its staff to use cheaper materials. They did so, only to find that these materials lasted for a much shorter time than the more expensive variety. The municipality found itself spending even more than it had done previously because it had to repair the potholes more frequently.

Measures should not drive improvements in one area at the expense of others or (especially) at the expense of the organization as a whole. To avoid this, organizations need to be aware of the way their operations interact. A major American HMO tried to keep a holistic perspective when it reengineered its primary-care delivery. This level of care was delivered to patients either over the phone or in a doctor's office. The managers were careful not to "optimize" the call center to the point of hyperefficiency. They set flexible targets for the length of time the nurses could stay on the phone with patients. They allowed longer calls because they knew that handling a patient's complaints by phone costs about one-tenth of the cost of giving the same advice in a doctor's office. Allowing longer calls enabled the nurses to handle a greater number of patient complaints and thus minimize the number of expensive visits to a doctor's office. By keeping their eye on the overall goal—the delivery of good-quality patient care at lower cost—the designers developed two separate operations—call center and office visits—that complemented and enhanced each other.

In other some instances, different measures can be used to evaluate different operations within the same organization. A large manufacturer, for example, might have the following operations:

- *Order Acquisition.* This is judged on revenue growth, high service levels, and number of new accounts.
- *New Product Development.* New product development is measured by the functionality of the product—the number of new features that it contains, the advanced level of the functions, or the number of new patents granted on developments contained in it.
- *Order Fulfillment.* This is judged on shipping costs, lead times, inventory level, and the simplicity and scope of the product range.

The differences in how each of the groups is judged will drive different behavior patterns: Order acquisition will want to offer as many product options as possible in order to attract more customers; new product development will want to offer products with the greatest possible functionality; and order fulfillment will be nudged into making fewer products in stable volumes in order to simplify its planning.

FOCUS ON THE FUTURE

Measures must describe not only what has happened, but also help determine what should happen in the future. A common fault of measurement architecture is to focus only on those things that have already occurred—the number of sales, total costs, and so on. These backward-looking measures are important, but they need to be balanced with forward-looking ones. For example, how many sales leads are in the pipeline? Which expenses are projected to be over- or underbudget? What proportion of customers intend to make repeat purchases?

When developing a measurement architecture, consider the ratio of backward-looking to forward-looking measures, and rethink the architecture if the ratio is too heavily weighted toward one or the other. Then, with a healthy stock of future-oriented measures in place, it is much easier for corrective action to be taken early and for problems to be addressed while they are still relatively small. A problem that is on the horizon can be fixed before it can cause any harm. Once a problem has already occurred, however, the damage has been done.

A team redesigning the primary-care delivery process at a large HMO found itself struggling to identify the right measures. Historically, the HMO had counted the number of procedures that doctors performed and what those procedures cost. In the future it wanted to measure things such as the overall health of its member population, the degree to which preventive health procedures were reaching the community, and the relative success of different protocols on a given health problem. The HMO knew that it was difficult to define measures for such things and that it would require extensive new procedures for collecting data. But it also knew that it had to have the new data in order to assess whether its desired outcomes (lower costs per member and better health for the member population) were being achieved, so it proceeded to develop the wider measures.

Future-oriented measures also help identify new opportunities. While they cannot actually measure the future, they can spot trends. For example, the recent shifts from the automobile to the sports utility vehicle, from beef to chicken, from vacations at home to vacations abroad all represented innovative business opportunities. The company that routinely measures where things are going stands a good chance of capitalizing on such trends before its competitors do.

LINK INCENTIVES TO OBJECTIVES

The organization's overall reward system must be aligned with the measures so that the implementers are motivated to perform. Individual compensation packages should be linked to outcomes. It is very easy to get this wrong. A computer software company, for example, found that paying 100 percent of a commission to its salespeople when they closed a sale tended to encourage an attitude of "take the money and run." That approach focused more on getting the next sale than on ensuring that its new customers were actually happy using the software that they had just bought. To change this attitude, the company modified its compensation scheme. Salespeople received 50 percent of their commission when the sale closed and the other 50 percent only when the customer paid the bill (which was taken as an indication of customer satisfaction). This improved the level of after-sales service and increased the number of accounts.

Compensation should be linked only to those things that employees can control and influence. They must be able to produce an improvement in the results by adjusting their behavior. It is unfair, and ultimately demotivating, to give people responsibility for results over which they have no control.

This is complicated, however, by the fact that in an organization that emphasizes excellent business operations there are many occasions when people are compelled to use their influence (rather than direct control) to achieve an objective. A well-known airline had to face this issue. It wanted the highest ranking for on-time departure of its flights, and it motivated its employees to meet its goal by offering them $60 bonuses for each month the airline received this accolade for on-time departures. The bonuses motivated employees not just to modify their own behavior, but also to encourage other employees to behave in ways that would help to achieve the desired results. It is worth noting that the pilots, whose prime concern has to be safety, were not part of this incentive scheme.

The focus on individual performance (and individual rewards) runs deep in some cultures. When a large U.S. utility became concerned that it was taking up to two years to get relatively simple new products to market, it realized that an individual product manager was in charge of designing, developing, and launching every new product single-handedly. But that manager invariably needed the cooperation of people from finance, sales, IT, training, and the legal department, and he often had to beg them for help. When they didn't deliver, the manager had to hunt them down and beg for cooperation. In the end, only the product manager was being held accountable for the product's timeliness and success. When its new-product procedures were redesigned, the company created cross-disciplinary product-development teams. An entire team was then held accountable for each product's success.

This kind of excellence depends vitally on teamwork. If a team fails to produce the expected outcomes, but individual members of that team receive stellar performance reviews, the foundation of the team and the prospects of success for the process will be undermined. Team members have to learn to succeed and fail together.

When a computer company set up a new call center, it arranged for 80 percent of the performance measures to be team-based rather than individually based. The 30-member team, motivated thus to support the work of their teammates, became so adept at working together that they only required the supervision of a manager for less than a half day a week.

But don't try and apply a formulaic approach to determining compensation. According to Jeff Skilling, president and chief operating officer of Enron, "That's asking for trouble, because you put an employee in the position where if they swing for the grandstand and they do great, they make a lot of money. They'll swing for the grandstand every time because they want to try to make a lot of money. But when they're swinging for the grandstand every time they might make a big mistake. And we're left holding the bag. So any kind of formulaic compensation in a business that's managing risk is asking for trouble."[4] Good advice from the company voted "the most innovative in America" five years in a row by *Fortune* magazine.

THE RESULTS AT PPL

Measures were a major driver of change at PPL, the former Pennsylvania Power and Light, a Fortune 500 company with 4.4 million customers in Europe and North and South America. A service company that depends for its competitive edge on the excellence of its customer care, PPL realized that if customers are not delighted by its high-quality service, shareholder value will not grow.

A key channel for delivering the company's services is the call center. When PPL's centers are disrupted, the organization's whole performance—future success—is put at risk. And the centers were thoroughly disrupted in February 1999 when the state-mandated policy of "electric choice" first came into effect. The policy opened up the electricity market to newcomers and inevitably made the average inquiry received by PPL's centers considerably more complicated. Worse, the company had decided at the same time to introduce a new customer service system. This was the result of a strategic decision to shift the focus of its customer care program from customer intimacy to operational excellence. The company decided that it is no good knowing all about your customers if one of the things you keep measuring is how fed up they are with PPL's inefficiencies.

The double disturbance caused by these two changes can be best appreciated by a look at the figures. In one typical week prior to the changes, the average handling time per inquiry at the call centers was 6 minutes 19 seconds; just over a year later it was 9 minutes 22 seconds, 48 percent slower. Something had to be done to improve matters. But it had to take place without causing any disruption to existing operations. The show had to go on, even while the players in it were learning new parts.

The answer was a program of change designed to take place in three distinct phases, each being carefully measured. The first phase, focused on planning, was to last for a couple of months. It established a series of regular measurements that were designed to monitor progress: there were 8 daily indicators, plus 16 balanced scorecard indicators, plus an "employee change-readiness inventory" of 25 factors. One purpose of gathering so much data was to see how different forms of intervention were statistically correlated with changes in service levels. Another new feature was a weekly customer survey designed to track six key indicators that showed how close the center was to the company's mission of "Quick, accurate, courteous service."

In the second phase, which also lasted about two months, the staff's skills were assessed and new teams were formed. These concentrated people's efforts on a limited set of tasks at which they had to become specialized. Supervisors were sent on a four-week training program; the call center's facilities were redesigned; and the call center's work space was reconfigured.

The third phase lasted little more than a month, but some key changes took place in that time. Call processes were revised and a system of monitoring agents was introduced. Supervisors were given targets, and the achievement (or otherwise) of those targets was linked to their final salary.

By the end of 1999, the average call-handling time had fallen to less than 6 minutes, and the average time that customers had to wait before their call was answered fell from more than 7 minutes in February to just 14 seconds in December. Reestablishing the center's high standards, and then exceeding them by a handsome margin, required a great deal of innovative thinking . . . and a great deal of hard work.

Several lessons were gained from the experience:

1. It helps to start by "driving out the stress." Techniques that can help here include the use of ranges instead of points for targets. Above all,

though, be patient. Nothing drives out stress like patience. Stress makes people stupid.

2. Culture change takes a long time. Though substantial gains can be made in less than six months, major enduring change takes much longer.

3. Try to focus on reducing ambiguity, not uncertainty. That is, make sure that everything you do is clear, even though the outcome may be uncertain.

4. Stick to the fundamentals. Reexamine all work and management processes and develop a proper strategy for using staff and other resources.

5. Finally, be respectful, trustworthy, and kind. Give people plenty of time and space to change, and keep key stakeholders informed.

Much thought and development have gone into measures in recent years, taking us well beyond the limited, simplistic, and misleading criteria of the financial model. More sophisticated measures can be a powerful stimulant for innovation while also revealing the true strength and weakness of a business operation. Multidimensional measures must be employed to track performance in all its permutations. Communicating the criteria to all employees, and linking measures to the goals of the company, will help ensure that senior management has the data to develop the business successfully.

Making It Happen

7

TARGETING
INNOVATION

"At too many companies, the boss shoots the arrow of man-
agerial performance and then hastily paints the bull's-eye
around the spot where it lands."

WARREN BUFFETT

O nce engaged in innovative change, an enthusiastic team runs the
risk of throwing off so many new concepts, ideas, and solutions
that management can be swamped and find itself unable to implement
them sensibly. The targeting of innovation comes to grips with this
problem. Evaluation of the urgency and potential gain of various
options is the key to starting off on the right foot. In this chapter, I offer
a matrix that will help make that impartial analysis possible—a
methodology for ranking options by order of priority. But I also caution
against overrunning the company with successive programs of change.
Nothing stops a well-planned reinvention program like "change
fatigue."

When I think about the need to target innovation, I am reminded of a story I was once told when I worked at UPS. At its Louisville, Kentucky, air hub, hundreds of thousands of packages go through the sorter every day. This critical operation is supported by a complex conveyor system. If the conveyors go down, packages can be late and significant time and money can be lost.

One day, the story goes, the conveyors stopped working for some unknown reason. The engineers tried to restart them, but to no avail. So they called in the best conveyor consultant around. He walked into the package center, looked around for about three minutes, walked to the far end of the building, opened an electrical box, turned one screw, and to everyone's delight, the conveyors started running again. The package center manager was thrilled, and asked the consultant for his bill. The consultant thought about it and said, "Ten thousand dollars." The manager was shocked, "Ten thousand dollars for five minutes' work? Give me an itemized bill." So the consultant pulled out his pen and wrote a two-item invoice. The first line read, "$500—turning the screw"; the second line read, "$9500—knowing which screw to turn." He got his fee.

This is the essence of targeting. Knowing which screw to turn within an organization to unleash its innovative potential. For if you know which screw to turn, and when to turn it, implementation will be greatly facilitated.

The conveyor-belt story is not a "true" story. A real example of why targeting and integrating are important is provided by a machine tool company in the Midwest. A few years ago, they found that they could achieve miracles by reorganizing the assembly of a complex electrical component, a key part of their business operations. But then the manufacturing chain got out of whack. After the first month, bottlenecks downstream resulted in a huge inventory buildup of that proliferating part—costing the company dearly. Yet the improved process was working so splendidly that management dared not demotivate the team by reverting to old practices. This company had been looking for innovation, and while the real solution still proved elusive, at least some creativity was being applied to the excess inventory problem. Management sent the team off to Honolulu for a three-week midwinter workshop-cum-vacation, a cheaper option than allowing costly inventory to continue to expand. While the miracle boys were away, downstream processes were brought into line and the inventory was worked down to normal levels. And the team returned to their workstations with big smiles, suntans, and loud shirts.

Although the solution to the immediate inventory problem was certainly innovative, the larger challenge of targeting innovation in a rational way had not been addressed. A company cannot possibly be innovative everywhere at the same time. There are not enough people, not enough money, and not enough energy to make it happen. But innovation in isolation can cause more problems than it solves. In the first chapter I suggested that par golf in a game of world-class players is insufficient. But this is only partly true. In fact, sometimes mere best practice in some functions *is* desirable. When, for example, would investing in having the most innovative payroll Capability be the right move, and when would a best-practice solution be desirable? In this chapter, I want to answer some of these questions by looking at how and where companies should focus their energies.

DETERMINING PRIORITIES

When I conduct executive training, one of my favorite activities requires participants to consider a typical set of Capabilities common in the insurance industry: Develop Products and Services, Customer Service, Manage Revenues, Manage Distribution Channels, Market Products and Services, Underwriting, Claims Fulfillment, Manage Provider Network, and Plan and Manage the Enterprise.

I ask the group to tell me which Capability is most important to an insurance company. Quite often, the first answer will be Claims Fulfillment. "Why?" I ask, and they will say, "Because this is why customers get insurance in the first place." I usually respond that Claims Fulfillment is a very important Capability, but I want to know which is the *most* important Capability. Someone will then suggest Manage Revenues because it is how the company makes money. Again, I commend them for their answer, but I still want to know the most important Capability. This goes on for a while, until nearly every Capability has been suggested. Eventually I stop the group and say, "Okay, I am going to give you the answer to this one: 'It depends.'"

I then tell them about the strategies of four insurance companies serving relatively similar markets.

- *Unum Insurance.* Unum is the market leader in disability insurance, a firm that differentiates itself by its skill in assessing and pricing risk. Unum claims, for example, to have such finely tuned data that it can distinguish the difference in risk between left-handed and right-handed doctors who drive Volvos and live in New Jersey.

- *Progressive Insurance.* This company has achieved a remarkable level of excellence in claims processing and, as a result, has become one of the most profitable firms in the industry. Progressive's loss adjusters operate from vans with cellular communication links and computer workstations. Driving around their assigned territories, they are often at the scene of an accident before the police. In many cases, claims are processed on the spot, and it has been known for a check to be handed over by the company's loss adjusters at the site of an accident.

- *State Farm*. Competitive positioning for State Farm depends on its exclusive (and extensive) network of agents and offices. Its wide geographic coverage is reinforced by the company's motto: "State Farm Is There." The firm differentiates itself from the rest of the pack by this type of branding.
- *USAA*. The customers of USAA are primarily in the transient, mobile military services. Because its customer base is so mobile, USAA tries to be as helpful as possible to its customers. In fact, at one time, USAA was the world's largest user of toll-free numbers, which it uses as the main means to communicate with customers. The company prides itself on being able to provide answers to most customer queries by means of a single toll-free phone call.

What is the most important Capability to Unum? It is Underwriting. For Progressive its source of differentiation is Claims Fulfillment. For State Farm, its Distribution Network is critical because the large volume it generates spreads its risk across a broad swath of the population. And USAA is focused on Customer Service. Capabilities that are strategic for one organization may well be less critical for another in the same industry. All four of these companies are essentially in the same business, but each concentrates on a different Capability to achieve its competitive advantage and its differentiation in the marketplace.

Evaluating change and innovation opportunities is best done with a cool analysis of value and opportunity. When assigning priorities in these areas, it is wise to keep the following points in mind:

- *Big Picture*. No subset of the company's work is an island. Changing one task is bound to have an effect on others. Once a Capability has been selected for change, try to identify at an early stage how it is going to fit in with other operations and with the business as a whole. Don't let yourself be forced to send your best people off to Hawaii while their output is digested.
- *Strategy*. Rank Capabilities on the basis of their strategic importance and the potential they offer for improvement. What is your source of differentiation?

- *Evaluation.* How much value does each part of the operation add? For this purpose, it is useful to divide work into two kinds: knowledge work and transaction work. Companies should try to offload transaction work to others (for example, giving it to clerks or customers or even embedding it in software), increasing their internal capacity for higher-value knowledge work.

- *Opportunity.* Where to focus energies and how to work out the strategies for specific Capabilities is dependent on how well the Capability is performing today. A Capability performing at world-class levels will certainly be treated differently than Capabilities with inferior performance.

The lesson is to focus innovation where it counts most, and avoid dissipating energies in areas less likely to produce either profits or differentiation. And keep in mind that the right Capabilities in today's rapidly changing environment will not necessarily be right for all time. They may not even be right for next week.

Deciding where innovation should be targeted can be tricky, but sometimes the choice is obvious. For instance, when the Belgian telecommunications company Belgacom began a program of improving the business in the early 1990s, its top priority was to improve its image with customers—for the simple reason that, at the time, its image was suffering after many years of comfortable monopoly and underinvestment. The average waiting time for an answer to a directory inquiry was between 1 minute and 1½ minutes, and customers sometimes had to wait over a year to get a telephone installed. And that was in a market that included among its customers the headquarters of NATO and the European Commission.

Belgacom therefore put two Capabilities at the top of its list of priorities—telephone installation and telephone repair. It was steered in this direction not only by the reaction of its own customers but also by the requirements of the state's contract within the overall deregulation of the industry.

And improve they have. In 1992 Belgacom took an average 40 days to install a new line. By the end of 1998, nearly all installations were made within 5 working days—an 88 percent improvement. In 1992, 55 percent of repairs were made within 48 hours. By 1998, 95 percent of customers had their service restored within 48 hours and 82 percent within 24 hours.

The order of priorities for American Express Financial Advisors (AEFA) was also quite clear. In the early 1990s, the company's market research found that the thing customers valued most highly was the personal relationship that they developed over time with individual AEFA advisors. But they also complained that advisors did not stay long enough (on average) for the relationship to deliver its full value. So AEFA launched a major initiative for a complete redesign of its sales processes. The company changed the technology it used, and it changed its pay scales, its hiring policy, and its training procedures. All these changes were designed to increase advisors' loyalty to AEFA, but the ultimate aim, of course, was to increase customers' loyalty to the company's services.

In most cases, the catalytic event—the wake-up call for change and innovation in a particular area—is not particularly dramatic. It can be a merger or an acquisition, an event that gives a company the opportunity to compare its way of doing things with the way its new partner operates, in some cases providing an opportunity to reinvent critical processes. A case in point is Glaxo Wellcome (now GlaxoSmithKline), which used the merger between the two companies as an opportunity to reinvent their critical product-development Capabilities. For a discussion of this merger, see Appendix A.

NOT ALL CAPABILITIES ARE CREATED EQUAL

If the focal point for innovation is not immediately apparent, it only means that the company has to think more carefully about how to order its priorities. To do that may require some reflection on just what the company's core values consist of. A senior executive at Owens Corning, the building materials manufacturer, once said that during his company's preparations for a major redesign, "We didn't just sit down and say, 'Gee, we need to reengineer something.' We first identified some very simple values on which we base everything else." They then went forward with confidence.

For companies that are floundering, a simple tool that can be used for guidance is the Innovation Targeting Matrix (ITM), a framework created as a way of helping companies identify those Capabilities from which they gain their competitive advantage (see Figure 7-1). These are the prime candidates for early attention—activities where you might want to start applying innovation. Along one axis of the matrix are plotted two very distinct types of Capability: transaction and knowledge. Transaction Capabilities are repetitive tasks which are performed in a more or less similar way every time, and which in many cases require little human intervention. Knowledge Capabilities on the other hand are nonrepetitive and require human insight.

The other axis is organized around strategic importance. Capabilities and processes are often categorized as core or supporting, core Capabilities being more strategic than tactical in nature. But not all core Capabilities are equal. Some have a greater bearing on an organization's ability to differen-

FIGURE 7-1. Innovation Targeting Matrix.

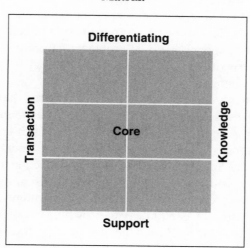

tiate itself strategically than others. We saw this in the insurance example above. Although claims processing is core to all insurance companies, it is a differentiator for Progressive. Thus there are actually types of Capability: *differentiating*, those that define the organization's special nature and differentiate them; *core*, those that are critical to the business but are not necessarily key differentiators; and *support*, those that are not peculiar to any one organization, such as HR and IT.

The matrix formed by these two axes can be used to provide an impartial view of where a company stands today. By indicating where on the matrix each of a company's current activities lies, a company can see its current Capability "position." In order to decide where to place each Capability on the matrix, people from different parts of the organization should be allowed to contribute and defend their views.

I often recommend that organizations also use the matrix to identify competitors' Cabability positions. Companies that are in similar businesses can have very different positions on the matrix. For one firm, internal research may be central to its differentiation, while a rival in the same business may depend on licensing arrangements for its new products. Such differences can make you aware that competitors know something you don't.

I once asked a group of executives from a client to map their Capabilities on the ITM. Some interesting debate broke out as the opinions, pet projects, and political hot potatoes were flung around the room. No one could agree. So I asked them, "What is your strategy? What is your key differentiator? What are your key measures?" Someone then responded, "We don't really have a clear strategy, and our list of strategic measures is two pages long." This company had real problems focusing its efforts. Before you can target areas of innovation, you need a strategy to define sources of competitive differentiation.

When activities are mapped properly on the matrix, the company's strategy will emerge. Let's take a look at two hypothetical pharmaceutical companies, company A and company B (both are composites of several real companies). Company A is the more traditional, big blockbuster firm, with goals of being the largest worldwide provider of ethical pharmaceutical products in all major disease categories distinguished through research and development, strong relations with the medical community, and operational excellence. Company B has a strategy of providing premier pharmaceutical solutions to patients in their chosen therapeutic areas through identification and acquisition of unique and effective solutions, recognized medical expertise, a strong network of partners, and limited capital investment. These companies are direct competitors with very different strategies.

Figure 7-2 shows the ITM mapping for both companies. The results are interesting. In the areas of research and licensing, Company A, with its long scientific history, does all its own research, while Company B depends on partners and aggressive licensing to acquire products. Company B's successful sales strategy and entrenched sales force make it an attractive licensing partner. In the areas of regulatory affairs and regulatory submissions, Company A views regulators as a necessary evil while Company B sees a proactive approach to regulators and submissions as a source of competitive advantage—if the result is faster product approvals. In the manufacturing and supply chain areas Company A does all of its own manufacturing and distribution. Company B does not see any competitive benefits in doing those activities internally, and has outsourced the entire supply chain, which is consistent with its philosophy of minimal capital investment. Company A takes the traditional view of HR, while Company B has outsourced the transactional aspects of HR and utilizes its HR group as in-house consultants to assist other areas in identifying, recruiting, and hiring the best resources. Company A views IT as a necessary cost, while Company B has outsourced the transactional aspects of IT and seeks to utilize technology as a source of competitive advantage in all areas of the company. These very different mappings are consistent with the two companies' different strategies. And both have proved effective, as both companies are successful.

FIGURE 7-2. Competitors with different ITM mappings.

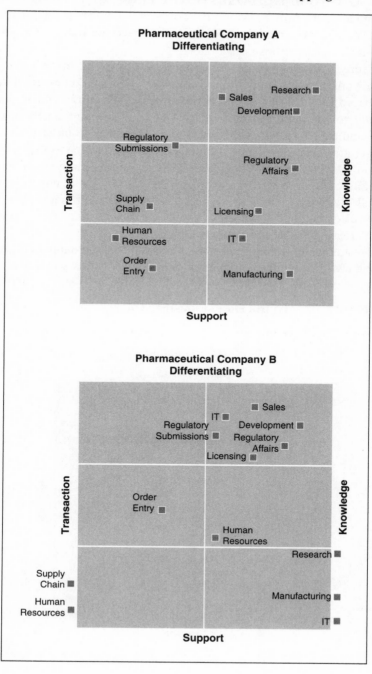

MOVING BEYOND THE BOXES TO THE LINES

Looking at your positions within the boxes of the matrix is only part of the story. The real power of the ITM is in the lines, the moves that you can make to change your business model.

Figure 7-3 shows some common moves you can make in order to change your business model. For example, you might down-skill a knowledge-based Capability and transactionalize it. This would enable you, for example, to hire your customer. Just a few years ago, in the complex electronics industry, experts were needed to pull together an order with a valid configuration. But now, using sophisticated configuration tools, customers can do this themselves, freeing your sales reps to do more valuable work. E-commerce is a great enabler of this trend. Or you could up-skill a transactional Capability, so that it becomes knowledge-based. This might involve using engineers, nurses, or social workers in call centers rather than clerks, creating higher levels of customer service.

Many other moves are possible. You might take a support Capability and make it differentiating. One national bank did this when it began to

FIGURE 7-3. Typical moves using the ITM.

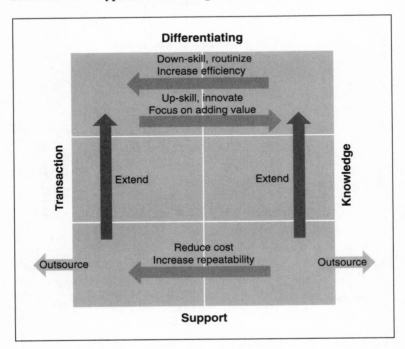

offer its indirect materials procurement Capability to its banking customers. (In Chapter 4, I discussed many companies, including Centrica and BT, that are doing just this.)

You could also try moving an activity to somewhere on the matrix that seems counterintuitive. The pharmaceutical Company B above (Figure 7-2) took R&D, typically a critical Capability, and outsourced it. Or take the example of Egghead, the well-known computer software retailer. A logical move would have been to routinize sales and fulfillment Capabilities so they could be offered on the Internet, without radically changing other Capabilities. This would have turned them from a bricks-and-mortar company into a clicks-and-mortar company, like every other retailer turned e-tailer. Instead, they took all of the bricks-related Capabilities and eliminated them. This turned Egghead directly into an Internet "pure play," and they have now moved into auctions.

Suggesting a seemingly illogical move will stimulate some interesting discussions. The implications of switching activities from what seems to be their "natural" position on the matrix to somewhere else can reveal insights into the rigidities of the existing structure and help uncover hidden assumptions.

After the discussions have died down and everyone agrees on a course of action, you need to step back and look at your artwork. Have you created something that will give you competitive advantage, or has it merely been an interesting intellectual exercise? I have found that a good ITM mapping, and hence a good operating strategy, often has the following attributes:

- Differentiating Capabilities should be a direct reflection of the company's strategy and should be prime targets for innovation. As a rule of thumb, these Capabilities tend to focus on knowledge work. Knowledge work should be improved by enabling people to carry it out more effectively. Some of the e-learning concepts discussed in Chapter 5 can be helpful here.

- Core Capabilities can also be targeted for innovation, but they should be transactionalized so that they are repeatable, streamlined, and automated. These often reflect supply chain or order management Capabilities that can be optimized.

- Support activities should be minimized or outsourced, unless, of course, you decided to extend them as new offerings, in which case they become differentiating Capabilities.

THE HUNT FOR EFFICIENCY

A third dimension can then be layered on top of our matrix: the opportunity for improvement. This could be illustrated in the matrix by varying the size of the circle representing the Capability. A larger circle could represent larger opportunity.

The eternal pursuit of efficiency and effectiveness tends to concentrate on cutting costs and on making operational improvements, by, for example, reducing cycle times. However, the search should be focused on the potential for growth. Innovate in areas that will help you not only to add more value to existing customers, but also to reach untapped markets.

When you put this all together, you end up with a number of strategies and guidelines that should guide your innovation investments.

- *Targeting.* Differentiating Capabilities with a high potential for improvement should be your logical choice for targeting innovation. Such Capabilities should attract a high level of resources and investment as soon as possible.

- *Extending.* Some Capabilities, which are differentiating or core Capabilities, have a low potential for improvement as they are already performing well. These should be the subject of a continuous search for improvement, because a well-performing Capability will deteriorate if left alone. And, since they are performing well, you should look for ways of extending them—that is, look at the lessons that these Capabilities are teaching and see how these lessons could be applied more widely throughout the organization. Or, better yet, look to potentially marketing these Capabilities to outside firms that can benefit from them.

    In one such case, the U.K. utility Thames Water went so far as to set up a separate company (called Connect 2020) to market one of its core Capabilities—supply chain management. Among the customers for this service were a number of other utilities that, like Thames Water, needed the services of an extensive workforce out in the field (and that workforce can sometimes be, literally, "out in the field"). These other utilities acknowledged that Thames Water's Capabilities in the area were superior to their own and that they were better off outsourcing the task to Thames than investing much time and money in trying to bring their own Capabilities up to a similar standard.

- *Outsourcing.* Capabilities that are candidates for outsourcing include Capabilities which are support in nature (i.e., they are not core to the business), but which offer a big opportunity for improvement. And since you may need to invest lots of time, money, and energy bringing these up to a sufficient level of performance, the best thing to do is outsource these to a specialist organization that knows how to create the most value from them. Web technologies are providing increasingly exciting ways to outsource. Two notable examples are ICG Commerce and epeopleserve: ICG Commerce provides online indirect materials procurement through a leveraged purchasing base; epeopleserve, a joint venture between BT and Accenture, delivers HR functions, such as recruitment, training, administration, and pensions services, through the Internet.

Nike, the sports shoe company, so well known for focusing on its differentiators—high-tech design and marketing—aims to outsource everything else.

- *Improving.* Capabilities that might be targeted for improvement may not be differentiating—they may not even be core—and they are already performing well enough. Seemingly, they do not present any great opportunity for improvement. But, as stated above, no Capability should be ignored, so continuous improvement is called for here. And, as I suggested earlier, look for opportunities to take these Capabilities out to the marketplace.

Although in this scheme of things support Capabilities might seem to be lesser beings, their significance must not be underestimated. Addressing underperforming support Capabilities can sometimes be the best thing a company can do. For example, fast-growing high-tech companies often have difficulty in finding the right technical skills to fill all the posts that they need. At such times, training and recruitment become critically important.

It is important to recognize that what is strategic in one organization may be merely tactical in another. Payroll services, for example, are secondary at most companies. But at Paycheck and ADP, companies that make their living from processing the paychecks of other companies, they are very definitely core Capabilities and of central strategic significance.

Paychecks and ADP also have their own employees and their own salaries to pay, so for them there is a sense in which payroll services are also tactical and secondary. It is a bit like Accenture and its IT services. Whereas these are core services that Accenture provides for its clients, they are also a service that the firm needs for itself internally, an enabling Capability that supports our ability to provide the same sort of services to its clients. In this case, such Capabilities are both strategic and tactical.

BEYOND THE STANDARD ITM

The ITM matrix has been used in a variety of unusual ways. At a large insurance company, it helped explain why political battles were brewing. The group in question is considered to be a support/knowledge–based Capability (the bottom right of the matrix; see Figure 7-1). They are claims experts, who are called in to solve really tough claims issues and to provide knowledge capital and best practices. For some reason, there seemed to be animosity between this group and the field offices. When they drew the ITM and filled it in with the Capabilities of the insurance company, they immediately realized that the department they were having problems with was performing differentiating/knowledge–based Capabilities (the upper right of the matrix). Of course, this makes perfect sense. Every time one of the claims experts overstepped the bounds by moving into a client-facing, differentiating role, the field offices felt threatened. The people whose necks are on the line to bring in money and serve the customer generally don't want the back-office cost center people telling them how to do it. They don't mind support but generally want to be left to themselves when determining these types of critical interactions. When the group of claims experts reviewed their department's mission statement, it had five bullet points. Four fit together nicely, but one stuck out like a sore thumb. It turns out that was the one that was driving them to the upper right corner. This an insight that they probably would not have reached had they not used the ITM.

A different use of the ITM was within Accenture's training organization. We are always assessing our investments in training to make sure we are getting value for our money. And the same approach has been used over the years for managing where training dollars are spent. Last year we decided to use the ITM as a tool for assessing these investments. For this purpose, the definition of the axes had to change slightly, but the intent was the same. A differentiating Capability was a distinctive Capability that *created value*; a supporting Capability was more commonplace, *enabled* the delivery of *value*. "Transaction" was redefined to mean something in the *public domain*, skills we could gain elsewhere in the marketplace, and "knowledge" was defined as Accenture's *proprietary knowledge*. The goal was to match the investment to the value it provided. The strategies for training development and conduct included:

- Completely outsource lower-value public domain training
- Design and partner with other companies on both lower-value Accenture proprietary training and high-value public domain training

- Design, build, and deliver high-value proprietary (upper right corner) training internally

When the training courses were mapped on the ITM, everyone quickly realized that most of the investment money and resources had traditionally gone to the internal development of lower-value public domain knowledge training, often targeting thousands of newer hires or younger consultants. Sometimes, as in this case, volume is confused with value. Such fundamental courses are important, but they are not a primary source of value. In contrast, the really high-value proprietary courses were often developed by a few experts in their spare time. Because the skills needed to develop these courses were rare, it was difficult to tap into the right resources to build the training. Yet this is where differentiating value can be derived. We found that very few courses were outsourced to companies that specialize in training around particular topics. As you can imagine, the insight gained through this analysis rapidly led to a shift in investments, and the appropriate strategies are now used for each training course.

AVOIDING THE PITFALLS

In my experience, there are a couple of traps that companies commonly fall into when trying to decide which Capabilities to target: the Playing It Safe trap and the Squeaky Wheel trap.

In the Playing It Safe trap, companies dip a toe in the water, so if it's too hot they won't get scalded. They set out to improve a Capability that is "safe"—that is, not of sufficient value for it to matter if it goes badly wrong. The problem with this approach is that it also won't matter if the improvement goes terribly well. Nobody will notice. And even if they do, the chances are that they will think that the Capability is of low value and therefore unimportant. As a result, no one will consider the improvement to be indicative of what could happen were a "real" Capability to be redesigned . . . which only goes to show that you can put a toe in the water and still get burned!

In the Squeaky Wheel trap, companies target those Capabilities about which the greatest number of people are making the greatest amount of noise. They rush in to fix the problem, believing that just because a wheel squeaks it must need oil the most. In the vast majority of cases, however, they need to consider carefully what the real benefits from improving that Capability will be. When oil is a scarce resource, there may be better uses for it than the mere removal of an aggravating noise.

Falling into traps like these can be extremely expensive. An American insurance company, for instance, became well known for its pioneering efforts at reengineering. As part of its trailblazing it extensively redesigned the way it issued new policies. To do this, the company had to divert considerable human and technological resources from other areas—in particular, from its investment management division. This led directly to the mismanagement of some critical risks in its real estate investment portfolio. The ultimate outcome of the company's pioneering was that it ended up in receivership. These unfortunate situations can be avoided by focusing efforts on critical Capabilities.

CREATING VALUE

In addition to strategy driven by admittedly somewhat subjective approaches, quantitative approaches can be used to help provide data points. There are many measures of value, however, and the one chosen for this purpose has to go beyond book value. Many companies are now trying to take into account more hard-to-measure elements of value. Skandia, a Swedish financial services group, was a pioneer in the 1990s in its attempts to measure its human capital and what it called its "structural capital." The results were regularly included in the company's annual report, alongside the more traditional yardsticks of performance.

Think of value in a company as analogous to the value of a diamond. A diamond's market price is not determined just by size and weight. It also depends on the stone's color, clarity, and cut, things that are much harder to measure. Likewise, corporate value depends not only on a company's profits and sales, but also on things such as the way it uses IT, the company's leadership, and of course, its perceived innovativeness. Shareholder value (the value placed on a company's shares by a recognized stock market) is one way to take almost all these elements into account. There are several measures for assessing shareholder value such as Economic Value Added (EVA, a proprietary method developed by Stern Stewart) and discounted cash flow (DCF), and there are many excellent books on how to value companies, and I won't re-create those discussions here. Instead I want to focus on how these measures can be used to help target innovation from a quantitative perspective.

Economic Value Added, for example, is essentially a measure of a company's after-tax net profit less its cost of capital (i.e., the cost of its debt and of its equity). Market value added (MVA), a close cousin, relates value to the change in a company's debt and the market value of its stock. It also factors in a number of adjustments for the distortions of traditional accounting. For example, it treats R&D as an investment rather than as an expense. Calculations of both EVA and DCF are based on information that is, for the most part, publicly available. But the calculations are not straightforward and should be left to experts. Only then can a company be sure that apples are being compared with apples, not with pears. Having plumped for one particular measure of shareholder value, the company can find out, on the basis of this measure, which are its high-value Capabilities.

SENSITIVITY ANALYSIS

To decide what steps to take next, companies have to know the effect a change in any activity will have on shareholder value. *Sensitivity analysis* measures the impact of different levers on overall performance, and it can be applied at almost any level of detail. The goal is to measure the effect of changing any one parameter by 1 percent while keeping all other parameters constant.

In one case, for example, a bank found that a 1 percent decrease in its noninterest expense had the biggest impact on improving its shareholder value. It also found that among its areas of noninterest expense, personnel was the major determinant of shareholder value: a 1 percent drop in personnel expenses resulted in a 4 percent improvement in EVA. At a major industrial client of mine, our analysis showed that a 1 percent reduction in cost of goods sold (COGS) would result in a 27 percent improvement in shareholder value, while a similar improvement in revenues or selling, general, and administrative expense (SG&A) would result in only a 7 percent improvement. The next step in the sensitivity analysis was to identify which Capabilities helped drive the company's COGS. We identified design and engineering, project management, manufacturing and assembly, and supply chain management as primary targets. We then assessed these in the context of the company's strategy and current performance levels to agree upon areas to target.

While sensitivity analysis is a powerful tool, its results should be balanced with other perspectives. Companies can, for example, try to put a value on the extent to which a Capability fits in with their overall strategy. And they can try to assess the risk involved in following any course of action.

THE BIGGER PICTURE

When targeting innovation, be sure to think about the bigger picture, about how a given Capability fits into the rest of your operations. To do that, you need to ask yourself these questions:

- *How might a change that is proposed for one Capability affect other Capabilities?* As I said earlier, no Capability is so isolated that nothing else will be affected when it are altered. This is where line thinking is critical. Remember the application of Braess's Paradox from Chapter 1? When box thinking is used, an improvement to one Capability has a 25 percent chance of improving the overall business, a 50 percent chance of not affecting the overall business at all, and a 25 percent chance of having a negative effect on the overall business.

- *Is the magnitude of the change proportional to the benefit?* It is often easy to identify an area where considerable value can be added. But if the cost of achieving that extra value is a massive internal reorganization, then it may well not be worth pursuing. As was said in Gilbert and Sullivan's *The Mikado*, "Make the punishment fit the crime"— or, in this case, make the value fit the effort.

- *Does the organization have the capacity to change at the pace required?* Many organizations identify Capabilities that are ripe for improvement and then set out to improve them, only to find somewhere along the line that the resources to complete the job are simply not available at the time they are required. It's no good writing a great trombone duet if you don't have two trombonists. In Chapter 3, I discussed the implications of change capacity in more detail.

These forces need to be considered together. Otherwise, certain moves that seem good on the surface may fall apart when you dig further. This is what happened in one celebrated case involving a troubled European telecom company. The CEO first addressed his cash crisis by trimming staff. Then, in a subsequent boardroom brawl, he found his commercial director unwilling to agree to targets for delivering a new client base in vertical sectors.

"I believe, I know, we can achieve this! I want you to believe it!" shouted the CEO, a short but vigorous American with a top-down management strategy.

The vice president for commercial affairs dared to stand up and take the floor.

"I know we *cannot* achieve this!" he said. "You have forced me to sack half of my staff. I simply do not have the horses. You'll have to back up and start over."

The rest of the management team looked on as the two men traded insults. As a direct result of the ensuing damage to their relationship, the commercial VP left the next day. Two weeks later the CEO abandoned his plan. Within a few months the company had been taken over and the impetuous CEO had left to pursue a new career.

This example is one where the dependencies were political in nature. Other connections may be more functional. And although with hindsight such connections seem obvious, they tend to be hidden before troubles start. One example of the obvious coming to light is a company that thought it could cut its costs by literally cutting the size of its bills. Billing is one of the most expensive activities for any telecom company, so any ideas for reducing that cost are taken seriously. In this case, the firm decided to reduce its billing costs by abbreviating the messages on its customers' bills, thus reducing its consumption of paper. But customers were so confused by the new cryptic messages they received that they flooded the company's call center with questions. In the end, billing costs fell, but overall costs rose.

Another thing to look out for is the case where the full benefits of improving an individual Capability are not gained unless other Capabilities are changed as well. An electronics manufacturer, for instance, redesigned its production Capabilities so that it was able to turn out finished goods in four hours (its competitors took weeks). But because other critical Capabilities—shipping, order entry, etc.—were not changed at the same time, the whistle-stop new products just sat in a company warehouse. The improvements in production, carried out in isolation, resulted only in higher inventory levels.

In order to manage the interrelationships between Capabilities, it is important to set up a systematic way of recognizing the connecting points, or integration points, between them and to have a means of making sure they're understood, agreed upon, and managed over time.

Some integration points are more obvious than others. If the product-development Capability is improved and shortened, for example, it is very likely to have an effect on the demand generation Capability. When planning to increase the flow of new products, for example, organizations should think simultaneously about how their sales forces are going to sell those products. Other integration points may not be so obvious. Suppose, for example, a company wants to design products in such a way to reduce total cost of ownership. For this effort to be successful, the links between product development and field service must be strengthened in specific ways, such as designing around field-serviceable parts, building in remote monitoring capabilities that include predictive notifications, providing the service company with advance warning of potential faults, and enabling remote repair of products.

Integration points always become obvious after the fact. But by then it is too late. Links between Capabilities will be easier to spot if the time is invested up front to think about the relationships. But cultural and competitive relationships are less tangible than functional relationships and hence more difficult to see. Companies are often torn between incremental and radical innovation, between focused and enterprise (or cross-enterprise) innovation. The competitive environment drives companies into thinking that they need to be the leaders in redefining their industry. But most companies (like most people) are instinctively limited in their appetite for this level of change, and their instincts tend to push them toward the incremental (and less painful) variety.

A PORTFOLIO OF CHANGE

Organizations need to be aware of the natural internal tension between incremental and radical innovation models, and they need to consider carefully what trade-off between the two conflicting forces they wish to make when choosing the right change program. One unfortunate way a number of companies have found to proceed is to aim for the moon (in terms of the magnitude of the change and the value to be gained) but not commit enough rocket fuel to reach the target (in terms of the scope of the change, the resources, and the risks to be taken). The result is not only a failure to reach the moon, but also a general disillusionment and cynicism throughout the organization toward all future rocket launches.

One American utility sought to achieve a $26 million cost reduction in its repair and maintenance Capabilities—quite an ambitious target for this company. Before it began, however, it declared to all those involved that any significant change in technology, organization, or compensation was off limits. The net result? The company managed to save just over $1 million.

Companies should also beware of falling into the "I have a hammer, so this must be a nail" attitude. Some become so attached to one particular technique (TQM, BPR, or whatever) that they try to apply it to every problem that faces them. This is not innovation, this is stupidity. As Ralph Waldo Emerson once said, "A foolish consistency is the hobgoblin of little minds."

Investing in innovation is much like deciding on your own personal investments. A smart investor puts some money in aggressive stocks, some in mutual funds, and some in bonds, creating a portfolio of investments. The same is true in business. You need a portfolio of innovations—different levels of innovation based on where the Capability is in the ITM matrix. For example, a mail order company that sells clothes by catalog might decide to radically change order fulfillment and at the same time outsource the call center. But it might also apply incremental innovations to the Capabilities associated with customer returns. No single approach could be applied to all these cases. The goal is to create a portfolio of change within the organization.

Chart 7-1 lists the implications of three levels of innovation—from incremental to radical but evolutionary to radical but transformational and revolutionary—for change issues, risk, and the potential for creation of value.

No template for targeting innovative change can be devised that will apply to all companies. The variety of challenges and opportunities in business is infinite and always will be. For starters, a firm's capacity for change is a potentially limiting factor that must be assessed. What I have laid out in this chapter is that innovation must be concentrated on activities where it counts most, where it is most likely to generate competitive advantage and shareholder value. Any other approach risks dissipating energies. Nor can a company expect a shift to different key Capabilities to be the best choice for all time. Such decisions need constant monitoring and verification. A changing competitive scene may mean that the Capabilities you identify as key today will not be right for next week. The ITM can help a company

Chart 7-1. Innovation Implications

	Incremental Innovation	Radical, Evolutionary Innovation	Radical, Transformational and Revolutionary Innovation
Scope of Change	Individual functions, departments, or other focused units	Core processes; enterprisewide	Throughout the value chain, including suppliers, partners, complementors, intermediaries, and customers
Change Capacity Issues	Low	High—significant political and culture issues to consider	Very high—internal and external political and cultural issues
Risk	Low to moderate	High	High to very high
Value-Creation Potential	Low—not a strategic differentiator	Medium to high—helps deliver quantum leaps in value	Very high—sustainable competitive differentiation

identify the Capabilities to focus on, and more importantly help suggest some moves that can lead to radical, revolutionary innovation. If targeting of innovation is carried out with care, and implemented in harmony with the full range of the company's Capabilities, the results can make the difference between being an industry also-ran and being an industry leader.

8

SIMULATING
NEW MODELS

"Results? Why man, I have gotten lots of results. I know several thousand things that won't work!"

—THOMAS EDISON

*U*p to now, we have been looking at ways of reshaping businesses to make them more innovative. Creative change offers the potential of great reward but necessarily carries with it considerable risk. Misguided innovation can be costly in time and money and in trust between manager and employee. How can these risks be contained? Many companies find that simulation is the answer. Although the concept of simulation has been around for quite some time, it is only in recent years that it has become sophisticated enough to fully test innovative solutions before actually implementing them in the business. In my experience, the refinement of an idea through computerized simulation is the best route to preimplementation testing. It allows us to approach, if not achieve, perfection prior to betting the business on it.

As a reasonably good jazz sax player, I am able to "jam" with a group of musicians without practicing. It's probably the most exciting way to make music. But more complicated music requires some rehearsal before putting on a show for a paying audience. Likewise, businesses need a way to be sure that their innovations—especially the big ones—are ready for prime time. For in the feverish pursuit of innovative change, it can be awfully costly to make wrong choices along the way. Resources are sure to be wasted, and, more importantly, goodwill toward further change within the organization can be squandered. Too often, I have seen employees start out enthusiastically over the prospect of innovations, then become intolerant of experimentation, especially when top-down management is imposing the change without sensitivity.

Companies are better off working out their changes in a safe environment with drawing board solutions before they put them into practice. The best way to do that is through Capability simulation, by imitating reality in a good computer model that can try out alternative business models as an animated sequence of changes. These "rehearsal" techniques offer an ideal opportunity for nondestructive innovation through the testing of various what-if scenarios. Because it is a safe environment, you can play with even the wildest ideas, potentially uncovering hidden jewels along the way.

The Capability simulations I am talking about here are different than the e-learning simulations I described in Chapter 5. E-learning simulation is more akin to flight simulation designed to train pilots. Designers of flight simulation know that the plane will fly when the pilot gets the hang of it. Capability simulations are designed to test *whether* innovations will "fly" when they are implemented.

To show the power of Capability simulation, consider a simple question I like to put to clients. Imagine a call center that receives on average 20 calls per minute and that, on average, each call takes 5 minutes to answer. Given that scenario, how many customer service reps (CSRs) are needed to have all calls answered immediately without queuing or waiting? The obvious answer would seem to be 100 CSRs, but this is not correct, because we are dealing with averages here and the real world is made up of peaks and valleys. The answer is that it is impossible to guarantee no waiting, regardless how many reps you hire. Instead of no waiting time, we might want to be more specific and say that we want callers to wait no more than an average of 30 seconds, that they should never have to wait more than 2 minutes, and that total service time should never be longer than 8 minutes. There is no way to know if this can be achieved without sophisticated computer tools that simulate the real, dynamic environment in all its complexity.

FIGURE 8-1.   Wait times and call completion times with 100 and 120 CSRs.

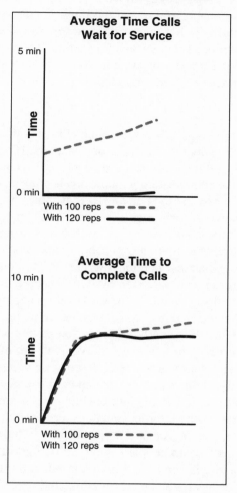

Figure 8-1 shows the results of a computer simulation with 100 CSRs and 120 CSRs. With 100 CSRs, wait times grow rapidly to well over 2 minutes for the average call; with 120 CSRs, the wait time is negligible. And call completion times continue to increase over time with 100 CSRs, but plateau at close to 5 minutes average time with 120 CSRs. So we know the "right" number of CSRs is somewhere between 100 and 120.

Computerized simulations allow the rapid modeling of ideas and testing of Capabilities as they would play out over time. They imitate real-world interactions as dynamic (moving) models rather than as static representations and enable you to see the lines that connect various components of a Capability rather than just the boxes. And the scope can be as wide as the imagination. They are techniques for discovery through quantifying the impact of changes on the business, and they provide a perfect environment for innovative experimentation.

BUILD, TRY, FIX

Now you may be thinking, "This stuff sounds like it is the opposite of what you have been talking about in the previous chapters. Here we are trying to design and test Capabilities before they are deployed. What gives?" As I have stated throughout the book, fostering innovation is more an art than a science. To some degree, we have to find our way by trial and error. And therefore the design and execution of Capabilities has to be a "Build it, try it, fix it" sort of thing—a gradual movement toward an ideal that is probably unattainable, unattainable because new technology, changing markets, and new skills are moving the goalposts almost continually. This is the concept behind 24/7 innovation: You zigzag your way, step by step, toward a moving target. And this is the point of Edison's quote at the start of this chapter.

When a company is making radical changes to its operating model, the rewards can be great—but so are the risks. You cannot afford to make big mistakes on big projects, or you may find yourself out of business. This is where Capability simulation is so useful. It will help you get your new business model as nearly right as possible. It can help you uncover new ways of thinking that were previously hidden, enabling yet more innovative solutions. And it addresses the interdependencies between the various components of the business to ensure compatibility. Underlying all these advantages, it helps free up people's minds to be innovative with the new business model, and this can have a dramatic effect on the outcome. Yet a simulation model is always an approximation, and it can only ever hope to reach within 10 to 15 percent of reality. Simulation is a decision-support tool. It is not a decision-making tool.

THE 80-20 RULE

The first 20 percent of the product development life cycle is where 80 percent of the big ideas are generated. The remaining 80 percent of the time is spent bringing the product to market. The same ratio holds for radical innovation. About 80 percent of the "value decisions" are made in the first 20

FIGURE 8-2.   Value decisions early in change Life Cycle.

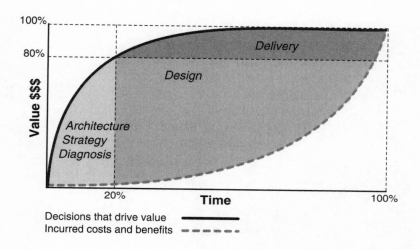

percent of a change effort. During this time, the focus is on strategy and architecture on trying to come up with the most innovative business model. The remaining 80 percent is about designing, developing, and deploying the change, as shown by the top curve in Figure 8-2. The lower curve in Figure 8-2 shows where costs are incurred, and as expected, the first 20 percent is where you incur the lowest costs. Unfortunately, too many companies like to get into the details—the 80 percent phase—without having nailed down the first 20 percent. This can be a costly mistake. Your ideas may turn out to be more expensive than you originally planned and ultimately force you to scrap them. Worse, the ideas that are implemented may be based on faulty assumptions and prove to be just plain bad for the business.

Most of the benefit of a good new model shows through in a short space of time, and—if handled right—this makes a powerful impression on employees and reinforces their commitment to the idea. They will realize that, as a means of looking into the future, computer modeling takes most of the guesswork out of the process.

BRINGING IT TO LIFE

The use of simulation and computer modeling for business purposes is almost as old as the first computer. But in the past, simulations were usually statistical models used to predict performance of a process. In recent years, the methods have grown much more sophisticated, in particular, through the

FIGURE 8-3.   Snapshot of an animated simulation.

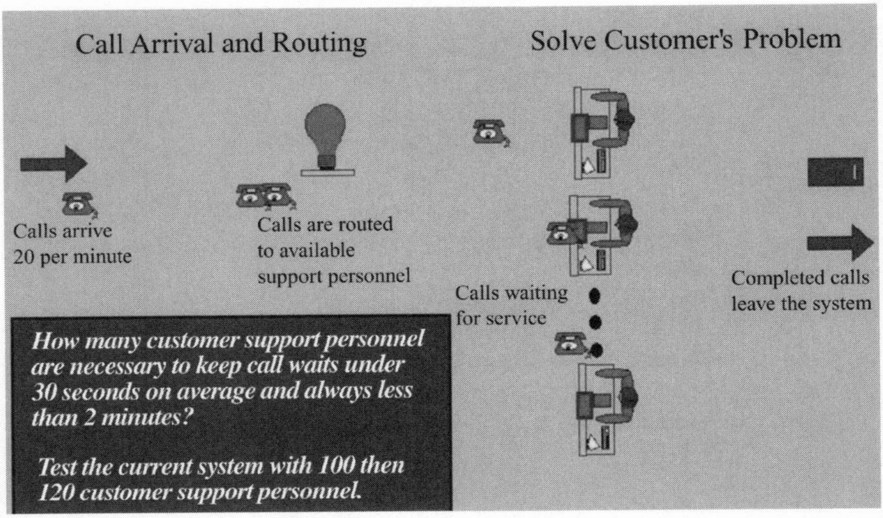

development of animation that allows managers to "see" the flow of activities as a moving on-screen experience. Animation has transformed simulations into a powerful tool for communication and change management. Complicated changes are demonstrated with remarkable clarity.

Animations (and state-of-the-art simulations) are created with sophisticated software designed specifically for this purpose. Imagine a flow diagram for a process like the simple call-center example above. Each box on the flow chart would represent an activity. But animations, instead of showing boring boxes, use pictures, for example, people, phones, and workstations. Figure 8-3 is a screenshot from such an animation. But remember, a simulation is more like a movie than a photograph. Everything on the screen moves. Calls, represented as phones, start to arrive at randomly generated intervals. And now the fun begins. Because when we plug in 100 CSRs, we can see the phones calls queuing up, representing the bottleneck and the increased wait times. If we wanted to get more sophisticated, we could add abandoned calls. We could expand the model further to show the impact of up-front voice response units, that help direct calls to the appropriate rep, and so on. I think you get the idea.

This moving picture is a powerful way of communicating the need for change and the benefit of undertaking specific change. In my work today, I use this tool whenever possible. At a meeting with one client, a design and manufacturing company, we were trying to convince key executives that it would be better to move some manufacturing activities into the design area, so that parts would be sent to manufacturing only after testing and programming into the tooling machines. This would help ensure that the parts *could* be manufactured, as well as give the design teams a better feel for how long it would take to make the part. And more importantly, it would give design a real test environment, allowing the design team to be even more innovative because they could try out variations to see which worked best.

Although this was a very reasonable thing to suggest, and I have convinced other clients of its value in the past, this particular client had a hard time visualizing at first what it would look like. So we created a simple animation that showed them how the process was working and where the bottlenecks were. Almost as if they were watching a Disney cartoon, they could see parts in the animation backing up exactly where they backed up in real life. We then ran the new model and showed how the queues disappeared, productivity was increased everywhere, and how they would now be able to push more parts through the pipeline. Although they had not believed it before, being able to visualize the interactions between design and manufacturing was proof enough. Spreadsheets could never have convinced them.

If animations are the movie, then simulation is the screenplay behind the movie. The animation example I used above was whipped together in a couple of days. It was representative but not statistically valuable. Really complex simulations can take months to build, but they are often statistically 90 percent accurate, just as a good script can give you a pretty good sense of what the movie will be like. Of course, the final result of a film depends on the quality of the actors, just as the results of business depend on the quality of its people.

In the past, managers who sought to test their designs tended to rely on static tools such as flow charts and spreadsheets to give them a feel of how their plans might unfold in reality. But the outcomes of static analyses produce an inaccurate view of the world. Businesses are too complex to be reduced to such a basic representation. A more sophisticated model is required to take into account all the changes brought about even by a simple modification in part of one process. Any change may have an effect on a number of other interconnected operations, and there is no way that the human mind, unaided, can grasp all the knock-on effects and dependencies.

Moreover, the interconnectedness of things has grown in recent years. In the silos of the functional age of business, activities could take place in isolation from what went on in the rest of the organization. Moving to a unified and coordinated view of the customer requires the organization to

foster a greater awareness of the impact that a small change in one operation can have on all the others. As the chaos theorists like to put it, the flap-
ping of a butterfly's wings in the rain forests of Brazil can displace larger
and larger air masses until a thunderstorm eventually erupts in Europe.

In the remainder of the chapter, I highlight a number of case studies
that show the power of Capability simulation in the context of innovation.
It can help launch new businesses, streamline existing business, model
informal processes, aid in change management, reduce time to market, and
facilitate scenario planning.

SIMULATING AT&T'S NEW LOCAL SERVICE

To provide a better understanding of how a Capability simulation works,
here is an example of an effort that included both the creation of new Capabilities as well as leveraging existing Capabilities within the business. The
case comes from AT&T, where the company was considering the launch of
local service within certain markets.[1] The simulation team needed to consider everything from ordering service to provisioning, billing, and customer service. Such launches would be risky and expensive, so they wanted
to be sure they were doing the right thing.

When starting out, no one could estimate the impact of interactions
between the customer experience in the order call center, the associated
infrastructure costs, the process cycle times, and the order cycle times. The
best answers were mere guesses. Consequently, budgeting would have been
a shot in the dark. So understanding these interactions was deemed critical
to success.

Another daunting issue involved the range of possible solutions. It was
known that three key areas—customer experience (e.g., time waiting and
service time), performance of business operations (e.g., throughput, activity-based cost, activity-based value, and reworking) and staffing and
resources (e.g., staffing required, utilization, and cycle time)—were interrelated, but the precise relationships were unknown. However, intuition led
one to realize that spending more (or less) money on one area, say staffing,
would have an impact upon both of the other areas. Of particular interest,
most executives wanted confidence in what the lowest cost per order would
be while meeting the service-level metrics in the other areas. The most
compelling question here was, "What would be the best balance between
the areas?"

There was also a concern about what would happen if all Capabilities
were not delivered on time. There existed in the new environment a number
of yet-to-be-designed information systems. The questions here were of prior-

ities. Which systems were most important from a cost perspective? Which systems were most important from a process perspective? What were the back-up processes if these systems were not implemented on schedule, and how effective and costly would these contingency operations be?

Capability simulation was deemed the only way to identify answers to these questions. The scope of the business to be analyzed is depicted in the high-level flow diagram in Figure 8-4.

The simulation was based on designs of four key business events and four operations. The four business events that would trigger employees to take action were:

1. *Outbound Calls*. When a service representative calls prospective customer.

2. *Targeted Inbound Calls*. When a customer who has been sent marketing materials for demographic or geographic reasons calls the ordering contact center.

3. *Nontargeted Inbound (NTI) Calls*. When a customer who has heard about the offering independently and would like the same offer (also known as a "me too" customer) calls the ordering contact center.

4. *Service Requests*. When a customer already signed up within the system needs a new copy of his or her bill or some other account service.

And the four key operations were:

1. *Ordering*. The contact center that focuses solely on taking orders from potential customers.

FIGURE 8-4.   AT&T business events and operations.

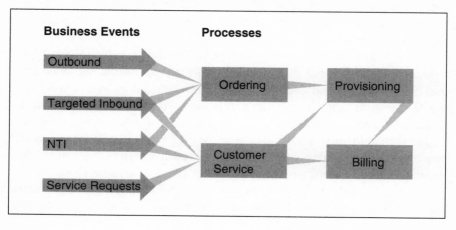

2. *Customer Service.* The contact center that responds to all service requests and approximately 20 percent of the order requests from new customers.
3. *Provisioning.* The service center that fulfills customer orders, such as wiring homes.
4. *Billing.* The service center that performs all billing functions, including receipt of cash.

Life within the process begins when one of the four business events occurs and ends when a potential customer declines the service or accepts service, has the service installed, and sends in the first payment. The way the team decided to move forward was to construct a simulation model of the entire order-to-cash process, experiment with different alternatives, then evaluate business objectives and customer service levels to balance the three areas.

As part of the design, they looked at various options for the solution. Some of these options were technological enablers, some were potential service levels to be delivered, and others were regulatory requirements that needed to be met. The power of simulation is that it allows you to see the impact on the overall Capability of some or all of these options. For example, what would be the impact of Internet-based service for customers? What would be the impact of automated provisioning?

At this point, AT&T had determined the scope, defined the objectives and measures, and raised the key questions that needed to be answered. Now it was time to describe the business Capabilities through more detailed flow diagrams. The level of detail depended in part upon the questions to be assessed in an area. If an area was key to the analysis and had a large number of existing problems or a large number of personnel, a more detailed description would be carried out. The level of detail had to be sufficient for the simulation team to gain a fairly complete understanding of the business operation at hand.

Next, the model was constructed and exhaustively worked to verify and validate it—in other words, to ensure that the right model had been built and that the model had been built right. Preidentified situations were then plugged into the model and the simulation results were compared to the expected outcomes. When differences occurred, further exploration was undertaken to identify what had caused the gap. When necessary, the model was modified accordingly. This process continued until all agreed that the model was indeed performing well.

The next step in the process was scenario analysis. After the most appropriate scenarios had been identified, the model was run long enough to yield an understanding of the issues and impacts. Through this process, a few additional scenarios are usually investigated that shed light on the operational requirements of the model. Scenario analysis generally takes two to four weeks. This is where the model is stretched to the limit, operationally speaking.

The analysis showed that the primary benefit drivers (issues to be investigated) in the ordering Capability were sales force automation, Web self-servicing, automated provisioning, front-end edits and validation checks, and streamlined order entry processes. If these were included as part of the Capability, it could be expected to meet their needs. The model looked at resources (types of personnel), the utilization of resources (how much time they actually work versus idle time), and head count. It then looked at the average speed of answer for each call—the total time it took to take care of both service requests (cycle time) and nonservice requests.

SIMULATION INSIGHTS AT AT&T

So far, this may sound very dry and clinical—about as much fun as going to the doctor for a full physical. But just as a battery of blood tests will provide insights into how well one's body is functioning, simulation analysis provides a sound analysis of how a business is functioning. At AT&T, one insight occurred during this piece of analysis. The local Public Service Commission (PSC) required that 95 percent of the calls into the contact center be answered within 30 seconds. Unbeknownst to the simulation designers, this particular service level significantly exceeded world-class call center performance and drove a five-second average speed of answer even during peak volume times.

The simulations showed that in order to achieve this level of performance, however, utilization of resources would have to be dismally low. That is, people would have to sit around waiting for calls to ensure that someone would be there to answer when a call came in. Of course, this would mean extra costs, and as there are no free lunches, these costs would ultimately be passed on to the customer. Armed with this information, AT&T petitioned the PSC for relief from this service-level requirement so that customers could be saved money. The PSC held firm on the service level, and now the decision was up to management—either absorb the additional costs or not enter this market. They decided to continue with their plans but did so armed with significant information that would drive different expectations, budgets, and revenues. Figure 8-5 shows the results of the simulation analysis for the ordering Capability.

FIGURE 8-5.   Simulation results for the ordering Capability at AT&T.

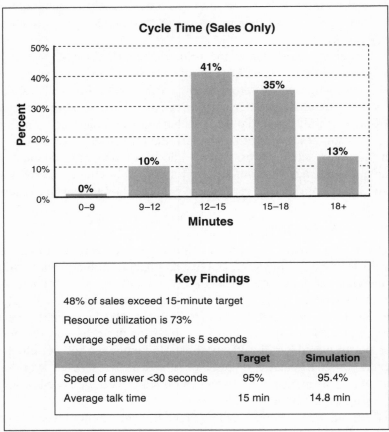

Now the team was on a roll, and the insights started to flow. For example, the marketing department had determined, through its homework, that 15-minute talk times during the ordering process with potential customers would yield a significantly improved "take rate" (the percentage of potential customers that accept the offer), and so a 15-minute talk time target was established. When the model was run, it showed that the average talk time would be 14.7 minutes for the way it had been designed. At that point, most people would declare victory and move on to the next issue. However, the model also showed that 48 percent of the calls would exceed the 15-minute target, which would result in an unacceptable waste of time and money. So they used the model and backward-engineered the system to determine the reasons for the 48 percent overshoot. When they found the root cause, that part of the process was redesigned, rechecked through the model, and "fixed" before the mistake ever saw the light of day. Simulations in other areas, such as provisioning, resulted in similar insights.

Sometimes, simulation can help deal with political challenges, as was found at AT&T during some sensitivity analysis. Soon after the sensitivity analysis was under way, a senior executive said she had a "gut feeling" that one metric—the channel mix—that usually drives implementation costs didn't really matter in this situation. She had no data to support her feelings, and therefore no one wanted to believe her. So the simulation team did some homework on the topic, and lo and behold, the analysis supported her intuition. No matter how the system was stressed, channel mix impacted it very minimally, only 1 percent. Further investigation determined why that was the case. Now, not only did the executive have data to support her intuition, she also understood the reason for the minimal impact and had the model to support her theory. People now believed her. Simulation can to be very useful in addressing situations like this and other political hurdles simply by providing data to support positions.

Although there were many other insights, I think you get the point by now. Needless to say, the simulation approach to prototyping business Capabilities proved to be a valuable technique for determining the feasibility of alternatives and exploring new, innovative opportunities for improvement. It improved the understanding of business Capabilities, revealed important success factors linked directly to the business case, and became a "living, breathing" tool that has been valuable throughout the change life cycle through to ongoing operations.

SIMULATION AND STREAMLINING
AT&T is a non-product-based industry. Simulation can be also very powerful when physical goods are involved. One example is provided by a major U.S. airline that streamlined the way it shunted planes back and forth from the boarding gates as a result of a new type of tug that came onto the market. The new vehicle could be used on more than one gate (with the old tugs, every gate had had to have its own dedicated vehicle), and it promised considerable efficiencies for all airlines.

The airline reckoned that by switching to the new tugs it could save money by reducing the number of tugs. But such a switch raised the possibility that an aircraft ready to depart would find itself having to wait for a tug to come from elsewhere to push it back. There was a danger that savings would be more than offset by delays in departure times. (As a frequent flier,

I was glad to see that the simulations took this into consideration.) So the company thought about the minimum conditions they needed to be certain to satisfy. In particular they wanted to be sure that 95 percent of all its pilots' requests to be pushed back would be handled without their plane having to wait for a tug. And they wanted to be certain that when delays did occur (in the other 5 percent of cases), they should never exceed five minutes.

The airline ran a computer simulation that incorporated these conditions. The model it developed for shunting planes back and forth allowed for changes to various parameters—including the number of tugs, the length of time between requesting a tug and departure, and the speed of the tug.

In the simulated operation, an aircraft would radio the tugs that it wished to be moved a certain number of minutes before its departure. The nearest available tug would then travel to the aircraft and push it back before moving on to the next request or to an empty gate. Two different models were created for two versions of the proposed operation, and each was run over the equivalent of 31 continuous days of operation.

The simulation indicated that a minimum of seven tugs would be required to service the airline's 15 gates in order to meet the predetermined conditions. It also revealed that the risk of delay would be increased by using tugs that operated on more than one bay. The key to keeping this risk to a minimum lay in designing a process that did not tie up a tug with an aircraft that was already delayed when that tug could be pushing another aircraft somewhere else.

Only with such a simulation was it possible for the airline to fully understand the knock-on effects of changing the variables in the process. It also helped to reveal which the really key variables were, and it gave a clear indication of where bottlenecks might occur—and how the reallocation of resources could help to get around those bottlenecks and streamline the business.

SIMULATING INFORMAL PROCESSES

Computer simulation is particularly suitable for operations that are both complex and to some extent formalized—i.e., subject to rigid rules and patterns. A good example is from Banque Generale de Luxembourg (BGL).[2] When they set out in early 1999 to simulate and analyze two of their core operations, they chose one formalized operation (delivery of credits) and one that was not so subject to set rules, a so-called informal process (recruitment of new employees).

The deliver-credits operation was the more obvious candidate for simulation. Delivering a loan to a client who has requested one is a fairly straightforward procedure that involves some standard steps that have been tried and tested over many years. A key element in it is time—the time between a client's request for a credit and the decision by the bank to disburse that credit. From a client's point of view, that is what the quality of a bank is all about.

The object of BGL's simulation was to provide management with information that would help to reduce the throughput time. And from the output of the simulation exercise, the bank came to realize two important things. Improving the quality of the information it held on its credit request files had a marked effect in reducing the average throughput times; and an increase in volumes of up to 3 percent could be handled under the present system without increasing throughput times. But volume increases of more than 3 percent had to be accompanied by an increase in capacity if the throughput times were to be maintained.

The company's recruit-new-employees Capability was not so easy to simulate because it was not subject to such easily definable rules. The processing of new recruits cannot be standardized to the same extent as the processing of a loan request. Like most organizations, BGL managed its recruitment on a more or less ad hoc basis, varying it according to the nature of the position and the availability of different managers. But the bank was growing rapidly at the time, and recruitment had become a key strategic issue. It needed good new recruits, and it needed them fast. The time it took to recruit new employees, however, was generally perceived by department managers to be too long.

The key outcome of the simulation was a number of suggestions as to how the recruiting time might be reduced without any decline in the quality of new employees. Simulation of various ideas for improvement led to a number of recommendations being followed. These included:

- The introduction of a plan to formalize and schedule in advance all the major steps in the operation—and especially the interactions between the HR department and other corporate departments. This, it was found, could help to reduce recruiting times by about 30 percent on average.

- A shift in the entire preselection of candidates to the HR department. This eliminated the need for any preselection by department managers (which in 90 percent of the cases merely confirmed the HR department's opinion), and thereby reduced the time for recruitment by an average of 2.8 weeks.

- The adoption of an increasingly proactive attitude toward the labor market. It was found that recruitment delays could be reduced if the

company were to keep an eye out for qualified people even before any
vacancies arose.

• The handling of incoming applications on a continuous basis rather
than in batches. This, it was estimated, could reduce the time needed
to find a suitable candidate by up to 35 percent.

SIMULATION AND CHANGE MANAGEMENT

As I said earlier, one the great strengths of simulation is its ability to
increase the acceptance of change throughout the organization. It can illustrate and explain the aims of a change program long before anything has
actually changed. It smoothes the way and helps to avert the skepticism that
tends to greet any project that appears to have been plucked out of thin air.

A major car manufacturer faced considerable skepticism when it decided
that it wanted to give priority to all its sold orders (vehicles that customers
had actually agreed to buy) over its stock orders (vehicles to be held in dealers' showrooms until customers for them could be found), irrespective of the
company's agreed allocations to dealers. It was not a popular idea with the
manufacturer's large dealers or with its own corporate sales department. The
dealers feared that they would be left without stock while small discounters
or Internet agents were given priority. However, the company was under pressure to reduce the time it took between an order and a delivery—the order to
delivery (OTD) time. And its main rivals were working hard to improve their
own OTD times, which increased the pressure.

A simulation of the proposed change was able to win over many
doubters by showing the benefits that would accrue from it. In particular,
the simulation showed that the average extra delay under the new system
from the time of order to the time of delivery would be only an additional
three days. Moreover, the simulation also showed that only a small percentage of all dealers' purchases for stock were actually sold within three
days of their arriving at the dealers' showroom, so the new operation would
involve only a very small percentage of stock orders being delayed beyond
their normal date of sale.

On the other hand, the simulation demonstrated that it would reduce
OTD time for sold orders by about 50 percent, a very significant benefit
that, it was clear to everybody, far outweighed the small additional delay in
the stock orders.

Simulation exercises like this consume considerable resources—both
human and technical—so it is inevitable that they are sometimes perceived
as an expensive toy that delivers results that could be obtained more
cheaply otherwise. To counter such perceptions, it is important to show that

simulation produces unique and innovative solutions that add value. For example, when BGL ran the deliver-credits simulation, a popular idea for a redesign was already in existence within the organization, and there was little desire to spend money in order to come up with yet another. When the simulation began to show the weak points of the existing solution and to indicate other possibilities, the results had at first to be defended against the established view. Only the clear evidence of the superior quality of the simulation's preferred option finally persuaded the company's managers to go for it.

In some cases, however, the problem is rather the reverse of this. Managers can come to have unreasonably high expectations about the outcome of a simulation. To avoid this, it is important that managers be made to understand from the beginning not only what simulation can achieve, but also what it cannot achieve. It is there as an aid for them, something to help them to do their job. It is not there to replace them and to make decisions for them.

REDUCING TIME TO MARKET

Simulation is often as much about saving time as it is about saving money. And saving time has become particularly important in recent years in the development and marketing of new products. Curtailing the time it takes to get new cars, pills, software, etc., from the drawing board to the shops enables companies to cut costs and to keep more in touch with customers' needs. In the past, it took five years to bring a new model of automobile to market, during which time the market could shift so much that the model could be obsolete before it ever appeared in the showrooms. This was one problem with Ford's infamous Edsel model in the 1950s.

Industries such as automotive, pharmaceuticals, and others that approach their product development in a fairly structured way are good candidates for simulation. For example, a leading pharmaceuticals and beauty products company realized that its attempts to use spreadsheets to analyze its product-development process were cumbersome and not very user-friendly and, when all was said and done, unsuccessful. It came to realize that the key to any mapping of the process lay in capturing exhaustive information on numerous areas of variability—phase lengths, attrition, resource requirements, and the arrival of new products, for example. Only when armed with this information could the company make informed decisions about the allocation of resources across its drug development program, and only sophisticated simulation could provide that information.

In the pharmaceuticals industry in particular, reducing product-development times is crucial. Because the life of a patent is limited, the faster a

company can bring a drug to market the longer it has to generate the revenue needed to pay off the cost of developing that drug. At the end of a
drug's patent life, there is very little additional revenue to be squeezed out.
With pharmaceuticals, almost more than with any other product, the benefit of accelerating a launch time by even a week can mean a multi-million-
dollar increase in net income.

The company in question was under great pressure to speed up its product-development processes. Competition in the industry was such that
companies were being forced to find ways to develop and launch two to
three times the number of new drugs that they had been handling. That
required quantum leaps, not marginal improvements, and to stand any
chance of matching (never mind beating) such leaps, companies had either
to increase the number of compounds in their drug-development phase or
they had to improve the success rate of the compounds that were moving
through the phase. Probably, they would have to do a bit of both. They set a
goal of doubling the output from their drug-development process over a
five-year period.

To find out how it could best reach this ambitious target, the company
built a simulation model with which a number of different options were
tested. The integration of new processes and of new technology that the
firm was introducing at the time required sophisticated analysis of this sort
because of the highly complex interactions and interdependencies between
the various elements.

One of the most useful outcomes of the simulation was that it helped
the company identify those points in time when additional resources would
be required if it were to meet the goal of doubling the output from its drug-
development process. But the simulation also showed that in order to meet
that goal the company would have to make a prohibitively high investment
in extra people and equipment. As a result, their only viable option was to
revise their goal downward to change where it intended its product-development process to be.

INNOVATION AND SCENARIO PLANNING

Simulation is about saving money—on the one hand, by avoiding expensive
mistakes and bringing new ideas to market faster, and on the other by coming up with Capabilities and innovations that are clearly superior to their predecessors. Throughout the book I have talked about different ways of
generating new, innovative ideas. In Chapter 2, I discussed the Seven Rs and
how they can help you define new processes. In Chapter 7, I discussed the
Innovation Targeting Matrix and how various moves through the matrix can

help bring to the surface different business models. Likewise, through simulation, different possible models will emerge from what-if analyses. A consideration of ways that the future might unfold and the effect it might have on the business is obviously fertile ground for innovation.

Much has been written on scenario planning, so I will only touch on it here. The reason I bring it up is because the combination of scenario planning and simulation is a powerful one-two punch. Scenario planning gives businesses a framework to think about the future and the uncertainties therein. It is often assumed that scenario planning is a simple exercise based on extrapolations from the past or on some sort of targeting of everybody else's averages. Obviously this would be insufficient in today's environment. In this world of quantum leaps, companies need to know where they want their businesses and its constituent processes to be in the future.

Scenario planning has its place in today's forecasting because in fact it does not start with the past. It begins with managers sitting round a table drawing out a small number of scenarios, telling each other stories about how the future might unfold and how it might affect the business issues that stand before them. A good session like this might have spared IBM one of its worst embarrassments of the 1980s when the company extrapolated data from the past to forecast PC sales, estimating that the world market for personal computers would rise to 265,000 machines by 1990. As it turned out, there were, in fact, 60 million PCs in use around the world by 1990.

Scenario planning is not an opportunity to indulge in wild fantasy. It is a formal exercise that usually begins with a general group discussion about how changes in society and technology might affect the issue under consideration. This leads the group to draw up a list of those things that will have the most effect on it, and the list then provides the basis for sketching out a rough picture of the future.

BC Hydro

One industry that is finding scenario planning particularly useful is the deregulated utilities industry. No one knows what's going to happen next. One company that I highlight in Appendix A is BC Hydro, a Canadian hydroelectric utility. The Utilities Commission of British Columbia is considering the creation of a competitive electricity market. BC Hydro's Grid Operations group has taken proactive measures to develop the business capabilities for a independent grid operator (IGO), an entity that would be responsible for managing the transmission grid and would be completely independent from the transmission, distribution, and power-generation companies. The IGO would need significantly new business Capabilities and would be faced with new operational and business roles, including management of network congestion, contract management, and customer relationships; reconciliation of physical energy consumption through financial settlements; and facilitation of the trading of energy.

To address these uncertainties, BC Hydro developed scenarios using a "building blocks" approach, identifying and analyzing several discrete components that would help define the shape of the changing market and suggest how BC Hydro would need to operate in this market. For each block, they defined possible outcomes for future business requirements. The building blocks were designed to be plug-and-play, meaning that some of them might not even be relevant for a particular scenario. Since the building blocks defined the characteristics of a desired end state, the scenarios became a starting point for evaluating pros and cons. Overall, three scenarios were defined and evaluated for pros and cons, helping BC Hydro prepare for a future that could go in various directions.

SIMULATION AND INNOVATION
I like to think of innovation as a precious metal. First, the ground or environment must be just right or it won't exist. Second, it's generally hard to find (even though it's possible to stumble upon it by chance). Third, diligent work is required or it will never see the light of day. Once it's found and extracted from the ground, the metal is indeed precious and its value is significantly more than the ground around it.

Innovation is like a precious metal in these three aspects. Most of us don't like to leave anything in our lives to chance. In fact, we usually do all we can to beat the odds. Looking for something that is hard to find can be a challenge, but, as with precious metals, great efforts often yield great results. The challenge is to be methodical, thus increasing the chances of finding something of value. Simulation is one avenue through which increased opportunity for successful innovation can be found.

Simulation's greatest contribution to innovation efforts is that, as noted in the examples, it helps build an environment conducive to innovation. It does this by focusing a team on those things that bring value to the subject at hand. This forces a team to define value and then build the inherent relations into a model that quantify the value proposition of the proposed solution. Through this process, team members often set aside their politics. This benefit alone is worth the added effort to foster and cultivate innovation.

It is in the area of doing the work required to realize the fruits of innovation that simulations can be both a tremendous asset and a liability. After identifying these relationships, building them into a valid model requires not only technical expertise and a solid grasp of statistics and probability but also a significant understanding of the proposal and its associated systems. In addition, considerable facilitation skills are needed to ensure collaboration, innovation, and confidence in the final solution. Bringing all of these skills to bear on a project thereby requires considerable experience in all of these areas, experience that is rarely found in one individual. However, investment in this set of skills improves the innovation environment, thereby increasing the level of innovation and the project's chances of success.

Simulation is, in effect, a way to stimulate ideas about how an organization might bridge the gap between how things are and how they might be, between the company's assessment of how it works at present and its vision of how it could work in the future. Simulation does not always come up with a surefire way of fulfilling that vision. It does, however, tend to show whether the vision is attainable or not. It's a bit like trying to reproduce a jazz tune electronically. It shows what's possible, but is no substitute for the real thing.

9

GETTING THERE

"The first step to failure is trying."

HOMER SIMPSON

*F*ew changes are as energizing in an organization as the move to an innovative mind-set. Making this happen requires organizations to revolutionize their structure and culture, and so leaders must take care to channel the energy in a positive direction. Employees and managers naturally cling to the familiar and fear the unknown. Resistance can emerge from those unaccustomed to life outside tidy, known functions. Over the years I have noticed several stages of this transition. In this chapter I show the way forward as it has worked for many companies I have been involved with. Strong leadership supported by technology, skills development, and performance measures can make the journey as successful as it is exciting.

As the Hall of Fame New York Yankee catcher Yogi Berra once said, "If things don't change, they'll probably stay the same." But staying the same is not an option in business, for change is the oxygen needed to grow and develop the company. Change defines new structures that support the ever-innovative organization. The key ingredient for developing a successful business today is innovation. And although innovation can be of the "falling apple" variety, in the context of everyday business, it is more often an incremental phenomenon, a series of gradual steps that employees are systematically encouraged to take.

Constant innovation is different from traditional stop-and-go change, where fatigue often sets in while the organization keeps trying to reach goalposts that are moving ever farther away. It is better to innovate continuously and instinctively rather than go through a series of wrenching periods of intense upheaval, inevitably followed by periods of lassitude and recovery. Organizations that do this will find themselves behind the eight ball once again as other companies, which are innovating continuously, have surged ahead.

I have likened continuous innovation to the improvisation of the jazz musician. Without improvisation, there is no jazz. Likewise, the capacity to innovate is an essential ingredient in an organization that wants to remain competitive in today's rapidly changing, e-enabled economy. Without change, no company will remain competitive. The big challenge is to make innovation pervade the organization to such an extent that it becomes, in effect, a core competence.

Unfortunately, unless a company possesses the powers of a superhero, it is nearly impossible to leap from disarray to innovation excellence in a single bound. Inevitably, the move toward innovation happens over time and through several stages. And typically, no two parts of the business can be expected to move at exactly the same pace. In some cases, a company may advance smoothly, without unexpected delay. Others may meet with strong resistance from one group of employees, and it will take a little longer to convince those employees of the benefits of focusing on improvements in their part of the business.

Different disciplines will develop at different speeds (Figure 9-1). This is why many companies start innovating in HR, finance, and supply chain processes. These tend to be more "tangible" processes, where the advantages of predictability are obvious. However, more "valuable" processes, such as sales and marketing or product development, are typically saved for later. This conclusion is supported by a recent survey I conducted of a num-

FIGURE 9-1.   Moving change at different speeds.

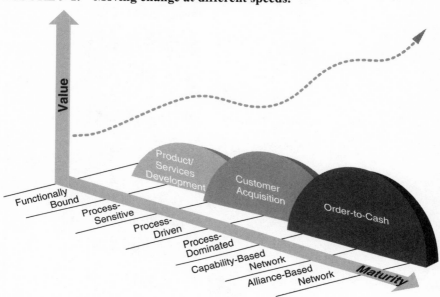

ber of leading European companies. I found that 70 percent reported excellent progress with their supply chain and support processes; only 40 percent said they had made reasonable progress with their product-development processes, and another 40 percent said they had made *no* progress on their product-development processes. Clearly these poor results are not caused by failure to target the right goals. They are caused by choosing the path of least resistance.

Since innovation will take root in different parts of the business at different times, organization and leadership structures must also be staged (Figure 9-2). At first, a company might appoint an isolated manager of a business operation or two as an experiment, as a first dipping of the corporate toe into the unfamiliar waters. During this experimental stage, the old-style functional owners remain the primary leaders, at least in the short term.

But then, as the benefits of the experiment become more apparent, the "owner" of the specific business process or Capability gains more formal responsibility and power, and the organization itself gradually becomes a hybrid—in which the two "perspectives" coexist. Finally, the owner becomes the more dominant party and the functional powers gradually diminish. Processes evolve into Capabilities, and these Capabilities are then interlinked for optimal performance. The owner of each Capability

FIGURE 9-2. Stages of organizational maturity.

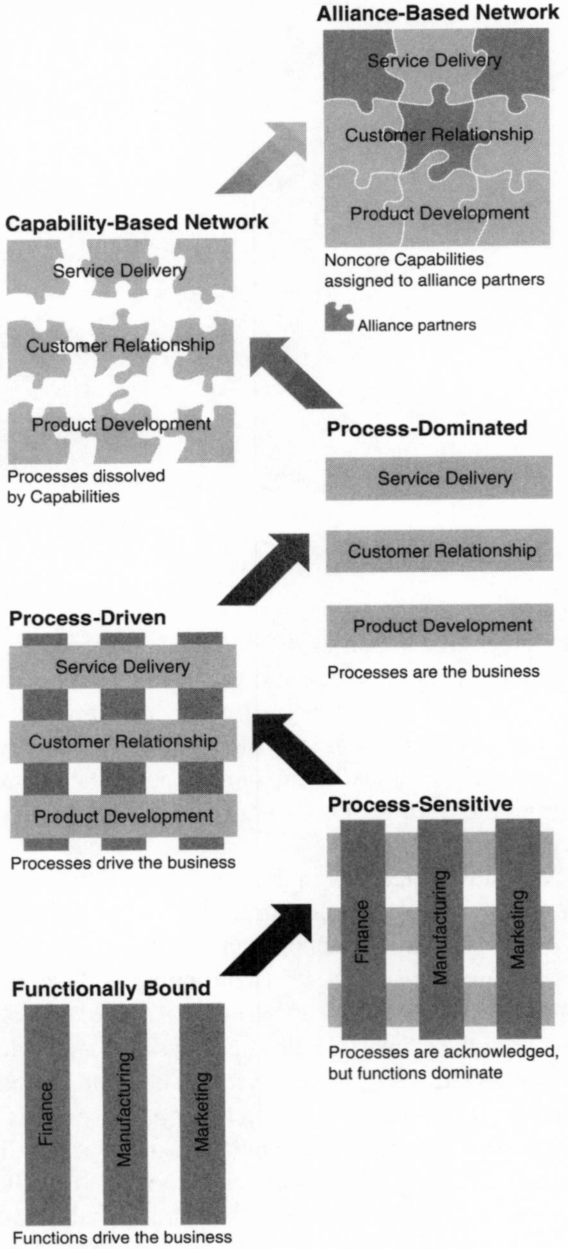

Alliance-Based Network

Service Delivery

Customer Relationship

Product Development

Noncore Capabilities
assigned to alliance partners

Alliance partners

Capability-Based Network

Service Delivery

Customer Relationship

Product Development

Processes dissolved
by Capabilities

Process-Dominated

Service Delivery

Customer Relationship

Product Development

Processes are the business

Process-Driven

Service Delivery

Customer Relationship

Product Development

Processes drive the business

Process-Sensitive

Finance

Manufacturing

Marketing

Processes are acknowledged,
but functions dominate

Functionally Bound

Finance

Manufacturing

Marketing

Functions drive the business

becomes the "voice of the customer," and the customer's interests are continually anticipated and satisfied through a culture of nonstop innovation. A team-based multidisciplinary environment has now taken over.

As I described briefly in Chapter 1, companies will pass through six distinct stages as they travel on the road to innovation maturity. The stages are not necessarily sequential. Often a company can begin a focus on Capabilities while it is still in the process-driven stage. And, as noted above, different parts of the business can be at different stages of maturity. The six stages are:

1. *Functionally Bound.* At this stage functions drive the business, and this is where most companies found themselves prior to the introduction of reengineering into the business vocabulary in the 1990s. There is very little that glues together the silos in such companies and there is usually minimal focus on customers and other stakeholders. Efforts are internally focused on each isolated piece of the business. In fact, most employees will have little awareness of what a business process is.

2. *Process-Sensitive.* Processes, which are laid over the existing organization, are acknowledged, but functions still dominate. Companies have begun to identify and design key end-to-end processes. This is a good first step, but rarely are massive benefits achieved. And, unless there is a strong commitment to moving forward, any gains tend to be unsustainable.

3. *Process-Driven.* Processes are emerging as a key driver of the business. Functions continue to exist, but in a subordinate role.

4. *Process-Dominated.* Processes are the primary driver of the business. Functions are reconstituted as centers of excellence, where the emphasis is on skills building around functional disciplines.

5. *Capability-Based.* Capabilities emerge as the primary driver of the business. Technology, organization, culture, and process are all addressed together.

6. *Alliance-Based.* At this stage, companies focus on Capabilities and address sourcing strategies and alliances. An alliance-based company is a global company with a mix of owned and allied Capabilities that know no national boundaries. Capabilities are arrayed in such a way that results can be measured, managed, and integrated.

The need for, and the ability of, companies to be innovative increases geometrically as they progress through these six stages. During the functionally bound stage, innovation is little more than a matter of trying what has been tried in the past—automating existing practices, for instance, or fixing what has been broken. At the process-sensitive stage, employees begin (probably for the first time) to look across functions for opportunities to innovate, and by the time a company is process-driven, innovation is applied to individual processes, while in a "process-dominated" business, innovation takes place across all processes. A Capability-based organization is able to look at innovative uses of technology, at e-commerce, and at changes to culture and human performance. Finally, an alliance-based organization has refocused on its core and is able to apply innovation pervasively throughout the organization. Of course, this is a rough guide, and companies can apply innovative concepts at any stage. However, the real value of innovation becomes increasingly apparent as a company moves through the stages, because the organization is focusing on lines and dependencies, not boxes. This is how you optimize the value of your efforts.

Mapping out the six stages is a useful tool for helping companies determine where they are today in terms of the development of the various aspects of their business. This can be very different for different processes. It is possible for you to be, say, functionally bound for production while already process-sensitive for marketing. This mapping also can help you decide where you want to be in the future. Areas of the business that are targeted for innovation will often require more "advanced" forms of organizational support. All of this results in a migration strategy that helps a business decide the steps to take toward the desired future state— bearing in mind, of course, that the business must continue to operate profitably during the transition.

FROM FUNCTIONS TO ALLIANCES

The stages I put forth below for the migration from a traditional organization to an innovative, alliance-based organization is a composite of research done over the years. I first mapped this out a couple of years ago as part of a research study I was leading at the time. And, more recently, Martha Batorski and Bill Hughes, two Accenture colleagues of mine, used this work as the basis for a recent survey, in which they studied 15 companies to see how they made the shift to process orientation.[1] This chapter combines my own observations with the findings of Martha and Bill's research.

The Functionally Bound Organization

This is the traditional organization. Most people in the company are unaware of end-to-end processes or Capabilities. The prevailing culture is often one of "getting things done" rather than one of creating value for the customer. The things that are done take place in corporate departments that are based on traditional management functions. Sales, for example, is a fiefdom with its own leader, and so too are manufacturing, customer service, and other areas. Hierarchies abound and seniority really matters.

The fiefdoms typically operate in isolation, often with little cooperation among them. In practice it is depressing to see how often they view each other as enemies and utterly fail to appreciate that they're all playing for the same team. Activities are characterized by the number of hand-offs there are between different functions, and there are numerous high-cost non-value-adding activities. Processes are undocumented and not explicitly assigned. Trying to serve the customer when each of the fiefdoms has a different game plan can be a losing battle.

Fortunately, few companies today are still at this stage as a whole. Almost all companies have pockets of process, where cross-functional work is taking place. However, some areas of the business in most organizations still operate in a siloed fashion.

The Process-Sensitive Organization

Most organizations move to this second stage when they have heard the wake-up call telling them that they are no longer competitive in their existing markets. Some organizations, of course, merely turn off the alarm and try to go back to sleep. But they tend to wake up a bit later in bankruptcy or in the arms of a predator.

By this stage, the typical organization has gotten a taste of the world of innovation through its new commitment to process orientation. Functions are still paramount, but processes are now defined and a champion has emerged who is going to lead the transition further. The organization has identified several end-to-end processes that need to be redesigned, but these processes have only a limited impact on the organization. I sometimes call this the "process veneer" stage, because although the company has laid a thin layer over the organization to make it look pretty, underneath the surface it is pretty much the same as it has always been. And although this may sound like I am suggesting that the changes at this level are purely cosmetic, that is certainly not the case. This stage allows an organization to begin the major changes necessary, behind the facade, to become more innovative.

Typically there are lots of change initiatives that are supported by cross-functional teams during this stage. Some companies call these "process improvement teams." But regardless of what they are called, within these teams, sales reps (for example) may find that they are talking to people in the marketing or logistics department for the first time ever. And that can have positive results, or it can have negative results. The individuals in the teams at this stage still view themselves as belonging to different teams with different goals—goals that are defined by their functionally oriented bosses. This is the first time when the lines and dependencies within the organization begin to emerge.

At this stage there is usually some outright resistance to the changes by a majority of the organization. In the worst cases, this can lead to a deep and long-lasting freeze on the progress of the whole initiative.

The Process-Driven Organization

An organization is process-driven when it is undergoing a full-scale implementation of process designs on a number of fronts. This is the time when processes really begin to take hold, but it is also a stage at which companies often get stuck, failing to move on to a process-dominated structure. At this point, companies are "betwixt and between." They are managed by both functions and by processes, a situation that is at best awkward and at worst dangerous.

Resources are typically owned by the functions and deployed to the processes. Now the role of the functions begins to shift away from that of accountability and move toward one of building deeper skills. A far wider range of employees begins to receive training in process skills, and employees begin to learn the specific details of what their roles will be when all the redesigned processes have been fully rolled out. Process owners are created who start to experiment with new performance measurement systems.

In effect, process owners find themselves in the position of having clear accountability for achieving outcomes, but through the use of borrowed resources, resources that are still to be found only in the functional fiefdoms. This requires excellent negotiating and diplomatic skills.

The culture of the organization changes markedly at this stage. For a start, there is a greater general awareness of process thinking, and there is a stronghold of supporters focused on scoring a few quick victories and on marketing their successes internally. But tension is commonplace as the often-conflicting needs of process owners and process coaches become increasingly apparent. On the positive side, out of this tension often come innovative solutions.

Being process-oriented is a key driver in creating a flexible, innovative organization. For example, Duke Energy improved its on-time fulfillment of customer requests for new services from 45 to 95 percent. Robin Manning of Duke Power remarked, "The power of process-centering is in flexibility—even more impressive, in my estimation, than 'before-and-after' performance success stories. We have introduced speed into an industry that is known for taking forever to change."

The Process-Dominated Organization

An organization is process-dominated when its own high-performing processes enable it to compete on a sustainable basis. At this stage, processes are continually being refined and improved, often with a high degree of innovation. Management has crystallized the company's strengths, and strategic processes have been targeted and are already being refined.

By this stage, the process owner has become king or queen. Work is now performed by multidisciplinary teams that are accountable to a process owner. The old-style functions have been disbanded and reconstituted as centers of excellence. These centers enable process performers to build up their skills by providing a community of experts who share experiences and the lessons they have learned. For example, logistics experts, regardless of the process they are supporting, get together regularly to share insights and ideas about their subject. Self-development of skills becomes the norm.

Innovative thinking begins to pervade the organization. The new way of working has become embedded in the company's culture, although there is still some resistance among people unaccustomed to working outside a functional structure. Quite often, the business has moved from being one that needs to be led toward change to being one where change takes place organically. Everyone is focused on serving the customer. Employees are treated as the critical resource for the company's success, and resources are invested wisely in the areas of the business that will have the greatest impact. The business is operated holistically, with all the processes working together toward a common goal. One challenge is making sure that the interdependencies between processes are well understood. Otherwise the company can go from functional silos to process tunnels—different versions of the same problem.

But as many have found, the processes are the easy part. Paul Goodrum, business process advisor for Shell Oil Products, commented on his organization's progress through the stages: "Although it didn't feel like it at the time, creating the process-centered organization structure was, perhaps, the easy bit. Aligning behaviors, skills, IT tools, management systems, and so forth along process lines is where the pain and gain really begin to kick in."

The Capability-Based Organization

We are now at the stage where companies compete on the basis of Capabilities. Processes are intertwined with technology, organization structure, culture, and competencies. Whereas the replication of an organization's redesigned process may be simple, the configuration of the components that make up the targeted capability is much harder to orchestrate. Consequently, well-designed Capabilities represent the new building blocks of competitive advantage.

A good example of a company that made the move in this direction is Eastern Electricity, a utility based in the United Kingdom that is now wholly owned by TXU Europe. In three years, they were able to cut overhead costs in half, a result that even exceeded their stretch targets. The key was that they did not stop at high-performing processes. Eastern changed and aligned all of the components of a business Capability. The Capability they developed is the "highly dynamic management of energy production to consistently high performance levels in an environment of fluctuating demand." They have become so effective at it that they now perform this Capability for other companies, including competitors.

A Capability focus recognizes the need to integrate all the various aspects of the business to achieve high performance. And this enables innovation to flourish. As the subtitle of this book says, this level of innovation is just what you need for "thriving in a world of change."

The Alliance-Based Organization

An alliance-based organization still competes on the basis of Capabilities. But they have also rigorously applied the targeting concepts I described in Chapter 7, so that there is now a mix of owned and allied or outsourced Capabilities. These Capabilities are arrayed in such a way that results can be measured, managed, and integrated. Related and dependent activities are kept in alignment. All of this is overlaid with a single leadership and culture, and linked via a common IT platform.

This is achievable because Capabilities are networked together in a form of plug-and-play architecture. The interdependencies of the Capabilities within the organization are defined in such a way that there is complete freedom within a given Capability to perform it any way, or to outsource it to someone else who can perform it better. An alliance-based organization is one where the company begins to divest itself of Capabilities that do not create value, that is, those Capabilities that are not differentiating or core.

Through these alliances, companies are able to address market opportunities that they would not have been able to address effectively alone. Consider New Energy, a Los Angeles–based company. As described in the Process Centering white paper, following the company's first year of operations in the deregulated California market, New Energy redesigned its processes to prepare for growth and to become operationally excellent. The company targeted radical changes in its operating strategy, culture, skills, performance measures, organization structure, systems, and facilities to build the business Capability of providing reliable, low-cost energy with timely and accurate bills. New Energy's strategy—to maintain a first-mover advantage providing integrated, high-value energy solutions—prompted it to seek out alliance partners with complementary Capabilities.

One such partner was Johnson Controls, which has the Capability to monitor and switch energy equipment remotely. This Capability, combined with New Energy's Capability, provides customers with a high-value energy solution called *peak shaving*. During peak hours, New Energy's customers are automatically switched off the electricity grid onto customer-owned site generators—which New Energy also sells—resulting in total energy savings. New Energy not only attained consistently improved levels of performance, but also created new markets for its energy solutions.

By targeting Capabilities that are the core of the business and partnering with other companies that provide complementary Capabilities, companies are providing truly innovative solutions.

ALL THE WORLD'S AT A STAGE

Although I am a strong advocate of Capabilities and alliances, not all companies necessarily want to or should go through all of the stages throughout the business. Functions do have roles in organizations. Every company needs to experiment to determine which stage gives it the best results for its business. A processed-foods company, for instance, may decide that because of its need for exceptional brand-management skills, it does not want to go any further than the process-driven stage. On the other hand, an electronics company with rapidly changing product lines may want to go all the way in order to keep it better focused on the customer and to remain agile.

Let's examine one company's experience of going through the stages in more detail. This is a joint Accenture and Economist Intelligence Unit study that I contributed to a few years ago.[2]

Lever Brothers is the soap and detergents arm of the Anglo-Dutch giant Unilever. It is a good example of an organization in which a major process redesign was sparked off by a wake-up call, by a dramatic development in the company's markets that created an urgent sense of the need for change. It is also a good example of how process change is usually driven by an individual or individuals in the corporation who have no particular commitment to the established way of doing things.

In the early 1990s, Lever Brothers was pursuing process change incrementally. One initiative in 1991 redesigned the company's supply chain process. Stuart Blinder, vice president in charge of supply chain, finance, and IT, had joined Lever only a year before from the U.K. company Thorn EMI. With years of experience of process change in companies such as General Electric, Cadbury Schweppes, and PepsiCo, Blinder had learned to question the established way of doing things.

The process change led by Blinder was known as total system effectiveness (TSE). It acknowledged (at a senior level and almost for the first time) that the company's traditional silo structure, based on the classic corporate functions, was a serious obstacle to progress in the last decade of the twentieth century. It was particularly damaging to the corporation's ability to take rapid decisions. Every idea had to go up and down each silo before being presented to the chief executive. This took too much time, and made it far too easy for groups that were resistant to change to derail proposals along the way. It had already become clear that speedy decision making was going to be a sine qua non for the successful organization of the twenty-first century. Blinder could see that there were great rigidity and waste in the existing Lever Brothers structure, and he believed that the only way to cut through it was to set up cross-functional teams that could pass through the barriers between the various silos.

Total system effectiveness was Lever Brothers' first real experience with high-powered cross-functional teams, but the benefits became apparent sufficiently quickly for the board to be in a position the following year (1992) to consider more general cross-functional training. The idea was to send a group of 100 managers from different parts of the company through a training program based on the lessons learned from the TSE experience, an experience that Blinder was able to show had chopped some $30 million off the cost of the company's supply chain process.

The board asked the company's "university"—its internal training center—to organize a curriculum for managers based around the core competencies that the TSE experience had shown were essential if people were to learn to think in this new way. In 1993, the initiative went into overdrive when a number of Lever Brothers' new (and supposedly breakthrough) products failed to find the market acceptance that had been hoped for. At the same time, the company's great rival of many years—Procter & Gamble—decided to slash its prices on a number of competing products by 14 percent. Lever Brothers' profits and market share suffered accordingly. It was a drastic situation that called for drastic action.

Product failures and price wars were not exactly unknown in Lever Brothers' history (over a century), but this time they seemed more serious. Almost overnight, pricing became the key competitive factor in a business that had long been known for its customers' brand loyalty. This was, after all, the industry that created the soap opera. But the soap opera itself was declining in popularity, which was a direct reflection of changing consumer behavior. Between 1991 and 2000, the audience for America's main daytime soaps fell by over 80 percent. Even long-running favorites like *Guiding Light* and *As the World Turns*—both of them sponsored by Procter & Gamble for over half a century—lost their audiences. The main reasons for the decline were thought to be an increase in the number of working women as well as more gripping daytime viewing for those who stayed at home, such as the spate of courtroom dramas that brought real-time court action into people's living rooms.

In fact, as discussed in Chapter 4, the decline in Lever Brothers' sales was a symptom of a deep-seated shift in the nature of consumer loyalty. In the 1990s, in many consumer goods markets, consumers felt newly empowered, and that encouraged them to shop around as never before. Sometimes the *only* consumer loyalty seemed to be to price. Long-established branded goods could find their name worth next to nothing when competing with a cut-price supermarket's house brand.

Lever Brothers was in no position to ignore the P&G price cuts. But when the company responded in kind with cuts of its own, it found that P&G's financial clout and dominant market position (in the United States) gave it a competitive edge that the Unilever unit just could not match. This edge, it realized, was being sharpened by the fact that P&G had quietly installed new supply chain and production techniques that were enabling the Cincinnati giant to sustain its profit margins even in the face of its dramatic price cuts.

Lever realized now that it was standing on a burning platform, and most people with hot feet tend to move. But the company was hindered by its own highly bureaucratic environment, an environment that was fiercely resistant to change. A new chief executive, Charles Strauss, was appointed in 1993, and he soon set about putting his stamp on the firm.

Strauss believed right from the beginning that Lever had to change dramatically or permanently lose the ground that had been slowly eroding. He used the adverse developments in the firm's markets as a catalyst to persuade the board of the need for all-around change, change that would alter for all time the organization's strategy, structure, processes, people, and culture. He proceeded to draw up a master plan that involved scrutinizing every aspect of the organization, looking for old rules that needed breaking, and examining external models of competition and operational excellence.

Included in the plan was a new vision for the company that focused on customers, on speed and flexibility, and on the power of its own employees. The new vision statement was: "To know our customers better than our competitors, to partner with our customers and suppliers more effectively than any other company, to better satisfy the consumer and meet customer needs through empowering Lever people to speed decisions in a team-based environment. We shall bring to market a sustained series of products and services such that we become known as the most successful, rapid innovator of packaged goods in the United States." At this point the company had moved into the process-driven stage of process maturity.

A new look appeared. In place of the established series of functional departments, the company set up two large market-based business groups—Personal Wash & Homecare and Fabrics. These two units were linked by five core processes that stretched right across the organization—customer management and service, supply chain, financial and IT, human resources, and legal services.

The reorganization was completed by the middle of 1994 and costs were reduced almost immediately through the closure of a plant and a reduction of almost 30 percent in the company's head count. The transition from old to new was led by three main groups:

1. The executive board charged with revising the overall vision and strategy, leading the changes, and monitoring progress.
2. A transition team of some 80 managers who were charged with redesigning the operational aspects of the business. This group was

broken up into specific project teams, each with its own sponsor on the board.

3. A special fast-cycle team responsible for the unique and separate task of managing the transition process itself, providing a vital link between the generals and the troops. This group prepared a route map of the journey of change that was to be undertaken, and then set out to explain to anxious managers that there was in fact a clear and decisive plan beneath the surface turbulence.

By the middle of 1996, the shift at Lever Brothers was almost complete, and the benefits were beginning to show through. The company was now at the process-dominated stage of transition, but was beginning to focus on Capabilities. It was already getting noticeably more feedback from its customers, and this information was being systematically pumped into a new innovation management system at the company's parent, Unilever. The goal had become to develop products that the market actually said it wanted, rather than products that Lever Brothers thought that it wanted (or, rather, thought that it should want).

The management of the flow of the company's products had been completely redesigned, and the various Capabilities affected by the redesign included inventory planning, production scheduling, and materials planning. The aim was to improve customer service, to establish optimal inventory levels at different times, and to lower supply chain costs.

A key part of the focus on Capabilities was the establishment of a means to measure the changes, to monitor progress, and to check that all the processes that had been redesigned (and not just a prominent few) were moving in the right direction. For this, Lever Brothers came up with a number of key performance indicators that were designed to identify specific areas that were not coming up to the mark.

In addition, because the company knew that one should not try to pour old wine into new bottles, it arranged an extensive program of training and coaching structured to make its employees' skills better suited to the new system. A special curriculum was designed at the Lever University to facilitate the acquisition of those cross-functional skills and competencies that are essential to success in a team-based environment. All of these are critical aspects of Capability thinking.

The ultimate proof of the effectiveness of the whole exercise lay in the company's financial results. In 1996, Lever Brothers had its best year ever and they have continued to be successful since.

SOME USEFUL TIPS

For years, I have been advocating that the success for any change effort like this is the "NOW Just Do IT" model. The "N" in NOW stands for need; a burning platform for change is communicated and well understood. The "O" is for opportunity; you have to be in a business that has a chance of succeeding. And the "W" is for the will of senior management; committed leadership with the intestinal fortitude to see the change through. And you need all three to be successful. Without the will of senior management, you are left with "NO": no, don't do it. Without opportunity, you are left with "NW": no way to succeed. And without the need being understood, you are left with "OW": a painful experience for all within the organization. "Just" stands for "justification"—a business case for change. "Do" means you need doers, not talkers. And, finally, "IT" stands for information technology. No change today stands a chance of making a difference without taking into consideration the important role of technology.

Many people like to talk about change management as if it were something separate from the rest of a change effort. Too often I see projects with a change management team that is separated from the rest of the effort. But this rarely leads to success. In my experience, I have found that the process of changing the process *is* change management. As you redesign the business, you must involve people, get them to buy in, and educate them as you go along. Communication alone is not change management.

The following 10 useful tips for the organization that is contemplating making the move away from a traditional functional organization to a more innovative model are gleaned from my own experience and the findings of the study on Process Centering cited on page 222.

1. The Need for a Burning Platform.   The existence of a burning platform—a real business need—and communicating of its existence to all employees helps to create the sense of urgency that is vital for mobilizing and energizing an organization over the longer term. Several companies in the study mentioned the fact that without a "burning platform" there was nothing to differentiate the transition to processes (or innovation) from other initiatives that were considerably less central to the success of the enterprise. Furthermore, in cases where a sound business reason for the transition existed, but where it was not well understood throughout the organization, or where it was perceived merely as an exercise in the latest management theory, the transition also delivered disappointing results.

So it is important to establish clear business reasons for setting out on the journey from the very beginning, and for those reasons then to be widely communicated from the very top of the organization. Only that way can the importance of the transition be well established in everybody's mind.

2. The Need to Educate All Employees about Processes and Capabilities.   Every organization in the study indicated that if they had to redo the exercise they would do two things differently: they would increase their general process education and they would improve their communication of the "to be" scenario, the vision of where the whole exercise was supposed to be taking them.

Companywide education on processes and innovation is essential before any change program is rolled out, if a company's Capabilities are to be kept running smoothly throughout the turmoil that such a program inevitably brings about. If employees are not sold on the idea, their natural conservatism will come into play. Most people innately prefer the status quo unless and until they are given some sound reason why an alternative is preferable.

3. Use the New Orientation to Bring Managers Closer to Customers.
Several participants in the study commented on the ease with which front-line personnel picked up the idea of process thinking. They also remarked on how sharply this contrasted with the general resistance of the company's managers to the change. This prompted the suggestion that the closer a company is to its customers, the easier it will be for it to make the journey.

Several of the organizations that found the change particularly challenging had leaders who had allowed a barrier to come up between their daily operational responsibilities and their customers. After they had had some firsthand exposure to customers and to customers' difficulties, these managers had an easier time taking on board the whole idea of end-to-end process orientation.

One of the lessons of this is that companies can speed up a sluggish start to their transition by nominating a few potential process champions at the top of the organization and at successive levels further down. These designated champions can then be sent out to experience firsthand some of the problems that face the organization's customers.

4. Leadership from the Top Ensures a Successful Outcome.   Organizations that have made a successful transition have invariably done so with the help of talented, committed, and compassionate leadership. Troubled transitions are almost always correlated with a lack of effective, visionary leaders. It is essential that an organization's leadership team understand and encourage the new way of thinking from the very beginning. Senior leaders should be clear about what can be expected from successful changeover, and also the commercial consequences of not making the transition.

Robin Manning of Duke Power, one of the 15 companies in the Accenture survey, confirms this. "Our senior leaders drove us mercilessly for three years," he says, "and going back was not an option. They created a real sense of urgency, and spent 75 percent of their time out on the road getting the messages understood. This had a significant impact on the success of our transition."

5. Buy Expertise That You Do Not Already Have In-House.   In many cases the idea—and the proposed route—of the journey is so strange that organizations do not have the in-house skills that are needed to make the transition. In such cases, they need to go out and find help in those areas where they have insufficient expertise—for example, with the techniques of change management, with developing training programs, with business architecture, or even with process design. Even the most successful organizations in the study contracted the help they needed or swapped notes with other organizations who had already undergone the transition. They were often driven by an awareness of how important it is to get the transition as nearly right as possible the first time around.

When looking for expertise, firms should leave no stone unturned. With Shell Oil Products, for example, alliance partners proved to be particularly helpful. Paul Goodrum, a manager with Shell Oil in Europe, says: "Shell has created a strategic benefit in the area of procurement through its alliances with partners that explicitly understand our processes. We manage the procurement process jointly and that provides us with more reliability and security."

6. Communicate Clearly, Continuously, and Repeatedly.   It is scarcely possible to exaggerate the need for information about the transition to be communicated clearly and regularly throughout the organization. If in doubt, remember the Rule of 50s. The first 50 times you tell people something, they don't hear you. The second 50 times you tell them the same thing, they don't believe you. Only during the third 50 times that you tell them do they begin to listen.

7. Try to Build in Safeguards That Prevent the Organization from Taking Backward Steps.   Senior managers who are not close to their customers can stall a transition that is already well under way and may even cause it to revert to a siloed orientation. This can sometimes occur because of an unexpected change of leadership. Incoming managers' allegiance to a traditional structure of fragmented departments can result in the company regressing to an earlier stage of process maturity. Two of the fifteen companies in the study barely survived the unexpected introduction of new leaders brought in after the resident champions who had worked through the early stages of the transition had retired, been promoted, or changed positions.

To minimize the risk from such a changeover, companies should develop several strong leaders on the team so that there is someone to carry on the role of champion if (and when) one of their number moves on. This removes the risk of the whole exercise being at the mercy of one person's career development.

8. Manage the Transition as a Series of Pilot Schemes.   When asked where their organization fell in the six-stage model, participants in the process centering study gave a number of different answers, depending on the particular process in question. Different processes within the same organization can be seen to be at different levels of maturity, correlated with the length of time that the redesign initiative has been under way. Hence the "develop products process" might be at the process-sensitive stage; the "acquire customer process" at the process-driven stage; and the "order-to-cash process" moving from the process-dominated stage to a Capability focus.

Most companies recommend taking a phased approach, one in which process initiatives are begun in sequence, with no more than one or two beginning at any one time. Taking on too much change all at once can be a shock to the organization and lead to a sort of traumatic inertia.

When different processes begin the transition at different times, however, it means that the company has to manage several levels of process maturity simultaneously. This requires excellent process management skills and measurement systems that allow for the different stages of development.

9. One Size Does Not Fit All.   Organizations should not try to follow any one case study too literally. No two companies will pass through the transition for the same reasons or by following the same sequence of events. Not only does one size not fit all; one size doesn't even fit two.

10. Target Process Owners Early On.   Companies that lost momentum during their transition did so because either:

- They had failed to identify a process/Capability owner who could refine and tend the process and ensure compliance with it.
- They did not counterbalance the process/Capability owner's role with that of the process coach, whose job it is to maintain accountability for resources and to build up the necessary skills through further training.

Identifying process owners early on helps to ensure that the whole transition takes place as smoothly as possible.

THE IMPORTANCE OF BUSINESS CAPABILITIES

Now we can see the full significance of innovation for corporations in the future. And we have a blueprint and a map for getting there. From my perspective, only organizations that embrace innovation as a core Capability will be able to compete in today's changing environment.

Business Capabilities are set to be the focus of competition in the future. As I explained in Chapter 1, a business Capability is defined as a collection of closely interrelated components that together deliver high performance on a repeatable basis. It takes a long time to build this up and, when well designed, it represents a formidable core competence that is not easily duplicated. A Capability like this demands a configuration of processes, systems, and skills that work together competitively (i.e., excellently), uniquely, and consistently.

An example of a company that went through a complete and successful transformation is YPF, an Argentine oil company. The eighth-largest oil and gas company in the world, YPF has built a very special electronic network that gives it a uniquely powerful pricing tool. The network links together customer information from the company's 1500 gas stations around the country and from 1700 of its competitors' sites. The company's local gas station operators are charged with monitoring their competitors' prices, and they regularly feed information about those prices into the company's central computer. The company centrally monitors every element of every retail gas operation so that it can keep its own prices competitive.

With all these processes, systems, and skills in place (the business Capability), the company is able to gauge consumers' buying patterns, to generate sales forecasts, and to electronically change the prices at individual gas pumps up to four times a day. But to get such extraordinary pricing flexibility, YPF has to tie in its accounts payable process with its outsourced electronic payment process. It also has to establish new relationships with the distributors of complementary products (such as food and beverages), and the only way it can do all that is via the Internet. Once its data is on the Internet, however, the company has to be sure that its Capabilities are truly excellent. Any inefficiencies will become known to rivals, who will be able to take immediate advantage of the information.

REFLECTION

As I said in the introduction, publishing a business book is risky these days, as leaders quickly become followers in this volatile marketplace. However, regardless where any one company might be 5 or 10 years from now, there are lessons to be learned that should be considered in the context of your own business. Try to use these to create new ideas for fostering innovation. Create and connect your own dots.

Consider Koch Industries, a company that thrives on a free market model. Koch has created a business of entrepreneurs throughout. This approach helped the company grow 200-fold over three decades, and helped it expand into new business areas previously not considered. Or consider Invensys, a company whose decentralized business model allows it to change its portfolio of business regularly. Through this model, Invensys has successfully merged two businesses, created a company with incredible geographic reach, and migrated its business from traditional industrial products to more high-tech solutions. WilliamsF1, the Formula One car manufacturer, is a consistent winner on the racetrack and an innovator of new technologies. This was done through passionate leadership, a clear focus, and a culture of innovation throughout the organization. The company operates as one team. Mölnlycke Health Care, the Swedish medical supplies manufacturer, was able to successfully transform itself in a few short years from a fragmented, prescriptive organization to a Capability-based company with innovation ingrained throughout. This shift was not without pain, as it involved significant changes in the employees and culture. But the payoff, as they get ready to float, has been a fourfold improvement in economic value. Or remember Universal Leven, which through alliance-based models was able to launch a new businesses rapidly with minimal capital expenditure. Universal Leven is a truly virtual company—with two employees—that has captured significant market share in a short period of time. Likewise, Global Village Telecom in Brazil was able to launch a new business from scratch in six months using a model that gives it flexibility to adapt as market conditions change. Or consider Fiat Barchettaweb, which changed the rules of the game by being the first OEM-to-consumer car that is handled entirely through the Web. And let's not forget the utilities industry, which is undergoing massive deregulation, new competition, and increasing uncertainty. Companies like Electrabel and BC Hydro have been able to create organizations that are flexible enough to meet changing market and regulatory conditions.

Each of these companies has attributes that make it innovative. Some have made innovative use of technology to create new business models. Others have created cultures of innovation that allow employees to make decisions in real time, as needed. Some have leveraged process change as a means of fostering innovation. Regardless, all of them focus on customers and markets, use measures to foster and assess innovation, and target what gives them competitive differentiation. And although these ideas can serve as a blueprint, they are certainly not a prescription. Each company will always have its unique needs, challenges, and opportunities.

Admittedly, getting there is never easy, especially for established companies that historically relied on standard business functions as their basic organizational structure. But as we have seen in this chapter and throughout the book, it can be done. Sometimes a burning platform starts the change, but following through almost always requires a strong, passionate leader to show the way. Whatever the circumstances, this takes vision, guts, and persistence. The change I am talking about is fundamental and pervasive. It affects everyone and everything in a company. It affects customers, suppliers, alliance partners, and anyone who touches the company. But in today's age of change, success requires nothing less. That's why 24/7 innovation is the only way to achieve a unique and enduring competitive advantage.

LOOKING TO THE FUTURE

I have discussed in some detail the importance of innovation and how to foster it in an organization. You now have a blueprint for thriving in a world of change, based on the concept of the Capability. And you have the map for getting there—the six stages a company goes through on the journey toward pervasive innovation. I have also described approaches for the targeting and simulation of change, so that efforts are focused properly before launching into the turmoil of a real-life change program.

In this Epilogue, I want to offer a couple of forward-looking ideas that will help crystallize the concepts we have been looking at in the previous nine chapters. One approach puts it all into fractal terms. The other looks forward to the next logical phase of the flexible organization that I have been advocating.

Interestingly, some of the content in this Epilogue dates back a few years when I was one of the early consultants to apply "new age" concepts to business. I presented some of these ideas to a group of managers then, and although they were interested, most felt my proposal was "a little ahead of its time." Maybe they were just being kind, but I don't think so. While writing this book, I realized that time had caught up with me, and now it seems a natural fit for twenty-first-century organizations striving to create the perpetual innovation machine.

Saying that a business needs to address its people, processes, and technology to deliver a strategy is not exactly compelling news, I admit. But throughout this book I have pushed the thinking a step further. I have discussed the concept of a business architecture, the blueprint for business that addresses people, processes, and technology. Unfortunately, the way most people develop a business architecture is to say that it is the sum of those three elements—a process architecture, a human performance architecture, and a technology architecture. Once again, however, this is a way of thinking about the boxes, the individual components, in isolation. The key is to intertwine these pieces and make sure they are aligned with the strategy, then to look at everything together. When you do that, you end up with a model that looks like the one shown in Figure E-1.

FIGURE E-1.   Capability overlay.

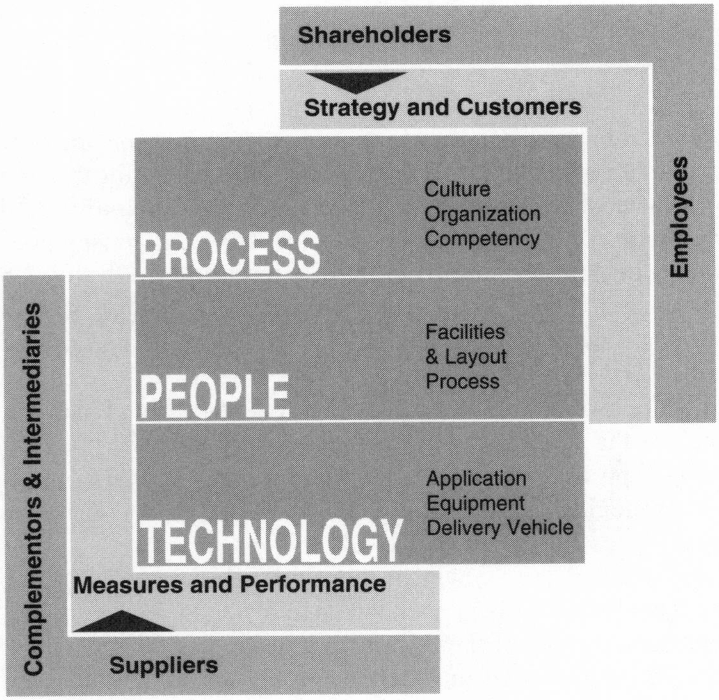

All the components in the figure must be set up to work together harmoniously, to address the tension between stakeholder wants and needs. The strategy must then be aligned with those stakeholder issues. Finally, the components of the Capability must be aligned to the strategy. And all of this needs to take into consideration the business and competitive climate in which the company is operating.

Let's look at how this is done. It seems that the typical way of designing a business is to deconstruct it into smaller parts. But in doing so, one must take care not to lose sight of the big picture. Some people suggest that implementing parts of chaos theory is a way forward, but I disagree. So little benefit has come from attempts to apply chaos research to business that pursuing this route seems futile. The chaos people have spun off interesting theories, and lots of book and articles, but few tangible business ideas.

I suggest the use of a different scientific concept, the fractal. I realize that since I initially created the content for this Epilogue, some other authors have also suggested fractals in business. But most of them have again been hung up on theory. I am proposing a pragmatic use of fractals in the context of Capabilities.

First, as always, it is useful to gain an understanding of what a fractal is. Webster's defines fractal as follows: "Any of various extremely irregular curves or shapes that repeat themselves at any scale on which they are examined and that are assigned fractional dimensions." In other words, a fractal is any geometric representation that replicates itself at lower levels of abstraction. In simple English, this means that if you zoom in on a fractal, you will see the entire design of the fractal re-created on a smaller scale. So no matter how far you zoom in on a piece of it, you will see the same pattern. A simple way to understand the fractal concept is to picture a television monitor videoing itself. Displayed on the monitor is the input from a video camera. If the camera is focused on the monitor, what you see is an image of the monitor inside of the monitor. Inside of that image would be another image of a yet smaller monitor, and so on, ad infinitum (see Figure E-2). Although this is not a completely accurate way of describing a fractal, it is sufficient for our purposes. For a more scientifically accurate illustration of a fractal, see Figure E-3.

Applying the fractal model to business and Capabilities allows us to represent the business in such a way that all aspects are repeated at each level of abstraction or "deconstruction."

For an organization to be tightly integrated and provide coordinated action throughout, each individual within an organization must be focused

FIGURE E-2. **A television camera pointed at its monitor yields a never-ending nesting of repeating images.**

on reaching a common goal, namely the strategy. To reiterate, a Capability is made up of:

- Strategy, including products, services, and distribution channels.
- Performance measures, used to drive behaviors, enable innovation, and help assess business performance against targets.
- Processes, describing how the work is to be done, including any physical infrastructure and assets.
- People, including organization structure, roles, jobs, competencies and skills, culture, and behaviors.
- Technology, including information, applications, and all of the technical infrastructure and equipment required to operate the applications.

Each of these Capability elements must take into consideration the full range of stakeholders, what their wants and needs are, and how they participate and contribute to the overall process. Most or all of the following groups make up the total range of a company's stakeholders:

- Employees
- Suppliers

FIGURE E-3.   A true fractal is a structure that repeats itself.

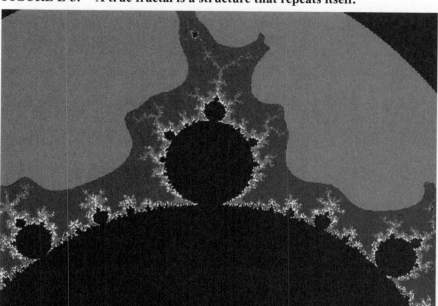

- Customers
- Shareholders
- Complementors
- Intermediaries
- Regulators

For an organization to be successful, all Capability components and stakeholders must be aligned at all levels. For example, a company as a whole will have a strategy, which I'll define as a manifestation of a company's mission or vision. For that strategy to be fully realized, each process, department, team, and individual must fully embrace and own the strategy. Whether or not an individual has an explicitly articulated personal mission statement, most have an internal compass that is used to guide them in their lives, including their work lives. For someone to be most effective in an organization, his or her personal mission and vision should be aligned with and consistent with the department's mission, which must be aligned with the overall business mission. When all parts are in sync, personal Capabilities are aligned with the overall company Capabilities. So, if you put it all together, you end up with something that looks like Figure E-4.

FIGURE E-4. **Cascading and recurring Capabilities.**

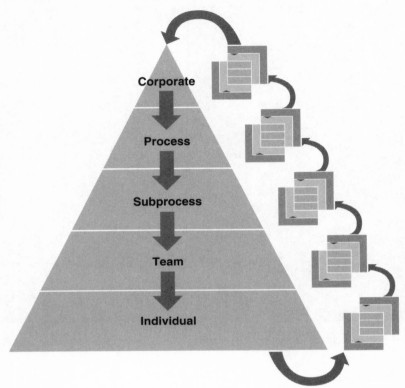

Another application of the fractal in the world of work involves the concept of staying in tune with customers and suppliers. Every process and subprocess within an organization has, consciously or otherwise, customers and suppliers. There are two challenges here. First, these internal customers and suppliers must be recognized and treated as such. Focus on those customers just as you would focus on your end customer. That is, never allow yourself to provide mediocre work to your customers (even internal ones), even if it makes some of your short-term measures look better. The second challenge when dealing with customers through the fractal framework is to recognize that every customer after you, immediate or other, is still *your* customer. Therefore, the company's end customer is still your customer, even if you work in manufacturing where there is usually little direct contact with the end customer.

There are two components of change within the business fractal:

- *Horizontal Expansion.* These are the components of the Capabilities and the stakeholders, the parts of the model that span the entire organization, across the value chain.

- *Vertical Expansion.* This aspect of the model deals with levels within the organization. The greater the depth within the organization, the greater the overall impact. To ensure success, *all* levels below must be part of the model.

This brings up a number of implications associated with using the fractal concept. The first is culture change. Most organizations create a mission or vision at the highest level within the company, but do not drive it down to the lowest levels. In terms of the fractal metaphor, each department and process, and each individual, would adopt a personal mission or vision consistent with the corporate mission or vision. The level of the change agent within the organization may limit the vertical implementation of the fractal. A change agent can only be truly responsible for the levels of abstraction below. Only the CEO is capable of implementing the entire vertical structure of the fractal.

Another implication involves system development. Although the model described above is more organizationally oriented, it also applies to different levels of detail in technology. System designs and requirements are driven down to lower levels of detail, and at some point in the expansion, code will be the result. And each level of abstraction should be a complete Capability, not another isolated deconstruction on the single dimension of technology. So as you move from broad application and technical architectures down to specific modules, be sure to consider the processes each module supports, the people who are going to use it, how it enables connections with customers and suppliers, and so on.

Finally, the fractal concept has implications for timing. Timing of the particular components of the model is critically important. If it were practical, everything would happen concurrently. But, unfortunately, this is not possible for a variety of reasons. Given that reality, which dimension should be given top priority and what should the relative timings of the other dimensions be?

Strategy is the first logical step. The purpose of the strategy is to move the organization in a particular direction, define critical success factors (both quantitative and qualitative), define boundaries for the organization to work with, and motivate and call to action the entire organization. In order for this to happen, everyone in the organization must be able to "find" him or herself in the company's strategic intent. The hierarchy as described by the model is different from the organizational hierarchy. That is, the highest level does not depict the vision of the CEO, but rather the collective vision of the company. In the vision chain, the CEO is at the bottom with all other employees. However, traditionally, because the CEO is a major influencer of the vision, the company's vision is quite consistent with the CEO's vision, sometimes at the expense of the other employees.

But for the fractal to be successful, all members of an organization must have personal visions that are consistent with the corporate vision. How can this be achieved? Certainly a corporatewide, concurrent effort to build a vision is impractical, and quite possibly undesirable. So what should come first—the personal visions or the corporate visions? The answer is simple: both. The senior executives within an organization should begin the process of developing the corporate vision, somewhat independent of the personal visions. Concurrently, everyone within the organization should be given the tools to develop his or her personal vision. There are many techniques for doing this. Accenture has used Steven Covey's principle-centered leadership (PCL) concepts for helping individuals create their personal mission. The key is to get people to look at their values and ideals and begin to create a vision statement for themselves. After the creation of the first cut of the corporate vision, people within the organization need to begin mapping their personal visions against it. The process of moving through the organization can be done one division, one group, or one team at a time. Eventually, after several iterations, the whole corporation will have the vision as a living, breathing entity that guides and motivates the organization.

The goal is to define the organization's culture in such a way that all employees can clearly see how they fit into the picture. It is the responsibility of each organization to take care of the people it displaces. People are any organization's greatest asset, and although they cannot be "reengineered," they can be motivated and given the incentive to perform in new ways. The greatest success within an organization comes when it is made plain to people why change is necessary and when they understand how exciting the process of change can be for them. When they accept that their behavior is part of a perfectly aligned bigger picture, they will do their best because they are being true to themselves. They will have become convinced that the corporate vision and strategy suits them, too.

In summary, the fractal is a useful way of conceptualizing how to build and develop Capabilities within an organization. When deconstructing the business, avoid breaking it into pieces (e.g., process, people, and technology), which would be like cutting a photograph in half. You end up with two halves of a picture. Instead, break it into small versions of the whole, similar to the way a hologram works. When cut in half, it becomes two complete, smaller-sized versions of the original picture, never losing the overall shape of the whole. By using this approach, you always have your eye, and your organization, focused on the big picture.

A LITTLE THEORY: THE ORGANIC ORGANIZATION

As I said, there is a lot of theory out there, but in this book I wanted to provide a pragmatic approach to creating sustainable business success. Still, I'm hoping you'll indulge me for a moment while I throw some theory at you, theory that I call the organic organization. I believe this could be a model for the Internet Age that we are all being sucked into. Once again, when I presented the concept to a group of executives, everyone said, "Interesting, but ahead of its time." The concept I presented was a structure for creating a truly flexible organization. It is the next logical step to the concepts I outline in this book. You can think of it as 24/7 innovation on steroids.

As with the other concepts in this book, my goal here is to provide a structure that enables rapid change, adaptability rather than optimization. To survive, you must always do better and faster than the competition. I am reminded of the story of two hikers who stumbled upon an angry bear. Immediately, one of them took off his hiking boots and put on his running shoes. The other hiker looked at him and said, "What are you doing? You can't outrun a bear!" The first hiker responded, "I know, but I only need to outrun you." So true. Stay ahead of the competition and you will win the race.

I define the *organic organization* as a network of interdependent goals that evolve to satisfy changing competitive needs. This network is orchestrated by some simple management mechanisms aimed at sourcing Capabilities to satisfy those goals. Figure E-5 shows what the organic organization might look like. It is guided by "radar" that looks for shifts in the business landscape. This is similar to a concept I described in Chapter 4 when discussing strategic management Capabilities. You need to constantly monitor changes in customers, competitors, and disruptive technologies, and define new goals that the business needs to achieve to stay ahead of the competition.

When a new goal is set, the next step is to determine how to source the Capabilities necessary to achieve the goal. Sourcing can be internal or external. Some potential approaches for identifying candidates to provide a given Capability include:

FIGURE E-5.   The organic organization model.

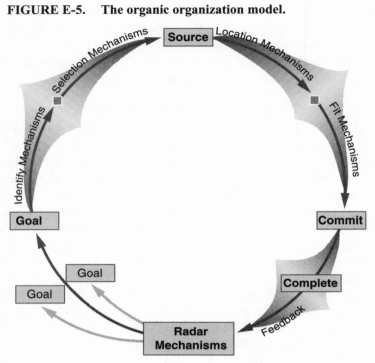

- *Preselection*. A company sends RFPs to a shortlist of companies that it thinks might be able to do the work.
- *Subscription*. Companies that are interested in receiving RFPs would subscribe. This can be done through the Internet, or through the mail, or any other means.
- *Publish*. The company publishes the request in a business magazine, in a newspaper, or over the Internet.
- *Sole Source*. The company has already identified preferred providers for specific Capabilities.
- *Automatic*. Certain Capabilities may be automatically triggered with no manual intervention.

After identifying potential parties to source the Capability, the next step is to select the partner. There are several mechanisms for doing that:

- *Direct*. This would be the approach for a sole source or automatic selection.

- *Via an Intermediary.* Use a third party to evaluate responses, or potentially even identify candidates in the first place.
- *Predefined.* Use predefined selection criteria.
- *First Come, First Served.* If speed is all that matters, maybe this is an appropriate selection mechanism.
- *Bidding.* Use the Internet or other vehicle for capturing bids.

Looking at the identification and selection process together, you can see some interesting concepts emerging, in particular, the idea of creating a B2B Capability exchange on the Internet. And, as I described in Chapter 1, the threat or ability of companies to source any Capability externally automatically creates a more competitive, entrepreneurial environment within the company. Or, the concepts in Chapter 7 on targeting can be used to determine which Capabilities should be sourced externally and which should be sourced internally.

Once you have identified the source of the Capability, the next step is to establish the location where the work will take place. In Chapter 2, I discussed the power of relocating work and some strategies for accomplishing that, and I won't repeat them all here. Possibilities include specifying one location, where everyone comes together (e.g., at the requestor's premises, as in the Volkswagen example in Chapter 2 where the suppliers came to the manufacturer); distributing the work to various locations; setting up a variable system (where work moves based on specific need); and coming up with a virtual solution (especially for electronic-based development, such as software or netsourcing).

The next step is critical—making sure that we are focusing on the lines, not the boxes. One line involves making sure that however the Capability is sourced, it fits in with other related and dependent Capabilities. For example, if we are dealing with a physical product that requires assembly, we want to be certain that it all works together. Some potential assembly models include:

- One company (supplier) does all assembly for all components.
- All companies assemble collaboratively. (This generally requires physical colocation if the products are tangible.)
- A third party can do assembly, even if they did not provide any of the Capabilities or components.
- The company in question can take the components created by the suppliers and put them together internally (self-assembly).
- The customer can do the assembly (the IKEA model).

Finally, all of the partners need to commit to a schedule for when they will get the work done, agree on who it is for, and, probably most important, agree on why it is being done—how it helps achieve the stated goal. Now, instead of managing the work, you only need to manage the commitments.

So the steps of this model are: set the goals, source the Capabilities, commit to the work, complete the work, and then feed back the results for future improvement.

Although this model is a still theoretical, I do believe it is the next logical step for companies as business learns to make the best use of the hugely important Internet phenomenon. It offers infinite flexibility. It addresses the lines rather than just the boxes. And with emerging Internet tools, this model is now achievable.

A TALE OF FOUR
COMPANIES

In this appendix, I provide four examples (GlaxoSmithKline, Invensys, The Real Estate Assessment Center of the U.S. Department of Housing and Urban Development, and BC Hydro) of companies that are doing innovative work within their own organizations. These illustrate innovation in different Capabilities (for example, product development, procurement, property management, and grid operations) and different industries (pharmaceuticals, high-tech, government, and utilities). These case studies illustrate that no matter what part of a business you are responsible for, or what industry your company is in, there are plenty of opportunities for innovation.

GLAXOSMITHKLINE

The consolidation of pharmaceutical companies worldwide has been prompted in part by the rising cost of research and development in the complex world of modern drugs. The trend is highlighted by the recent merger of SmithKline and Glaxo Wellcome. Glaxo Wellcome, itself the result of a merger in 1995, is highlighted in this case study.

A major catalyst for the Glaxo Wellcome merger had been the fact that two of their drugs accounted for 40 percent of the merged companies' sales, and one of them, the antiulcer drug Zantac, was about to come off patent. It was a critical situation that required the company to take a number of urgent steps, one of which was to accelerate overall product-development procedures.

The companies' dependence on these two best-sellers was a symptom of both success and failure—the global success of Zantac, a story that was to become one of the great stories of the industry, and the failure of the inventor (Glaxo) to keep its pipeline of new drugs sufficiently well stocked so that they could offer another blockbuster drug that would take over from Zantac when its patent expired.

Patents are usually awarded for 20 years from the moment a company first files for protection. Companies need to file early to protect their new inventions, but, as soon as they file, the clock starts ticking. They need to get their product to market as rapidly as possible in order to maximize their revenues while the product remains under patent protection.

The largest part of the time that it takes to get a new drug to market is taken up by compulsory clinical trials in which the drug is tested for efficacy and side effects. If they are lucky, companies end up with about 10 or 11 years between regulatory approval and the expiration of a patent. In this time they have to sell the product aggressively to recoup the development costs and make a profit. Clearly, any opportunity to reduce the time that it takes to carry out clinical trials by, for example, improving the processes involved, gives the company extra time to recoup its costs.

Before the merger of Glaxo and Wellcome, the two companies had identified rapidly rising costs and the lengthening time of clinical trials as areas for special attention. Costs were rising partly because of the increasing complexity of the industry and partly because of more aggressive regulation.

Although the merger created opportunities to look for economies of scale in R&D, where combined annual expenditures were in excess of £1.2 billion ($1.7 billion), it also created complications. There were large cultural differences between the two organizations, including distinctive cultural differences in their clinical trial processes. "We knew after the merger that if we were going to get the best out of both organizations we had to create a new way of working that was Glaxo Wellcome, rather than Glaxo or Wellcome," explained Dr. James Palmer, a senior vice president.

Early in 1996 the new company identified improvements in the drug-development process, and in clinical trials in particular, as critical to its success. It concluded that operational performance had to be raised to a level where it could handle 20 new compounds coming out of its exploratory research each year. This, it was estimated, would lead to the launch of three new medicines every year after 2000.

Glaxo Wellcome embarked on improvement to its drug-development process so it could achieve the goal of delivering three significant new medicines annually. But it also realized that capacity and cycle times would have to be changed in order to reach all its goals.

The outcome was a clinical process redesign (CPR) initiative, which was expected to increase the company's capacity to conduct trials on potential new drugs by 50 percent and to reduce the time required for such trials by one-third. The redesign had four distinct phases: diagnosis, solution development, implementation, and consolidation.

Diagnosis.   This phase involved extensive consultation throughout the organization, carried out through face-to-face interviews and workshops. It identified some major differences between previous Glaxo and Wellcome employees and between their teams in the United States and the United Kingdom. It also highlighted the areas that seemed to offer significant opportunities for improvement, one of which was planning and performance measurement.

Also in this first phase, a senior executive was appointed to lead the redesign through its other phases. Appointment of Dr. Trevor Gibbs, a high-level executive, signaled the degree of top management's commitment to the redesign.

At a fairly early stage, Dr. Gibbs decided that it was important to deal with the short-term issues, but to do so "in the context of a long-term implementable five-year vision of medical development." With that split in mind, the project was divided into two main streams: medical process redesign (MPR) and new paradigm (NP). The purpose of the former was to improve existing processes while the latter aimed to look three to five years into the future to identify opportunities to implement step changes to the development process. Supporting both was a metrics team and a change management and communications team.

Solution Development.   The challenge for the MPR team in the second phase was to find improvements in those areas identified in the first phase as offering the most opportunities. All the while, the teams had to keep a close eye on the core drivers of the project—improving customer focus and increasing credibility, efficiency, and productivity.

In their search, each team interviewed a wide range of staff, held workshops, and reviewed operating procedures and existing best practices. Their aim was to come up with innovative approaches that would give the company a competitive edge.

At the same time, the metrics team was developing new approaches to measuring and targeting the clinical trials process, while the communications team was looking for the best ways to involve and inform staff during the program.

Implementation.   The most critical aspect of the project was the method and style of implementing the solutions that had emerged from phase two. Previous change initiatives had generated solutions, but the complexity and sheer magnitude of the combined organizations had foiled attempts to implement them. And the task in this instance was no less immense: it called for training 7000 people—in 56 different roles, 2 centers, and 24 operating companies—to carry out 42 new "solutions," new ways of performing old processes.

An organizational matrix was devised consisting of two sets of teams: one set was responsible for delivering the detailed contents of the solutions across the board, while the other was responsible for seeing that different geographic areas were fully covered. At times, these efforts involved more than 150 people.

In addition, a number of special tools were adopted to ensure that news of the redesign was spread as widely as possible. One of these was a so-called "model office," a central point at the company's principal headquarters created to raise the profile of the redesign effort and to facilitate ad hoc training and awareness. This was supported by separate help desk phone lines in both the United States and the United Kingdom.

From the outset, explaining the "why" of the changes was seen as being just as important as communicating the "how" and the "when." In addition to extensive staff training, an electronic document library was made available in 26 countries to provide access to over 100 key documents that described the new ways of working.

Consolidation.   The final phase of redesign involved the implementation of the systems and an intensification of the campaign to win the hearts and minds of all the company's employees. In most such cases, the mind adapts to new ways long before the heart does. Widespread demonstration of the redesign's goals at this stage helped to win further support and to maintain the program's momentum.

By the end of 1997, 80 percent of the solutions identified in phase two had been implemented. Dr. James Palmer said, "The strength of medical process redesign was that we created practical solutions that could provide real benefits and we delivered them into the business on a time scale no one had achieved before."

The impact of the clinical-process redesign solutions has been felt at many different levels within Glaxo Wellcome. At the clinical trial level, for example, the company has seen a reduction of about one-third in trial cycle times and a reduction of over 10 percent in the resources required for each trial. Improvements such as these inevitably ripple throughout the organization.

Given that clinical research is key to the success of pharmaceutical companies, as part of the NP work stream of CPR, Glaxo Wellcome looked at the key issue of motivation to drive improvements. Historically (until the end of 1998), a limited number of Glaxo Wellcome operating companies had received funds to support a predetermined clinical research head count. Payment was not clearly related to the activities performed by the designated head count. Allocation of work was not transparent, and operating companies did not have the operational flexibility to respond to the variable workload that is inherent in clinical development. So Glaxo Wellcome introduced the concept of an "internal market" to increase transparency in funding and provide greater opportunity to operating companies who performed well on time, cost, and quality. The objective of the internal market is to select operating companies to conduct group studies and allocate to them appropriate funding to complete these studies. The group therapeutic development teams (TDGs) fund operating companies with monies to cover all costs, including clinical and data management staff, internal overheads (e.g., medical information systems and R&D operating costs), and external costs such as investigator payments.

Well before the start of a program of work, the TDG team initiates discussions on an agreement with each selected operating company. The agreement specifies the target number of subjects to be recruited by the operating company, and the time scales for development. It defines the internal resources required (full-time equivalent months) to run the study (clinical monitoring and data management), and payment is made for those resources. Payment only changes if it is agreed that the resource requirement has changed. In other words, payment is based on activity.

Glaxo Wellcome's internal market has been in operation (outside the United States) since November 1998. In 1999, the internal market sent 394 individual bid request packs to the operating companies seeking their bids to participate in the studies. In total, £3.1 million ($4.4 million) was paid to the operating companies as internal market revenue. And in the first quarter of 2000, £2.6 million ($3.7 million) was paid to the operating companies as internal market revenue, and £5.8 million ($8.1 million) had been committed to the operating companies for the remainder of that year.

So, has this investment paid off? Although the set-up time for internal market studies is 14 percent longer than the set-up time for the studies done according to past models (due to the more complex contractual arrangement), the recruitment time is 50 percent better (18 weeks for internal market studies versus 36 weeks for non–internal market studies). And average fully loaded full-time employment costs decreased by 5.5 percent in 2000 compared with 1999.

Overall the improvements have strengthened Glaxo Wellcome's drug pipeline in terms of both capacity and speed. And these improved processes will allow GlaxoSmithKline to produce innovative drugs faster and meet the increasingly intense global competition head-on.

INVENSYS
Throughout the book, but mainly in Chapter 2, I have referred to Invensys. Although they have received quite a bit of airtime so far, there is still more of the story that is worth telling. After the merger of BTR and Siebe to create Invensys, the new company looked for ways that it could make some substantial operational savings from the marriage of the two organizations. One of the areas that it identified was purchasing; it reckoned that within three years it should be able to save over $100 million annually by improving and rationalizing its purchasing processes. Its hopes were raised by the fact that in both premerger organizations purchasing had been carried out at the business unit level. And, since before the merger both companies had been unable to take advantage of many opportunities to gain economies of scale, it was assumed that both the opportunities and the ability to take advantage of them would be much greater after the merger.

A new chief purchasing officer for the whole group was put in place, who introduced a system of "commodity teams," small, dedicated teams that were solely responsible for purchasing each of the major commodities that the firm required, no matter where in the world they came from or where they were destined to go. Hence the first step in redesigning Invensys' purchasing process was a change in the organization itself.

At first glance, a switch to commodity teams might seem a retrograde step, one that centralizes the purchasing function unduly. In fact, however, it leaves responsibility for purchasing where it was. Its advantage over the old system is that it ensures that purchasing is coordinated effectively, and only through such coordination can a large organization hope to gain the full benefit of its purchasing power.

Invensys set up 44 different commodity teams in all, each team headed by an experienced commodity manager. On top of the 44 commodity teams was a supplier development team whose job it was to work with all the individual business units and to help them find and introduce new suppliers who could further reduce costs. The company planned to get all its commodity managers together as a group every six weeks, but that was not easy. Many of them traveled extensively. If there were problems with a particular supplier in China, for instance, the commodity manager would probably have to go to China to sort it out on the spot.

Putting together effective purchasing teams was only one part of the attempt to reduce costs. In addition, Invensys set about redesigning its global purchasing process; during this redesign effort, the company's commodity managers worked with teams from the various business units. Each team was multidisciplinary and included representatives from the engineering, legal, quality, and finance functions. One particularly important aspect of the redesign was the restructuring and standardizing of the contractual framework within which the company operated. This saved money by helping Invensys accelerate the speed at which it closed contracts with suppliers.

Another aspect of the purchasing process redesign was an attempt to improve the processes of Invensys suppliers. In a network of dependent entities, each is only as strong as the weakest member. Invensys could only go up to a certain point in improving its own processes if its suppliers failed to get to the same point in theirs. The value of an electronic order-processing system, for example, is limited if the company's suppliers are using paper-based systems.

To encourage suppliers to follow its example, Invensys defined the standards that it expected them to achieve in their own processes. A special supplier development team now reinforces these standards with regular, on-the-spot quality audits. Where standards are low, it encourages the supplier to make improvements by sending personnel to onsite training at Invensys' own plants.

Another way that they improved supplier performance was by setting up a team of a dozen supplier development engineers. These people work with suppliers, commodity managers, and product developers to ensure that everything is working smoothly. In many cases they are troubleshooters. In other cases, they get involved early in the supplier certification process, looking at potential suppliers and approving them. They work on a global basis, traveling around the world going from supplier to supplier. And in this role, which is both proactive and reactive, examples of creativity abound.

At one stage Invensys was having problems with a part that was being produced by a casting manufacturer. The finish on the part was not adhering as it should. In the past Invensys would probably beat up on the supplier, forcing them into submission, even if it meant that the supplier would lose money and be less able to perform effectively in the future. In the new environment, they would be likely to help the supplier to locate the flaws in the manufacturing process, thus enabling them to solve the problem more effectively. All Invensys development engineers are Six Sigma master blackbelts.

Communication is vital to the success of any process change, but it is particularly vital with one as complicated as this. Invensys' new purchasing processes, and the technology and postmerger organization that made them possible, were all explained at a Purchasing Summit held by the company in Orlando, Florida. Alun Evans, an Accenture colleague of mine, was responsible for pulling together the content of the Summit. As he put it, "There was a terrific feeling of excitement over all three days—it was the first time that 300 of the key purchasing people from all over the globe came together in one place, with one purpose. The breakout sessions were the most creative I've ever seen and generated the action plans for the next 3 years." The summit helped to reinforce the sense of urgency and purpose that was necessary if the promised benefits were to be delivered on time. The goal was to optimize savings not for departments, but for Invensys. At the end of the day, it's all about creating shareholder value. This is line thinking at its best.

THE REAL ESTATE ASSESSMENT CENTER OF THE U.S. DEPARTMENT OF HOUSING AND URBAN DEVELOPMENT (REAC)

It is particularly satisfying to watch a deeply conservative, traditional organization open itself up to the possibilities of change, and there are few organizations more traditional and conservative than government departments. So when the U.S. Department of Housing and Urban Development (HUD) decided in 1997, as part of its management reform, that it must try to reform its antiquated bureaucracy, it had a unique opportunity to reinvent itself as a customer-focused, performance-oriented organization. And it welcomed that opportunity with open arms. It used leading-edge electronic technology to turn one part of itself into an innovative e-business that has become a role model for other U.S. government departments.

The Department of Housing and Urban Development is responsible for the management of some 3 million rental units across the United States. In

1998 the organization had no reliable information about the condition of these properties and no comprehensive system for inspecting them. Assessment was carried out in 50 different centers with 50 different sets of managers and 50 different authorization processes. It was extremely difficult to track where properties were deteriorating, or where fraud, waste, and abuse were taking place.

Not only was HUD unable to pursue owners who failed to properly maintain their properties, but it was also unable to track whether families living in HUD-subsidized or -insured properties were living in decent, safe, and sanitary conditions.

As part of the answer to its problems, the department set up a separate agency called the Real Estate Assessment Center (REAC), which was to be a single focal point for keeping an inventory of all the properties in which HUD had a financial interest; REAC was also to be responsible for inspecting and classifying those properties.

Early on HUD decided that it wanted to free REAC from the classic problem facing government agencies: namely, paperwork. With the help of the chief executive, REAC set out from the start to design a totally new system based on a paperless e-business model. Using advanced IT and new redesigned processes, REAC enabled everybody in the organization to have online access to objective quantifiable measurements of HUD-supported properties. Not only does HUD now know where the properties that it supports are located, but it also has a much better understanding of those properties' physical and financial condition.

The REAC inspectors use handheld tools to enter property inspection data and then they upload it (via the Internet) to the organization's central databases. Because the new systems rely so heavily on technology, REAC had to provide initial technical assistance and training to housing owners and agents, and to housing authorities, to help them become e-literate. Many of them were unfamiliar with the Internet, for example. Providing technical support they needed in order to feel comfortable with the technology and the systems was one of the keys to REAC's success.

With the help of the new systems and processes, REAC was able, in just over a year, to:

1. Complete the first ever physical inspection of all 29,000 HUD-assisted multifamily housing properties.

2. Assess (for potential financial risks) more than 18,000 financial statements submitted by the owners of multifamily housing projects.

3. Carry out a survey of more than 250,000 public housing residents to find out their levels of satisfaction. The survey solicited an

extraordinarily high 50 percent response rate, and 89 percent of those responding indicated that they were "satisfied" with their living conditions.

The data gathered in this way was used as a regulatory tool to reward good performers and to sanction poor ones. Properties that came in the top tier would not have another inspection for three years; the next tier would be inspected every two years; while the bottom tier would continue to be inspected annually.

The system is now in the process of being adapted by the U.S. Department of Agriculture, and other agencies (such as the Internal Revenue Service and the U.S. Marshals Service) are looking at what it might do for them. The director of REAC, Donald J. LaVoy, says that this shows how "all of government is starting to understand the importance of e-commerce in doing their transactions."

The fact that the leaders of REAC had unusual backgrounds (and complementary ones at that) helped the organization to come up with innovative answers to HUD's problems. LaVoy himself was a former Naval aviator and unit leader with the U.S. Marine Corps. He had had no experience with HUD before his appointment, but his deputy, Barbara Burkhalter, had worked with the department for eight years. Burkhalter's professional background was as a financial manager with a large public accounting firm; LaVoy's background was in change management and building IT systems. While LaVoy focused on the external affairs of the agency, Burkhalter looked after the financial and internal matters.

Being set up essentially as an e-business means that REAC has a very different structure from other government entities. It is a flat organization in which all employees report directly to LaVoy and Burkhalter. Everybody knows what his or her job is, and everyone is empowered to produce what is required. Common business processes are in place across the organization. "We make everybody follow the same model," says Burkhalter. "We've even named all of our business systems with common-sounding names. We just change the first letter." The result is a standard process that achieves reliable results.

The Real Estate Assessment Center's workplace is an open environment designed to encourage teamwork. For many government employees, of course, this atmosphere was disturbing at first. "They're used to attending meetings, and they're used to advising and guiding somebody else, and we're totally not about that," says Burkhalter. "We're about production, output, and outcomes."

LaVoy emphasizes that the open workplace helps to stimulate innovation: "We have a lot of government employees who are very knowledgeable about resources and programs in the traditional areas, but who are not perhaps completely up to speed on the latest uses of technology. On the other hand we have a bunch of young people who are very, very up to speed on all the tools accessible via that medium. Our approach teams these two constituencies together, if you will, sitting side by side in an open environment."

Despite initial difficulties in adapting to the strange culture, the employees have eventually come to thrive on it. Burkhalter thinks they are happy once they change because this is a more job-satisfaction type of work environment. A lot of them have ultimately ended up giving the agency "110 percent."

When the private consulting company Public Strategies Group Inc. reported on the progress of REAC in the autumn of 2000, it said that REAC "has provided HUD with the kind of information that makes its entire vision of a reinvented HUD possible." LaVoy went even further: "REAC is the model of what the future HUD needs to look like, as well as other government agencies."

BC HYDRO

With the deregulation of the utilities markets in many countries, there is increasing uncertainty over how things will shake out in the coming years. But utilities already understand that this will mean learning to survive in a competitive environment. It will also mean learning to be more flexible in how they go about change, because whatever they do may need to be fine-tuned or even replaced in the future.

So how does a company survive in that new world of competition and unpredictability? One company that is living up to the challenge is BC Hydro, a hydroelectric utility that supplies 90 percent of the power to the province of British Columbia in Canada. Over the past few years, the B.C. Utilities Commission has been investigating the possibility of establishing a competitive electricity market. To date, the predominant scenario for promoting open access has been the creation of a separate system operator function. In light of these events, BC Hydro's Grid Operations group is taking measures to develop the business Capabilities for an independent grid operator (IGO). Independent grid operators are responsible for managing the transmission grid independently from the transmission, distribution, and power generation companies. In the past, this role was purely technical and was taken on by a grid operations group within the vertically integrated monopoly utility. A typical responsibility was balancing transmission-line energy flows to ensure network stability.

In the future, the IGO will need significant new business Capabilities and will be faced with a much more complex operational role. On the business side, the IGO will need to handle contract management, develop and maintain customer relationships, reconcile physical energy consumption through financial settlements, and facilitate the trading of energy. On the operational side, it will need to coordinate scheduling and manage network congestion for an increasingly complex environment where industrial companies, power marketers, and generators will all be looking for the best deal. Put simply, the IGO will need to do a lot more than grid operations do today.

The prospect of this new environment created some concern for BC Hydro's Transmission and Distribution (T&D) business unit. As discussed in Chapter 8, to address the uncertainty, BC Hydro developed market scenarios using a building block approach. The building blocks are discrete components that help define the shape of the changing market as well as how BC Hydro will confront it. By considering and assessing each building block, assumptions can be made that define the most likely characteristics of the future marketplace. The company identified and analyzed 14 building blocks.

- *Market Transition*. The timing of the transition from the current state to a wholesale and full-competition market.
- *Energy Market*. The structure of the energy market: Power Exchange, bilateral, or mixed.
- *Ancillary Services Market Structure*. How ancillary services are acquired: long-term contracts or through a Power Exchange managed by the IGO.
- *Power Exchange Participation*. Voluntary versus mandatory participation in the Power Exchange.
- *Geographic Scope*. Local operation of a BC IGO or participation as part of another regional system operator.
- *Structural Scope*. Whether the IGO operates independently of the Power Exchange or is combined with the Power Exchange as one entity.
- *System Operations Scope*. IGO's responsibility for the operation of transmission and distribution assets.
- *Asset Management and Ownership*. The allocation of asset management responsibilities and ownership.
- *Market Power*. IGO's responsibility in monitoring and mitigating market power.

- *Corporate Ownership*. Ownership as an independent company or as part of a holding company.
- *Governance*. Governance structure to ensure perception of independence.
- *Corporate Services*. IGO approach to obtaining corporate services.
- *Funding*. Means for recovering IGO set-up and operating costs.
- *Incentives*. Incentives available to the IGO organization which do not violate Federal Energy Regulatory Commission–defined conflicts of interest.

For each building block, BC Hydro defined a range of possible outcomes for future business requirements. The concept behind the building block was to develop scenarios based on potential outcomes. The building blocks were designed to be plug-and-play, meaning that some of them could be discarded if proved to be irrelevant. Since the building blocks basically defined the characteristics of the end state, the scenarios became a starting point for evaluating pros and cons. The target outcomes as well as issues were first defined for each building block. Overall, three scenarios were defined and evaluated for pros and cons.

Given that they needed to start moving before things were finalized, decision trees were used to determine the most likely initial scenarios. They then conducted a high-level Capability fit analysis, comparing current Capabilities in the areas of operations, customer contact, asset management, and corporate services to those likely to be required by a system operator in the future. At the end of the process, the program sponsor and his key team selected the potential end state based on the scenario which had the most relevance. At the conclusion of the analysis, they had formulated this question: "What are the priority Capabilities for limited competition and what do we need to do to acquire them?"

To address that question, BC Hydro developed a conceptual business architecture for a system operator in British Columbia. In order to do this, they first created an extensive market model detailing the expected participants and their interactions, working from the outside in. They then identified the priority Capabilities required to support limited competition.

When they had defined the Capabilities, they defined them as a whole, rather than piecemeal. The result of this effort was a holistic blueprint equally reflective of the people, process, and technology characteristics for a viable system operator in British Columbia. The key characteristics of the blueprint were as follows:

- The organization was divided into centers of responsibility.

- Based on the jobs and roles within the centers of responsibility, a linkage was made to the processes (or portions thereof) the individuals within each center were responsible for.
- The technology and tools needed to perform the processes were then defined and associated with the processes.

This method of identifying and presenting a business architecture allowed the company to start from the question that most often seems to be foremost in their minds: "What's in it for me?" It allowed them to look at the architecture from the perspective of themselves and their people and confirm that all aspects have been analyzed. And this is the epitome of line thinking.

B

INNOVATION CAPABILITY MATURITY

The following chart is not intended as an exhaustive diagnostic tool, but it should give you a good idea of whether your company is in the ad hoc, basic, advanced, or pervasive stage of innovation for each blueprint element.

Blueprint Element	Question/Topic	Ad Hoc
Strategy	*When is innovation used?*	To avert crisis
Performance Measures	*Who is measured?*	One person becomes scapegoat when innovation fails; project manager is rewarded when innovation succeeds, not based on innovation but rather on great "management" skills
	What kinds of measures are used (see Chapter 6)?	Did it solve a crisis?
Process	*Position in four-step innovation process (see Chapter 3)*	Idea generation only
	Converge/diverge processes	No distinction between converge and diverge processes
	Target selection	Reactive, based on current problem
	Solution selection	Low rigor, "seems" right

Basic	Advanced	Pervasive
Time- and budget-constrained Optimize processes	Innovation is more than just seeking to optimize Innovate on high-value stuff (see Chapter 7) Innovation is a valued Capability	Innovation as centrifugal metaphysical, quantum force Innovation as currency
One person "acknowledged" for role but not measured/rewarded	One person is measured and accountable for "team innovation" Performance appraisals include innovation contribution	Everyone measured relative to career progression, core skills
Did we meet "innovation budget"?	"Amount" of innovation is part of project success Explicitly link innovation to bottom line	Main focus on business outcomes, less focus on innovation's contribution Redefine what is measured
Identify problem—idea generation	Mastery of four-step process	Four-step improvisation—beyond four-step process
Using diverge techniques	Using both	Beyond, use freely in every decision
Somewhat proactive approach to selecting innovation targets Identify/focus on the "right" problem	ROI-based target selection	Based on current and future problems
Compared against cost/budget constraints	Considering all seven Rs (see Chapter 2) and impact on ROI	New synergies between solutions

Blueprint Element	Question/Topic	Ad Hoc
Process	*How/when innovation is built into process*	Not considered until a problem comes up
	Environment	Lots of walls; little space for innovation or collaboration
People	*Culture: Confidence in innovation*	Pray it will work
	Culture: Attitudes toward innovation	Innovation viewed as artsy-fartsy
	Organization: Who leads?	Last one to step back
	Organization: Who participates?	Whoever is dragged into process
	Competency: Innovation skills	Curiosity, no deep skills
	Competency: Teaming skills	People focused on individual performance and contribution, lack of listening

Basic	Advanced	Pervasive
Scheduled on an ongoing basis, a little in advance but not part of original plans	All work is planned to include time for innovation	Implicit in all tasks, solutions, processes, and activities
Open design of workspace	Purposefully designed innovation "spaces"/rooms Teams colocated to facilitate communication	Set up to facilitate innovation—innovation feng shui
Hope it will work	Innovation works	Innovation is necessary
Skepticism about innovation	Innovation as focal point	Innovation without thinking about it—no longer a separate thing
Innovation champion (person really excited about innovation, but with no authority, not accountable)	Single-person accountability	Group accountability, everyone innovates all the time
Innovation among subteams	Whole team responsible	Internal and external project team members (across the value chain)
Isolated, good skills Ability to employ a rainbow of good tools and techniques	Understanding of rationale for tools and techniques and their application; integrated skills	Innovation skills no longer stand alone, but are merged with other core competencies (e.g., problem-solving skills are inherently innovative)
Small group, one-on-one facilitation; forced teaming	Expert facilitation	Expert at facilitating and participating—high-performance teams

Blueprint Element	Question/Topic	Ad Hoc
Technology	*Tools for idea generating*	Random brainstorming techniques using paper and pen
	Tools for idea capturing	None beyond duration of meeting

Basic	Advanced	Pervasive
Individual tools: Mind mapping software	Collaboration tools in innovation rooms	Virtual collaboration tools for generation and selection
Flip-charts, folded up for "later" use	Idea bank—intrateam	Idea bank (inter- and intrateam and external); integrated feedback loop

APPLYING THE
SEVEN Rs

The following chart can be helpful in deciding when to apply some of the Seven Rs when developing new business models. Some of the questions associated with each "R" can be found in Chapter 2 and some were not described earlier in the text. This is only to get the thinking started. Go wild, and use them all of the time, in counterintuitive ways. That's where real innovation will emerge.

Questions for Each R Effort	Apply When...
RETHINK	ALWAYS!
RECONFIGURE	
How can this activity be eliminated?	• They are low-value or waste activities. • Processes have a low-value density. • Value received from activity is minimal (e.g., approving small amounts).
How can common activities be consolidated?	• Common activities are performed in multiple locations. • Common activities are performed inconsistently. • There are economies of scale (e.g., shared services).
How can reconciliation be reduced by putting quality at the source?	• A lot of time is spent reconciling paperwork and correcting errors. • There is little accountability for errors.
How can information sharing with suppliers and customers improve the process?	• Demand is uncertain or unpredictable. • Stock-outs are frequent. • Inventories are excessive.
How can intermediaries and non-value-added work be eliminated?	• Intermediaries add no value and just relay goods or services.
How can best practices from other industries be borrowed and improved upon?	• You are looking for new ideas (i.e., always).
RESEQUENCE	
How can predicting increase efficiency?	• Accurate information on customer demand is available early. • Forecasting models have proved reliable. • Time compression is more critical than accuracy or inventory costs. • Product or service variations are relatively low.

Questions for Each R Effort	Apply When...
How can postponement increase flexibility?	• Customers want customized products or services. • Inventory carrying costs are too high. • Forecasting models have proved inaccurate.
How can parallelism reduce time?	• There are limited timing dependencies between activities. • Time compression is critical. • Rework is necessary due to late error detection.
How can the number of interconnections and dependencies be minimized?	• Where there are bottlenecks, large queues, or frequent hand-offs.

RELOCATE

How can the activity be moved closer to the customer or supplier to improve effectiveness?	• Distance from the customer or supplier has introduced delay, miscommunication, or error. • Customer convenience is critical. • Customer volume is large enough and transportation lead times or costs are high.
How can the activity be moved closer to related activities to improve communication?	• Activities require a high level of teamwork or collaboration. • Rework and errors are hard to trace back to the source.
How can we decrease cycle time by reducing travel time and distance?	• Travel is a significant proportion of the process. • Goods are shipped multiple times (from plant to warehouse to customer).
How can geographically virtual organizations be created?	• Resources are geographically dispersed, but don't need to be physically nearby to produce an outcome. • Groupware technologies can be leveraged effectively. • Costs of doing business may be lower in a different geographical area (e.g., moving call centers to remote areas).

Questions for Each R Effort	Apply When...
REDUCE	
How can the frequency of the activity be reduced or increased?	• An activity is non-value-added but necessary. • There is low variation in the process or product. • There are high variability and low setup costs and times (e.g., small lot sizes).
How would more information enable greater effectiveness?	• Greater accuracy is needed. • Greater segmentation would yield greater marketing effectiveness.
How would less information or fewer controls simplify and improve efficiency?	• A high proportion of costs goes to data collection or controls. • The value received from information or controls is minimal. • Absolute accuracy is not necessary.
How can critical resources be used more effectively?	• Utilization of key resources is low. • Critical resources are performing non-value-added or waste work.
REASSIGN	
How can existing activities and decisions be moved to a different organization?	• Another organization has skills or resources you lack. • You want different branding. • It is too difficult to change the previous operating model or culture.
How can the activity be outsourced?	• You don't perform the activity at world-class levels. • The activity is neither a core competency, nor is it critical. • Another organization performs this activity at world-class levels. • You have limited resources and want to focus on core competencies.

Questions for Each R Effort	Apply When...
How can the customer perform this activity?	• Customers want to be empowered to help themselves (self-serve). • Certain customer segments are not profitable. • Costs need to be reduced.
How can the organization perform an activity that the customer is already performing?	• The customer wants more value and/or convenience. • The organization wants to get closer to the customer.
How can cross-training integrate and compress tasks?	• Multiple tasks are needed to produce an outcome. • Processes are not complex enough to justify a specialist. • Only 20 percent of cases or less require special expertise.
How can suppliers or partners perform this activity?	• The supplier or partner has skills, assets, or economies of scale that you lack. • The activity is not a core competency. • The activity is in an area of the business that may change rapidly in the future; and you need added flexibility.
RETOOL	
How can technology transform the process?	• You want to make time, location, or performer irrelevant.
How can the activity be automated?	• The current process is paper-based or manual and cannot be eliminated. • The activity suffers from errors, inconsistency, or reconciliation problems. • Greater transaction volumes are needed.
How can assets or competencies be leveraged to create competitive advantage?	• You have world-class competencies. • Growth potential in the existing business looks bleak.

Questions for Each R Effort	Apply When...
How can up-skilling, down-skilling, or multi-skilling improve the process?	• Customer satisfaction is low (up-skilling). • Multiple specialists are needed to produce an outcome (multi-skilling). • Technology can create knowledge workers (down-skilling).

D

INNOVATION DIAGNOSTIC

Innovation can be, and should be, fun. Here is a diagnostic tool to help you assess just how innovative you are. It is, I admit, quite tongue in cheek. But who knows, you might just learn something.

1. When someone comes up with an innovative idea on your project, they:

☐ Are called into the boss's office and told that that sort of thing isn't done around here

☐ Receive quite a few askance glances, but people think about their ideas in private

☐ Are regarded with the same serious decorum that would be afforded any contributor

☐ Are publicly recognized for their efforts

2. You overhear two people talking about your project at lunch. They say:
   - ☐ "The people on this project are about as creative as a brick."
   - ☐ "If we have one more brainstorming meeting I will hurl chunks."
   - ☐ "They have come up with a lot of good ideas on that project."
   - ☐ "Everything that I see coming out of that project is fresh and innovative. It seems like a great place to work."

3. If you were to schedule an idea-generating session tomorrow for your project, what equipment would be readily available?
   - ☐ Flip-charts and pens
   - ☐ Audio (to play CDs to set the tone for the meeting)
   - ☐ Digital imaging (to capture ideas in their creative context)
   - ☐ Conference room specifically designed for idea-generating sessions

4. You propose to the project manager that you schedule a two-day idea-generating session for developing a key capability architecture. He or she:
   - ☐ Says (after he or she has stopped laughing), "How's that again?"
   - ☐ Explains, "We didn't plan for that in our project scope and work plan. If you can find the time in another deliverable, let me know how it goes."
   - ☐ Says, "I think that's a great idea. We have a small contingency budget set up specifically for this type of thing."
   - ☐ Says, "That's a great idea. I know you haven't been on the project long . . ." and then pulls out a project plan that demonstrates idea-generating sessions woven strategically into the preparation of each deliverable.

5. If your team were the three musketeers, what would your motto be?
   - ☐ One for one
   - ☐ One for all
   - ☐ All for one
   - ☐ All for one and one for all

6. You have conceived a very innovative idea for your project. Your cynical friend starts a pool that tracks the odds of a successful implementation. The resulting odds are:

☐ One in a million

☐ One in a hundred

☐ Even

☐ Sell your Amazon stock and put it here (well, at least when Amazon's stock was worth something)

7. Your work area is like:

☐ An assembly line

☐ A library

☐ A bakery

☐ A design studio

8. You have just walked out of an innovation meeting on your project and bump into a co-worker you haven't seen for a while. He or she asks, "So how did you get picked for this?" You reply:

☐ "I screwed up on my last deliverable, and this is my penance."

☐ "I was standing by the water cooler one minute too long."

☐ "I was selected from a list of volunteers."

☐ "They liked my idea so much, they wanted me to lead the effort to flesh it out."

9. If you had a question about innovation on your project, who would you talk to?

☐ Yourself

☐ The goofy guy with the scented markers and koosh balls on his desk

☐ The designated innovation leader

☐ Anyone

10. Check the phrase that best describes the level of innovative skills on your project:

☐ Brainstormed a few times

☐ Know a few good techniques or activities to spark innovation

☐ Have a lot of tools and know when to apply them

☐ Know how to integrate innovation techniques into other process techniques (i.e., the two are not separate)

11. You use innovation on your project:

☐   When I am so instructed

☐   When I trip over it

☐   When the project plan says I should be innovative

☐   All the time

12. Which 1960s TV show best illustrates how innovation is used on your project?

☐   The Three Stooges

☐   I Dream of Jeannie

☐   Gilligan's Island

☐   The Man from U.N.C.L.E.

13. How do you know when you have a good idea on your project?

☐   Insufficient data to respond to this question

☐   If it looks just like our last good idea

☐   Everyone thinks it sounds good

☐   It grew from the other 99 ideas that weren't as good

14. Which TV character would be most comfortable in your work environment?

☐   Sergeant Joe Friday ("Just the facts, ma'am")

☐   Sherlock Holmes ("Whatever remains, however improbable, must be the truth")

☐   Columbo ("There's just one more thing I'm not quite comfortable with . . .")

☐   MacGyver ("Have you got a paper clip so I can defuse this bomb, program the auto-motion tracker, and cook dinner?")

15. What kind of tools do you regularly use to support innovation?

☐   Flip-charts and pens for brainstorming

☐   PowerPoint or other office software to record and manage "ideas"

☐   "Innovation" software, such as Mindman or Idea Fisher

☐   Collaborative workgroup software

16. You are conducting a man-on-the-street interview with a random
selection of people on your project. You thrust your microphone into
each person's face, and aggressively ask, "What is the role of innovation on our project?" Most of them say:

☐   "Huh?"

☐   "It may be worth trying, but I don't think it will add much value."

☐   "I think we need to make it a part of all we do."

☐   "We make it a part of all we do."

I am sure some of the more curious of you (and if you got this far, you must
be curious) are wondering what your IQ (innovation quotient) is. Here's
how to figure your score: All the first boxes are worth 5 points; all the second boxes are worth 10 points; all the third boxes are worth 15 points; all
the fourth boxes are worth 20 points.

If you scored less than 100 points:
- You need an innovation ambulance; check yourself into the innovation ICU.

If you scored between 100 and 160:
- This book may be just what you need to get your company into
  better health.

If you scored between 160 and 240:
- You are quite advanced, but could still learn a trick or two from
  this book.

If you scored more than 240:
- Give me a call, as I want to learn from you.

Notes

Introduction

1. *Jazz: The Rough Guide*, Ian Carr, Brian Priestley, and Digby Fairweather, Rough Guides, March 2000.

2. Jerry Hirshberg, *The Creative Priority: Putting Innovation to Work in Your Business,* HarperBusiness, New York, 1998.

Chapter 1

1. Basco on Braess's Paradox, a phenomenon discovered by Dietrich Braess in which increasing the capacity in congested electronic networks can paradoxically decrease the network's performance throughput.

2. *Four-Hour House*, San Diego Building Industry Association, 1983.

3. *Building Process Excellence—Lessons from the Leaders*, The Economist Intelligence Unit Limited and Accenture, 1996.

4. John Seely Brown and Paul Duguid, *The Social Life of Information*, Harvard Business School Press, Boston, 2000.

5. Gary Hamel, "Killer strategies that make shareholders rich," *Fortune*, June 23, 1997.

6. Letters to the Editor, *Evening Standard* (London), February 28, 2000. Letter from Gary Pentland.

Chapter 2

1. *Roxanne*, dir. Fred Schepisi, Columbia/Tristar Studios, 1987.

2. Net lore consists of urban legends (folklore) that are handed down over the Internet, the origins of which are often hard to identify. And they are quite often untrue or largely embellished. I have seen this story circulating around the

Internet for a few years now. Although I have not personally taken the time to debunk the myth, there are two interesting Web sites that offer perspectives on this story. One is from the National Academy of Sciences and is part of a book, *Advanced Engineering Environment: Phase 2—Design in the New Millennium.* This seems to provide an accurate, historical view of the history of American rail lines. The Web site is *www.nap.edu/html/adv_eng_env_p2/ch4.html.* The other interesting site, *www.straightdope.com/columns/000218.html*, takes the story a little further.

3. Source: *www.Benetton.com.*

4. "Technology is 'demolishing' time, distance," *USA Today*, February 29, 1999.

5. Source: *www.chrysler.com.*

6. Source: *www.williamscommunications.com.*

Chapter 3

1. Peter K. Hammerschmidt, "The Kirton Adaption Innovation Inventory and group problem solving success rates," *Journal of Creative Behavior*, vol. 30, no. 1, first quarter 1996. Peter Hammerschmidt provided me with some additional perspective on his research study. "I derived another conclusion in addition to what you offer. The "planning" environment was very rule bound (seven rules to follow in completing the task) and the implementing instructions had virtually no rules at all (just sit and wait). What I observed was that the adaptors worked most effectively in a rule-oriented environment and that the innovators worked most effectively in an environment where the rules were not clear. By aligning people with their most preferred environment they excelled, but when I placed them in a nonpreferred environment, their success rates dropped at a significant level. In short, there were two primary factors impacting the success rates: role preference and communicating with others of differering styles. Both groups were equally "creative," but their styles of creativity were very different."

2. This four-step process was developed mainly by Brad Kolar and Mark Haffner, two colleagues of mine as part of an innovation research study that I commissioned while heading the Center for Process Excellence.

3. "Kellogg cranks up its idea machine," *Fortune*, July 5, 1999.

4. George Land and Beth Jarman, *Breaking Point and Beyond,* HarperBusiness, New York, 1993.

Chapter 4

1. Peter F. Drucker, *Management: Tasks, Responsibilities, Practices*, Harper & Row, New York, 1973, p. 61.

2. Gail Odom, a colleague of mine at Accenture, provided me with these two examples. They are from a white paper of hers on customer collaboration and innovation.

3. Quoted in Tom Peters, "Lessons in leadership," *Strategic Planning R.I.P.*, TPG Communications, February 28, 1994, p. 9.

4. Source: *www.lendingtree.com.*

5. Source: *www.seti-inst.edu/science/setiathome.html.*

Chapter 5

1. Michael Porter, "What is strategy?" *Harvard Business Review*, November–December 1996.

2. *E-Europe: Connecting the Dots*, Accenture, 2001.

3. *BusinessWeek* once estimated that the initial purchase price of a corporate personal computer accounts for only 10 percent of its lifetime cost (which it estimated at $42,000). The rest of the cost goes toward troubleshooting, administration, software, and training.

Chapter 6

1. Chris Adams, Neha Kapashi (Accenture), Andy Neely, Bernard Marr (Cranfield School of Management), *Managing with Measures—Measuring eBusiness Performance*, 2000. Available at *www.accenture.com.*

2. Robert Kaplan and David Norton, "The balanced scorecard—Measures that drive performance," *Harvard Business Review*, January–February 1992.

3. The Performance Prism was born out of a joint collaboration between Accenture and The Center for Business Performance. There are some excellent articles on the topic, including Andy Neely and Chris Adams, "Perspectives on Performance: The Performance Prism," *Journal of Cost Management*, 2001; and Andrew Neely and Chris Adams, "The Performance Prism Perspective," *Journal of Cost Management*, vol. 15, no. 1, January/February 2001. Neely and Adams are also publishing a book on the topic: Andrew Neely, Chris Adams, and Mike Kennerly, *Analysing and Improving Business Performance: The Performance Prism*. Financial Times Prentice Hall, London (available January 2002).

4. "When change is a matter of survival," *Outlook*, vol. XIII, no. 1, January 2001.

Chapter 8

1. This example from AT&T was provided to me by Dave Ferrin, a colleague of mine who is an expert in Capability simulation.

2. Marc Aguilar, Tankred Rautert, and Alexander J. G. Pater, *Business Process Simulation: A Fundamental Step Supporting Process Centered Management*, Accenture, 2000.

Chapter 9

1. Martha M. Batorski and William J. Hughes, *Process Centering: New Relevance for the eEconomy*. Accenture, 2000.
2. *Building Process Excellence—Lessons from the Leader*, The Economist Intelligence Unit Limited and Accenture, 1996.

Bibliography

Accenture. *eEurope Takes Off.* Accenture, London, 2000.

Accenture. *eEurope: Connecting the Dots.* Accenture, London, 2001.

Aguilar, Marc, Tankred Rautert, and Alexander J. G. Pater. *Business Process Simulation: A Fundamental Step Supporting Process Centred Management.* Accenture, 2000.

Batorski, Martha M., and William J. Hughes. *Process Centered: New Relevance for the eEconomy.* Accenture, 2000.

Brown, John Seely, and Paul Duguid. *The Social Life of Information.* Harvard Business School Press, Boston, 2000.

Davenport, Thomas H. *Process Innovation: Reengineering Work through Information Technology.* Harvard Business School Press, Boston, 1993.

The Economist Intelligence Unit and Accenture. *Building Process Excellence: Lessons from the Leaders.* The Economist Intelligence Unit, New York, 1996.

Gladwell, Malcolm. *The Tipping Point: How Little Things Can Make a Big Difference.* Little Brown, 2000.

Hammer, Michael. *Beyond Reengineering: How the Process-Centered Organization Is Changing Our Work and Our Lives.* HarperCollins, New York, 1996.

Hammerschmidt, Peter K. "The Kirton Adaption Innovation Inventory and group problem solving success rates," *Journal of Creative Behavior,* vol. 30, no. 1, 1996.

Hirshberg, Jerry. *The Creative Priority: Putting Innovation to Work in Your Business.* HarperBusiness, New York, 1998.

Kao, John. *JAMMING: The Art and Discipline of Business Creativity.* HarperBusiness, New York, 1997.

Keen, Peter G.W., and Mark P. McDonald. *The eProcess Edge: Creating Customer Value and Business Wealth in the Internet Era.* Osborne/McGraw-Hill, Berkeley, Calif., 2000.

Land, George, and Beth Jarman. *Break Point and Beyond: Mastering the Future Today.* HarperBusiness, New York, 1993.

Neely, Andy, Chris G. Adams, and Michael Kennerly. *Analysing and Improving Business Performance: The Performance Prism.* Financial Times Prentice Hall, London, to be published January 2002.

About the Author

After 15 years in Accenture's New York office, **Stephen M. Shapiro** moved to London to lead the firm's Process Excellence practice in Europe. He has consulted with global leaders from BMW WilliamsF1, ABB, and UPS to Lucent and Xerox, and he was one of the founders of Accenture's Process Excellence practice in 1996. Shapiro has worked with external thought leaders including Michael Hammer and Peter Keen and is recognized as one of today's most influential consultants in the area of process capabilities.

Index